Badfellas

Badfellas

Crime, Tradition and New Masculinities

Simon Winlow

Oxford • New York

First published in 2001 by
Berg
Editorial offices:
150 Cowley Road, Oxford, OX4 1JJ, UK
838 Broadway, Third Floor, New York, NY 10003-4812, USA

Berg is an imprint of Oxford International Publishers Ltd.

Library of Congress Cataloging-in-Publication Data
A catalogue record for this book is available from the Library of Congress.

British Library Cataloguing-in-Publication Data
A catalogue record for this book is available from the British Library.

ISBN 1 85973 409 X (Cloth)
1 85973 414 6 (Paper)

Typeset by JS Typesetting, Wellingborough, Northants.
Printed in the United Kingdom by Biddles Ltd, Guildford and King's Lynn.

To Gran, without whose help this book would
never have begun.

To Mam and Dad, without whose guidance I would have
been the subject of this book rather than its author.

Contents

Contents

Acknowledgements

While researching and writing this book I have often thought about writing this page, being, as it is, the final part in what has been a long, hard and exceptionally rewarding period of my life. Over this period I have accumulated many debts, and in some small way I hope my effusive thanks on this page go some way to reassuring those who have helped me that their generosity will not be forgotten.

On the academic side, my most pressing debt is owed to Professor Dick Hobbs at the University of Durham, my mentor and guide into the world of academia. It was with his encouragement and guidance that I actually began to think that I had what it takes to be an academic, and that somebody might actually be interested in what I had to say. He supervised the PhD thesis on which this book is based, and was also good enough to read through various drafts of my work, and with brutal honesty tell me what was 'shit' and what was 'okay'. Perhaps more importantly he imbued me with an appreciation that being an academic still required a strong work ethic and a commitment to actually producing some publishable data. I'd also like to thank Steve Hall from the University of Northumbria for continually pushing me to think more deeply about theory, and Gary Armstrong for examining and passing my PhD and being broad minded enough to appreciate that ethnography still has a part to play in informing us about our social world and changing working-class culture. I'd also like to thank Kevin Stenson, Chris Crowther, Chris Greer, Max Travers, David Welsh, Diana Medlicott and Marisa Silvestri at Buckinghamshire Chilterns University College for helping to get me my first full-time academic post, making me welcome and providing a friendly working environment, and all in the Department of Criminology at the University of Teesside, especially Mark Simpson, Peter Harper, John Harrison, Colin Webster, Colin Dunnighan, Roger Moore, Jill Radford and Sarah Soppitt. I would also like to express my sincere thanks to Malcolm Young for favourably reviewing my manuscript and offering an insightful and realistic critique of my work, and Berg Publishers for publishing this book.

There are also many outside of academia to whom I owe a great deal. Firstly I need to thank all those who gave up their valuable time to talk to me, and all those who participated, knowingly or unknowingly, in the ethnography. Few people who engage in any form of criminal activity have anything at all to gain by speaking to academics, and I greatly appreciate their generosity and honesty. I learnt a great deal from doing this research and I owe them my eternal gratitude. Unfortunately, the cheque isn't in the post. I would also like to thank a wide and varied circle of friends who have given me more laughs than anybody has a right to. They've also had a significant impact upon my work by just being regular participants in what we sociologists might call a 'specific urban milieu'. I'd especially like to thank Nel, Ju and Gav, for just being great friends and great entertainment. Others worth a mention include Gos, Dez (still Ford Estate's most eligible bachelor), Damo, Dan, Derek, Pricey and Mad Dog and all the other usual suspects who are still hanging about and getting up to mischief. Space restricts me from adding to the list. I must also thank my brother Chris for getting the good looks instead of the brains, and Carol for producing Emily and Jonathan, the two most perfect children to walk the earth.

But most of all I'd like to thank my perfect family.

Introduction

One quarter of us is good. Three quarters is bad. That's a tough fight, three against one.

(Meyer Lansky)

Background

Civilization is not 'reasonable'; not 'rational', any more than it is 'irrational'. It is set in motion blindly, and kept in motion by the autonomous dynamics of a web of relationships, by specific changes in the way people are bound to live together.

(Elias 1982: 232)

This study describes and explains clearly perceptible economic, social and cultural transition in the North East of England since the late 1970s. In detailing these global changes, I will focus on the effect that they have had upon a specific locality and how those changes have manifested themselves upon changing masculinities and associated criminal practice and opportunity.

I will go on to detail the methodological structure and research strategy of this study in the coming pages, but first will attempt to frame the study in terms of its theoretical basis and place its structure and findings within a wider sociological context.

In this study I attempt to describe the social, economic and cultural processes that have resulted in the changing social action I have witnessed. As I will show, the social structures that exemplified the industrial modern age throughout much of the twentieth century up until, roughly, 1980, have lost their solidity and relevance to contemporary society, and behaviour and culture have altered to fit in with new social and economic circumstances. These processes, de-industrialization, global-ization and the arrival of post-modernity, have resulted in changing masculinities and the evolution of criminal trends in the North East.

Ideas and issues associated with what can generally be termed 'the post-modern' are central to the theoretical basis of this book. I use theoretical developments associated with post-modernity throughout this study, and rely heavily on issues and theory that are associated with the process of Western de-industrialization, and that are often seen as being symptomatic of post-modernity or are in some way tagged on to the debate. I do not take any direct position in relation to this theoretical debate and attempt no definition, but I find the general idea of the post-modern and the decline of structure and meta-narratives useful in explaining what is a rapidly changing region in a rapidly changing world.

As I indicate above, the social action and criminality described in these pages is explained in terms of its social roots, and I have placed 'special emphasis on firsthand acquaintance with social life' (Platt 1994: 57). In this regard, this study takes a good deal of its theoretical inheritance from the work of the Chicago School of criminology, especially in terms of methodological foundations and the desire to detail aspects of city life. As I will discuss later, participant observation was a central research tool in this study (although not all of the ethnography appears here), and as I have employed this apparently fast-disappearing research tactic, I am the inheritor of the Chicago School tradition (Downes and Rock 1988, Chapter 6).

Like many members of the Chicago School (such as Shaw 1930 or Shaw and McKay 1972), I have also attempted to study a specific area that is in the throws of considerable change. During the 1920s and 1930s Chicago underwent waves of immigration and a resulting population boom, and became for ever associated with big time gangsters, prohibition and lawlessness (see, for example, Landesco 1929; Allsop 1961). In this study, carried out in the mid to late 1990s, the North East of England is portrayed as being caught up in the post-modern condition, having been subject to massive de-industrialization and wholesale social and economic upheaval. As I indicate throughout this volume, this locale is also experiencing the arrival and entrenchment of entrepreneurial and hierarchical criminality, a development that has merged with the conflict-orientated criminal culture of the industrial North East.

Like the members of the Chicago School, I attempt to place these powerful changes at the root of the changing social action studied, and like them I focus upon a specific location. For the most part Chicago School scholars focused purely on criminality caused by environment (see, for example, Raushenbush 1979; Shaw 1930). However, I have expanded the remit of this study to include non-criminal behaviour, and indeed a great deal of the material offered here relates to the description and explanation of changing masculinities in a specific location. That said, I have placed crime clearly at the heart of this study, and use changing criminal practice and opportunity in the North East of England as symptomatic of the social, economic and cultural changes I later describe in detail.

My research can be seen in part as a continuation of the Chicago School's concerns, and also as an extension of their analysis from the modern to the post-modern. As Park (1916; 1952), Shaw (1929; 1930 and so forth), Wirth (1928; 1938) and others described the social realities that they encountered, they were also detailing social situations specific in time and space; and as they lived and worked in the modern era, it was aspects of that era that they described. This study details aspects of change in a specific locality, from the modern to the post-modern, and focuses attention on how this manifests itself upon contemporary social realities. In doing this I take into account global transformations and explore factors outside the immediate locality which have infiltrated and affected the North East of England, rather than focusing purely on the city and its ecology as influences upon behaviour.

Other influences upon the structure and content of this book are numerous and will become apparent. In particular, the work of Hobbs on professional crime and entrepreneurship (for example, 1988, 1995) is noteworthy, as are the contributions of Bauman (1989, 1992) and Baudrillard (1975, 1981, 1988 and so forth) to the post-modernity debate. The work of Dave Byrne has also been useful in shedding light on the North East's experience of de-industrialization (1983, 1989, 1993) and added the necessary quantitative evidence to my qualitative endeavours.

Globalization, Locality and Dialectical Dynamics

It makes no good sense to define the global as if the global excludes the local . . . defining the global in such a way suggests that the global lies beyond all localities, as having systematic properties over and beyond the attributes of units within a global system

(Robertson 1995: 34)

If 'modernity is [was] inherently globalising' (Giddens 1990: 63), post-modernity has continued to direct attention towards the globe as a unit of analysis in its own right (see, for example, Albrow 1992). Much of the work relating to globalization has focused on globalization as a 'process whereby the population of the world is increasingly bonded into a single society' (Albrow 1992: 248). It is often argued there is a particular dominant culture within this society (for instance by Featherstone 1990; Murphy 1983; McGrew and Lewis 1992), although this is far from universally accepted (for example, Webster 1988; Strinati and Wagg 1992).

On the basis of what I have witnessed, I propose that post-modernity has led to a fragmentation and diversity of culture rather than to cultural uniformity. As Friedman claims, 'ethnic and cultural fragmentation and modernist homogenization are not two arguments, two opposing views of what is happening in the world today, but two constitutive trends in global reality' (Friedman 1990: 311). I accept there are elements of culture that have been absorbed around the globe, but these influences are not always treated, accepted or understood in the same way. The amalgamation of the global and local is resolved in different ways in different spaces at different times.

Clearly, the media and other global institutions have infiltrated the lives of young North Eastern men, but as I shall go on to describe, how these new means of under-standing and expression have merged with local cultural histories and social action is not always immediately apparent. A dialectical progression of cultural formation has resulted, as local understandings merge with global influences, creating new forms of action and understanding (see Giddens 1990, 1991). Analyses similar to the one I offer here have used the apt term 'glocal' to help depict the relationship between the local and global (for example, Appadurai 1990; Swyngedouw 1992; Hobbs 1998).

More insightful readings of globalization have acknowledged that we are not necessarily progressing down a path from the particular to the universal, and that globalization and specificity can go hand in hand. In a similar vein to Friedman (1990), Robertson has pointed out that 'we are, in the late twentieth century, witness to – and participants in – a massive, twofold process involving the interpenetration of the universalization of particularism and the particularization of universalism' (Robertson 1992: 100). Seen from this point of view globalization is characterized by 'the organization of diversity rather than by a replication of uniformity' (Hannerz 1990: 237).

In this study I examine a culture that is being transformed by globalizing and post-modern forces and is moulding new cultural understandings from a synthesis between these forces and local interpretations of their outcomes. The North East of England, while clearly showing the signs and results of global upheavals, maintains a specific sense of locality, and the transformations I will discuss within working class masculinities in this locality are the result of a complex interaction between the local and the global. The population of the North East of England has not blindly accepted global cultural input; rather it has absorbed them into the local culture and attached its own understandings to global influences.

One example of this, which I offer in this study, is that of changing criminal structures and practice. Entrepreneurial criminality in the North East has maintained aspects of criminal cultural heritage, absorbed global images of these endeavours and put a specific local spin on things.

In attempting to depict aspects of changing culture in the North East, I offer the dialectical relationship between the global and the local as a central dynamic. As Appadurai has pointed out: 'The critical point is that both sides of the coin of global cultural process today are products of the infinitely varied mutual contest of sameness and difference on a stage characterised by radical disjunctures between different sons of global flows and the uncertain landscapes created in and through these disjunctures' (1990: 308). Any attempt to describe the current state of this culture with traditional modern cultural and subcultural analysis would have been worthless since the boundaries and content of that culture have been transformed (Horne and Hall 1995). Local and global influences merge, re-emerge and remould themselves to the extent that, at this stage, one is unsure of their precise point of emergence (see Chapter 4).

Background Discussion

From the outset it is important for the reader to note that this research is inescapably bound up with my personal history at a number of levels.

Primarily, the reader should be aware that I am a product of the very culture I attempt to describe in this thesis, although a continued stay in academia has served to distance me from it slightly. I was born and raised in the city of Sunderland and subject to a working-class upbringing and other socializing experiences similar to many of the respondents in this study. Most notably, I learnt just what it means to be 'a man' in this environment. I learnt the cultural importance of violence and came to recognize its aesthetic attraction as well as the skills and ineptitude with which it is variously deployed. I learnt about the subconscious influence of peer pressure and the desire to achieve status within the established modes of attainment (I am not talking about the education system). However, the reason you are reading this book is that I began to read sociology.

Sociology, even in its most basic application, began to allow me to explain the social and cultural structures that I had experienced and witnessed and to contrast them sharply with my new academic setting in the sedate and historic city of Durham. I did not easily adapt to this new environment and sought to flee the short distance back to the place where I knew instinctively how to act and where I would not have to repeat myself two or three times in order to have my accent understood by the southern, middle-class invaders who make up the vast majority of Durham's undergraduate and teaching population. They had not experienced what I had, and would, I felt, be hard pushed to understand deviance theories with the clarity which I felt I was able to attain. For I was able to compare concepts and theory with actual social action. When researchers talked about football hooligans, drug dealers, fences, cheque forgers and so on, I saw the faces of people I knew were involved in these activities; and when theorists wrote about differential association, anomie, strain and deviant subcultures and so on, I felt able to test these concepts upon groups with which I was acquainted (which I do here to an extent: see Bryman 1988 on the ability of participant observation to test explicitly formulated theories). The result of this was a desire to write my own research on the culture and deviant action to which I had access.

Along with these influences, I had seen the region of my birth change dramatically over time. For though I was born after the industrial heyday of the North East, upon reaching adulthood I saw clearly that my home city and the surrounding region had transformed substantially in the brief period during which I had been old enough to notice. I had watched with interest the dramatic decline and eventual closure of the shipyards, an industry so bound up with the shared social consciousness and self-image of the population of the city of Sunderland that few non-participants can fully understand the effects and influence of their eventual closure (see Roberts 1993).

The majority of the coal mines in the area had already closed before 1972, the year of my birth, and employment patterns changed (see Byrne 1989, 1993). Intergenerational unemployment began to take hold and 'problem estates' gained periodic media coverage, culminating in 1991 when CNN reported the riots on the Meadowell estate in Newcastle to a global audience. Crime was increasingly reported in a manner that hinted at a coming age of anomie among young people in the North East, and, for the first time, news began to break of organized gangs, drug dealers and even drug importers. Tales of money laundering and multi-million pound deals emerged; North Eastern gangsters were now apparently an actuality, and arrests, trials, jailbreaks and gangland hits sparked the imagination of a rapt public (see, for example, Morton 1994, especially Chapter 5) and signified a considerable shift in the boundaries of criminal success.

Again my education gave me a sense of perspective; I read about post-modernity, post-structuralism, de-industrialization, disorganized capitalism, globalization and the development of an underclass. I also began to witness the cultural effects of these changes; most importantly here, those criminal trends and gender structures within the working class which began to change palpably, sometimes visibly (see especially Chapter 3). My attention was gradually drawn away from the traditional masculine working-class role models in the North East and their deviant by-product and I began to focus more on criminal entrepreneurship and the beginnings of a deviant enterprise culture (the importance and nature of this change will be examined later, in detail). Many young men in the North East were now not destined to follow a life course similar to that of their fathers, and the social, economic and cultural structures that had existed throughout modernity were clearly losing their solidity. I began to use, and will use here, theoretical concepts concerning vast social and economic change as a foundation for examining the shifting cultural trends I was beginning to recognize, and slowly but surely began to mould my theoretical readings with what I had witnessed into a viable study format.

A theoretical base, and the sheer amount of time I spent in the field, allowed me to adapt my analysis and understanding of the interaction I witnessed as well as allowing for documentation of the ever-increasing criminal entrepreneurial trend in the region. I had first viewed this growing trend as a simulation (see Baudrillard 1983, 1988) of deviant business to which these young men had access through the mass media. External cultural inputs, it seemed, began to merge with local tradition and masculine modes of expression, and these young men began to witness and appreciate the attractiveness of the illicit deal and recognize and bestow subtle status upon those with criminal competency. Some young men, it seemed, engaged in illegal trading that produced only a tiny amount of profit, simply to be part of a coming image of a sexy subterranean environment of shady deals and hidden knowledge. Some seemed willing to buy goods because of the 'fell off the back of a lorry', nudge-nudge-wink-wink, salesman's pitch usually confined to episodes of *Only Fools and Horses* or *Minder*. It seemed as if the prospect of dealing in, or simply having access to, illicit goods became an end in itself, which was equally as powerful as the prospect of saving money on a variety of purchasable consumer goods.

With aspects of the newly emerging cultural formations being used to mould viable forms of meaning and understanding, illegal entrepreneurial endeavour became placed in a wider social context where all the potentially favourable definitions of legal entrepreneurship blurred with the seductive elements of criminality. Engaging in the illicit marketplace implied you were in the know, you had access to a hidden world of profit and privilege, that you weren't a 'mug punter . . . simply asking to be taken' (Taylor 1984: 169). This is how it seemed to start, as a simulation of the deviant marketplace, but over the course of my research I saw key respondents' business competency grow in an environment increasingly focused on getting the money rather than being seen to get the money (see also Chapter 2). As successful manipulation of the marketplace grew and professional criminals came to the fore, the seductive qualities of this milieu seemed to multiply and acknowledge the now real and flourishing deviant marketplace. Criminal entrepreneurs saw them-selves and were seen by their admiring public as 'men of action' (Goffman 1967) who 'have seen through the system – they are above the piffling mundanities of everyday society and stand apart from its petty aspirations' (Hobbs 1995: 116) and have 'more or less secret contempt for those with safe and secure jobs who need never face real tests of themselves . . . [and] have deliberately sought out this environment, declining to accept safe alternatives, being able, willing, and even inclined to live life in a challenge' (Goffman 1967: 182).

The arrival of a large and diverse deviant marketplace based on entrepreneurship and financial gain, and the changing criminal practices contained within that market-place, represent a departure from the dominant criminal precedents in the region, and this change is linked to changes in the economy, society and culture. Criminality in the region had previously mirrored the economic order of highly structured industrial production and was often, although not always, restricted to conflict-orientated crime rather than potential financial gain. In the terms of this study, it corresponds closely with changing working-class masculinities in the North East of England.

Cultural Inheritance in Context

> Many similarities between the lower-class Negro father and son (or mother and daughter) do not result from 'cultural transmission', but from the fact that the son goes out and independently experiences the same failures, in the same areas, and for much the same reasons as his father. What appears as a dynamic, self-sustaining cultural process is, in part at least, a relatively simple piece of social machinery which turns out, in rather mechanical fashion, independently produced look alikes.
>
> (Liebow 1967: 223)

The situation that Liebow describes above is pertinent in this study, for his arguments appear correct in relation to North-Eastern working-class men in the modern industrial age. During this period social, cultural and economic structures were powerful and social relations and behaviour could be predicted and explained in those terms. In contemporary society things have changed and in the 1990s – a period of immense upheaval – we can no longer prognosticate that lower class sons will go out and independently experience the same social realities as their fathers. Nor can we reliably claim that 'cultural transmission' between generations of males remains such an influential predictor of life course. I shall go on to discuss these matters in depth, but the following should here be noted:

This is a work of sociology. I state this obvious fact as I wish it to be recognized that what follows is an account and analysis of a changing cultural and economic environment, and those involved in that environment. The analysis therefore will be 'sociological' in that it will concentrate on social, economic and cultural change, and specifically that experienced by working-class males in the North East of England. This is not an attempt at a 'theory of everything'; I have avoided generalizations where possible and have used theory only in relation to that which I have witnessed.

I make little reference to the 'wooden dichotomy' (Horowitz 1990: 47) of actions based on rational choice versus actions determined by circumstance, as it is my belief that similar life experiences may lead one individual to see his or her life as a series of choices and another to see his or her life as controlled or even predestined; even so, how an individual sees his or her life may have little to do with actuality. Both hypothetical individuals are subject to their social and cultural environment and may change from one means of explanation to another throughout their lives; and I use this as my starting point in explaining the behaviour of those included in this study. This, I would argue, is not the place to enter into an epistemological and ontological discussion as to the nature of social action. Those issues can be addressed elsewhere and I wish this study to be judged on its individual merits, rather than seen as being a component of a wider theoretical debate.

At times I shall offer a type of cultural deviance theory, linking criminal practice to cultural change and specific cultural formations, yet the deviance often refers to deviance from middle class sensibilities rather than from legal norms. For example, violence as a cultural characteristic, whereby people acquire 'favourable attitudes toward . . . the use of violence' through a 'process of differential learning, association, or identification' is often mentioned. As a result, 'the use of violence . . . is not necessarily viewed as illicit conduct, and the users do not have to deal with feelings of guilt about their aggression' (Wolfgang and Ferracuti 1982: 314). Closely linked to these ideas of deviant subcultures is Sutherland's idea of differential association (see Sutherland 1937) and Akers social learning theory (Akers 1977), both of which shed useful light on the subject matter in question.

I will often use the idea of a working-class North-Eastern 'subculture', whose characteristics I will detail later, but use this term to indicate a set of norms, values and desires that are different from those held by other sections of society. These other sections of society are not accorded detailed analysis in this document as, unlike many other subcultural theorists, I did not witness any real degree of 'alienation' or 'status frustration' or 'strain' between wider society and those who inhabit that subculture (see also Downes 1966; Wilmott 1966). I will, however, detail a changing culture as it is 'lived', and my use of the term aims to address more general aspects of this culture, although I often go to pains to stress its fluidity and its change over recent decades. I also use the term 'lifestyle' (see Chaney 1996) to refer to more specific strands of behaviour born from the general subculture. For example, I speak of those involved in a deviant 'lifestyle' within the general subculture.

Matza has argued that subcultural theory 'over-predicts' delinquency by accounting for far more than actually exists (1969), and indeed there seems to be a move away from using the term in recent sociological literature (see, for example, Jenkins 1983; Willis 1990). I hope to avoid this, pointing out that many of those who are subject to the fluctuating culture I will describe do not act criminally (see the above discussion of the use of the term 'lifestyle') but remain subject to the nature of the their changing cultural environment and masculine ideology. They may also recognize the various aspects of and paths to high status within that culture, but choose, or feel compelled, to comport themselves in a way that does not contravene legal strictures. Such men are not fighting a battle to deny their metamorphosing cultural inheritance, but are engaged in a process of accentuating the emerging non-law-breaking aspects of that culture to which they still have access.

With regard to violence, the masculinities of the culture can be sustained by merely maintaining a position of not being subject to the will of other males, rather than by attempting to boost a masculine image by attempting to impose their will on others (see Connell 1995). Simply put, they are attempting to maintain a persona not of toughness, but of not being 'soft'. Complex systems of identity and self-perception are at stake: honour, shame, status and a working appreciation of the seductions and repellent aspects of violence necessitate negotiation. This pattern is not, of course, restricted to North-Eastern working-class males, although it should be noted that males in this environment and others like it quickly learn to 'deal' with violence and potentially dangerous situations because they encounter them far more regularly than their middle-class counterparts. Familiarity with any form of social action inevitably brings an understanding of its uses and meanings, and violence is no different. I am not attempting to imply that violent situations are treated as a mundane aspect of working-class reality, but violence and a working knowledge of the intricacies of the social interaction that surrounds and incorporates it leads to the formulation of defence (and attack) strategies that can be employed as and when required.

One can 'deal' with dangerous situations in numerous ways. Sometimes violent challenges will be met head on, at other times negotiation can be used successfully. Protective friendships can be cultivated; humour can be employed; situations can be spotted early and avoided; body language can be tailored so that one avoids seeming weak and yet still comes across as unthreatening. Complex dialectics of knowledge and an understanding of the social and cultural environment can be employed as multi-variants of the fight-or-flight principle. The minutiae of the progression of any potentially violent situation immediately serve to inform those with the necessary knowledge of subtle or dramatic changes in circumstances and their various effects upon potential outcomes. For those who have witnessed and participated in extremely violent incidents, the 'hyped-up sensation' (Hobbs and Robins 1991: 569) one feels during their preamble and progression are not manifested as a loss of social understanding. Extreme instinctual fear, the knotted stomach and pounding heart, do not blind the knowing participant, nor stop him calculating odds and formulating socially informed strategies. Whether or not the participant understands this in terms of a recognized social understanding of how knowledge resides on a sub-conscious level matters little when violence enters the social equation. Reactions are important; adaptability and speed of thought and action are the tools with which one extricates oneself, in one way or another, from the threat of physical and cultural harm.

In this study I will focus on men who are more likely to meet potentially violent situations head on, and on those who have acknowledged the adaptive nature of their culture, thus accentuating those aspects that may result in their breaking the law. In doing so I hope to explain some of the reasoning of those who choose this course of action and the benefits that they may obtain.

Those who are included in this study (Chapters 2 and 3), and the groups to which I refer, find themselves living in a period of great economic, social and cultural change. They are now playing out 'a diverse narrative of self' (Giddens 1991: 54), moulding and remoulding self-images and characteristics informed by global influences and local interpretations. Moreover, because of the declining influence of modern social structures, they are now living in a very different world from that of their fathers, and these issues will be addressed in detail.

Research Methods: Description and Discussion

The choice of research method was never really open to debate. The sociological and anthropological texts that caught my imagination have often embodied some form of ethnographic endeavour (Sutherland 1937; Downes 1966; Liebow 1967;

Whyte republished 1993; Polsky 1971; Patrick 1973; Parker 1974; Hobbs 1988, 1995; Williams 1990). Many have dealt with similar subject matter to that which I wished to study. I appreciate the sheer determination it takes to gain the trust of deviant groups, the tact and hard work, the long hours, the frustrations and the financial burden and, of course, the empathy and insight needed to understand the world from the perspectives of these groups (see Blumer 1969). I recognize the advantages of more quantitative research methods, but circumstance, as well as my epistemological leaning, pushed me towards the research strategies I was eventually to employ. From the outset it was my wish to produce a document that portrayed and explained the foundations and dynamics of a social and cultural life world which exists in the post-traditional, post-industrial North Eastern urban milieu. I wanted to provide 'a clear, firsthand picture' of the 'life of ordinary people, on their grounds and on their terms' (Liebow 1967). To gain the detail and depth of understanding I sought, it was necessary to engage in fieldwork.

The disadvantages of fieldwork have been well documented elsewhere (for example, Cicourel 1964; Bryman 1988; see also Guba and Lincoln 1982 and Evered and Louis 1981 for a different slant on the debate), and I do not intend to reproduce the same arguments in a debate which will never be resolved. My own outlook upon this debate is captured effectively by Bryman (1992: 173), who believes

> rather than the somewhat doctrinaire posturing of a great deal of the literature dealing with the epistemological leanings of quantitative and qualitative research, there should be a greater recognition in discussions of the general aspects of social research methodology of the need to generate good research. This injunction means attending to the full complexity of the social world such that methods are chosen in relation to the research problems posed.

I am unable to predict whether or not this book will be considered 'good research', but I can say without fear of contradiction that those research methods I did employ were the most sensible given the initial aims of the research and the circumstances surrounding its inception.

What should be primarily noted by the reader when considering this epistemological debate and the methods employed in this piece of research is the level of access that I was able to achieve with a relatively small amount of effort (see, for instance, Spiegel 1969; Liebow 1967 for a very different account of the problem of access). From the first tentative steps I was aware that I would be able to gain access to some deviant activities just by 'turning up', as it were. The potential material that I was sure I could retrieve made ethnography the most obvious choice. It was these methods that would enable me to gain illuminating details and the partly hidden nuances of a 'deviant social scene' (Adler 1985: 2) in social, economic and cultural transition.

I felt sure that I already had a detailed understand of the culture I was to study, and of the social understandings that those involved in this environment brought to their actions. For the most part I knew the area quite well, I knew the people, I knew the complicated systems of behaviour and understanding, what could be said, and when and to whom; and I knew about illegal business. Some of those who unknowingly helped to form my theoretical points had been close friends before I even knew what sociology was, and others were aware that I was know-ledgeable about accepted modes of behaviour in the developing trading culture.

Becoming conversant with the illegal economy was never a primary goal, but being around people always on the look out to make a deal was always useful for my research goals. The time spent doing this research not only widened my frame of analysis and research opportunities but also established checkable credentials that were to serve me well for a number years.

Other researchers have used previous knowledge of the culture they have studied to good effect (for example, Polsky 1971; Parker 1974; Hobbs 1988, 1995) and I was confident I could do the same. From my standpoint this was a piece of research just waiting to be done.

Access

As few white researchers could now successfully research sections of black American society (Spiegel 1969), so few of the educated, middle-class and middle-aged British researchers could engage with those sections of society to which we are drawn as criminologists and sociologists. This, of course, is no fault of their own; for even those who do not enter academia fulfilling the above criteria will eventually do so if they remain there long enough; and thus it can be argued that the most ground-breaking ethnography has largely been conducted by researchers at the start of their academic careers (for example, Hobbs 1985; Adler 1985; Whyte 1993). I was lucky enough to have the opportunity to conduct this piece of research in my early twenties, an all-too-brief time of life when my age and physical appear-ance did not contrast with those of the subjects researched. None of the academics it has been my pleasure to meet could have successfully gained access to the culture I describe, and in a sense this makes the study unique (see Whyte 1993). In essence, then, circumstance seemed to create a situation in which all the tools necessary to conduct this research were placed before me. My previous detailed knowledge of the culture, and my continued contacts within it, my age, my physical appearance, my own imperative to do ethnography, and the academic backup at the University of Durham, and even my accent, all helped. As Fleisher (1993) has pointed out, many scholars who discuss and analyse the lives and beliefs of criminals have not spent enough time on the streets among their subjects to understand the cultural and semantic context of their speech. To use a linguistic analogy, outside researchers often report the phonetics of crime without understanding its syntax and semantics. I was able to avoid this problem as, for the most part, I had the same accent as those I was studying, recognized their accepted and occasionally highly complex speech codes and structures, and spoke just like them. As the saying goes, a bad workman blames his tools, and it seems I will be denied this convenient excuse. Any deficiency in this piece of research must therefore be placed firmly at my door.

Techniques

I employed both covert and overt techniques of observation, and on a small number of occasions conducted unstructured interviews, some of which I taped. These neat categories of ethnographic endeavour seem however to minimize the fluidity of the research as it was actually conducted. As Gans (1967) has indicated, the role of the participant observer is never clear cut; he participated in activities that cast him 'in three types of research roles: *total researcher, researcher participant, and total participant.'* Gans (1967: 440) describes his role as researcher: 'As total researcher I observed events in which I participated minimally or not at all . . . As a researcher participant, I participated in an event but as a researcher . . . As a total participant, I acted spontaneously as a friend . . . and subsequently analysed the activities in which I had so participated.' However, even Gans's subdivisions do not fully describe my various participant roles. I generally did not enter social situations with a preconceived idea of which role I would cast myself in; adaptability was necessary throughout the period of research, and I would choose whichever role would seem most likely to benefit my research.

For instance, 'Artie' and 'Michael' (who feature in Chapter 2) had been introduced to me some time before the research began and knew who and what I was, and consequently I asked them to submit to interviews in order to get as full a picture of their activities and their imperatives to action as they understood them. For the possibility of gaining a great deal of information about adaptive deviancy with such a minimal amount of effort was too good an 'opportunity' to miss (Riemer 1977). I was also able to conduct a type of overt/covert research into their behaviour; and although they knew of my occupation, I remain convinced their behaviour did not change to allow for my presence. I could and did come and go to their homes and places of business, I attended football matches, played in football matches, attended boxing events, weddings and funerals, and went on two stag weekends and drank with them in all of these settings. As Liebow (1967) has claimed, 'taking this inside view makes it easier to avoid structuring the material in ways that might be alien to the material itself', and this, to an extent, allowed me to 'learn the answers to questions I would not have had the sense to ask if I had been getting my information solely on an interview basis' (Whyte 1993).

I conducted covert research on a number of individuals engaged in a wide range of criminal activity, especially at the start of my research when the study was still to find a firm focus, for I did not feel they would be at ease with the presence of an outsider. An ability to understand the social environment and act unobtrusively was, of course, crucial to my ability to carry out covert research successfully, but my level of access was everything. I am not the first researcher to admit that there were times when I forgot the primary reason why I was actually there, as my research seemed increasingly to focus on my own social environment. Hobbs (1988: 6) sums up this research predicament perfectly, admitting for the most part that he

> spoke, acted, drank, and generally behaved as though [he] was not doing research. Indeed, [he] often had to remind [himself] that [he] was not in a pub to enjoy [himself], but to conduct an academic inquiry and repeatedly woke up the following morning with an incredible hangover facing the dilemma of whether to bring it up or write it up.

My research into the social organization of bouncing, which was later to focus more specifically on post-modern masculinities and deviant opportunity, was also solely covert, but was slightly different (see Winlow et al, forthcoming, for wider discussion of covert ethnography on bouncers). For those who are unsure just what a bouncer is or does, they are men or women employed to keep order in licensed premises. In this connection, they are usually expected to deal with any behaviour that the licensee deems unsatisfactory, and this can involve a vast array of acts, the most obvious of which is being violent. This occupation comes in for a good deal of analysis throughout this book, but at this juncture suffice it to say that it calls for a specific form of robust masculinity. Bouncers are not new. They have been around in various guises for generations, although I focus on the post-modern realities of their occupation, the environments in which they work, and the changing modes masculine expression they exhibit and embody.

Again, in this bouncing milieu, I was fortunate to be able to exploit contacts but less so than had I focused on some other site of the social and cultural change that has occurred in the North East. One of these contacts was able to briefly procure for me a job which you will never see advertised in the local job centre, and it was because of this that I was able to widen my circle of unwitting respondents, and in so doing engage in a new form of 'opportunistic' research (Riemer 1977). Once in these environments I was able to observe, participate and build relationships by doing what Becker (1963), Polsky (1971) and Douglas (1972) advocated: I gave the respondents a chance to get to know me and form judgements about my trustworthiness by being around me. I did not, however, feel they would necessarily be favourably disposed towards me if I was to reveal my role as researcher.

Much of my research into bouncers and the developing night-time economy overlapped with paid research for the Economic and Social Research Council.

This research also concerned bouncers, changing masculinities, the night-time economy and the regulation of this problematic market, and I was employed primarily to conduct participant observation in these locations. I obtained a licence and a regular job on the door of a bar and got on with it.

Being accepted as a bouncer rested on my ability to do the job, to prove myself to be 'one of them' and inculcate myself into the milieu. Acquaintances were all-important: 'Do you know x? I know y who often hung around with x. You say you know z? You must know w then.' In a roundabout way, those who did not know me were checking me out, but were also trying to find some common ground with a person they had just met. When I was engaged in conversations such as this it became apparent to me just how insular the 'deviant social scene' (Adler 1985: 2) that I describe really is. Everyone seemed to know everyone else, or, at least, there existed some link based on friendship and acquaintance. Again I fell on my feet as my credentials stood up.

Becoming a bouncer is not an easy task for a researcher. I have already mentioned the importance of access and my good fortune in this regard, but this is by no means the end of the researcher's problems. Again I was lucky in that it was easy for me to blend into the social scene because of my knowledge and understanding of the culture; however, once this point is reached, further hurdles arise which the researcher must address, for location, strategy and the nature of the 'bouncing' meant (see Chapter 3) that the threat of violence was constant. Many of my colleagues talked a great deal about violence and its application, and to become fully accepted by those studied I felt it necessary to engage in a type of masculine bravado with which I was not entirely comfortable. I had to offer my opinion on hundreds of passing women and I had to swear a lot. It was simply impractical to 'keep my mouth shut' (Polsky 1971: 126–7), as this behaviour alone would have served 'to chill the scene' (Polsky 1971: 132) and force those whom I aimed to understand to restrain their behaviour in front of this strange person who just stood there with his mouth shut and kept an unnaturally close eye on their behaviour. This apart, I had to face the realistic prospect of being a victim of violence because the clientele of the establishments where I worked were young and consumed a lot of alcohol, moving from one pub to another before going on to a nightclub. In these circum-stances one felt violence was never very far away, and indeed I witnessed violent conflicts relatively often in these environments. Being sober among masses of drunken men and women can create feelings of vulnerability, and indeed I often felt on edge, even with the imposing figures of my colleagues next to me (Fagan 1990; see also Field 1990 on the relationship between alcohol consumption and violence, and Tuck 1989 on violent incidents occurring as young people gather when leaving drinking places).

Violence was common, and though it became apparent that some individuals were prone to erratic violence, this tendency was also accentuated in others by the use of amphetamines and/or steroids (see Carey's 1972 research into amphetamine users and their potential for violence).

Further problems existed. It was obvious from the very start of my research that I would be unable to directly record specific incidents or encounters as I attempted to maintain a covert research role working as a bouncer. As Williams (1990: 3) had done, I took to jotting 'key words and phrases immediately after each visit, and reconstructing conversations or a scene from those notes the next day. It was not unusual to spend a day or more writing up an hour or two's field observations.' I found this method to be reliable, although it was really my only option as I wasn't about to retire to the lavatory to take notes (Ditton 1977). Research ethics also needed to be addressed.

Ethics

> We do not for a moment wish that we could rid ourselves of deviant phenomena. We are intrigued by them. They are an intrinsic, ineradicable, and vital part of human society
>
> (Matza 1969: 17)

All research can pose ethical dilemmas (Barnes 1979) and the research for this book was no different. Even at a most basic level I was not entirely truthful with some of those researched because I did not reveal my role as a sociologist/criminologist (see also, for example, Wallis 1976). I do not feel overly guilty about this, as my brief sortie into their life world had little or no effect upon their lives, and I hope I have disguised their identities and locations adequately and have therefore protected them from unwanted publicity. I also hope it will be apparent that it has never been my intention to portray any of those researched in either a negative or a positive light, for I attempted to be value free and described the social scene as I found it. I hope therefore I have not offended any of those researched by my portrayal of them.

More significantly, and as the reader will gather, I was present at or aware of a good deal of criminal activity as it unfolded, and was informed about a good deal more after the fact. Because of my background I found none of the activities of those researched particularly offensive, and, as my aim was to depict a 'deviant social scene' (Adler 1985) in all its richness, I was 'willing to skirt the boundaries of criminality on several occasions' (Hobbs 1988: 7).

Not all the criminal activities of which I was aware, or at which I was present, appear in these pages. This is partly due to my desire to maintain the central theoretical basis of this work, partly due to discretion and the desire to hide the activities of various individuals, and partly due to my previously expressed wish not to offend any of those who participated, either knowingly or unknowingly.

As Polsky (1971: 138) correctly noted, studying criminals in their natural setting requires the researcher to break the law, even if this is merely through the possession of 'guilty knowledge'. The possibility of arrest sometimes did rear its head, and claiming participant observer's rights would no doubt have earned me no more than a laugh from the arresting officers. Such is the lot of the ethnographic researcher, and at the time I believed the risk to be worth it for, as Hobbs 'considered it crucial to be willingly involved in "normal" business transactions, legal and otherwise' (Hobbs 1988: 7), I too found it necessary not to be immediately dismissive of business propositions. For instance, I could be asked if I could 'get rid' of a range of fake designer goods. Doing this allowed me to immerse myself further into the culture and gain a depth of understanding that would otherwise be hard to obtain. Again, in a similar vein to Hobbs, I do not consider this admission renders my research 'unethical' (Hobbs 1988: 7–8) for I found it necessary to become almost fully immersed in the culture in order to see the structural organization of a wide range of delinquent activities. 'Cultures are fluid, adaptive responses and as a researcher I too was fluid and adaptive' (Hobbs 1988: 11).

Acting as a bouncer for the purposes of this research created ethical issues. For even though much of my research on and contact with crime and criminals was not overly problematic, being a bouncer was. Polsky (1971) has written that 'you damned well better not pretend to be one of them, because they will test this out and one of two things will happen: either you will . . . get sucked into "participant" observation of the sort you would not wish to undertake, or you will be exposed, with still greater negative consequences.' And though most of the bouncers with whom I worked were not engaged in criminal activity (at least not when the were at work), they too tested me out and *I damned well did have to pretend to be one of them*. The nature of the work meant that if you were not going to carry out the job in the manner their experience deemed necessary, there was no point in your being there. *Not* pretending to be one of them would have created negative consequences, and not just for my research on bouncers but for my wider research interests.

Once I began the job I found it remarkably easy to pretend to be one of them, but from the outset I did not find being a bouncer particularly appealing, although I believed the opportunity too good to pass up. (Observing bouncers in their natural setting while not participating was far easier and more enjoyable, but simply hanging around in bars was unlikely to uncover the depth of understanding I sought.) I felt perfectly comfortable with the idea of standing around a busy pub door talking and laughing with my colleagues and portraying myself as a tough guy, though, at first, I was not quite at ease with the likelihood of the actuality of having to throw someone out of the pub or club. For much of the time this was not a problem, as many nights passed without incident. However one had to be involved in all the disturbances even if only peripherally, and once the first incident had come and passed I actually felt like a real bouncer (which of course I was). Jumping into the middle of a group of fighting men is a powerful bonding activity for young men and bouncers alike, and once this was completed my access and status were considerably enhanced, further aiding my research.

During the time I was at work on various pub and club doors both in and outside of the North East, the aims of my research took a back seat. At first I was more concerned with merely getting through the nights intact, but as my experience of the occupation grew I became more comfortable with the component parts of the work and was keen to do a good job. Weakness would not be tolerated by my colleagues or the licensee, and would immediately be seized upon by customers of the premises. Proving myself with a view to furthering my access was not always at the front of my mind. In a situation such as this, what is in one's immediate social environment commands the attention. Plans for further enhancing my research opportunities were laid to rest while I was at work, for when I was at work it would have been detrimental to the research and to my health to have been anything other than a bouncer.

Violence did occur, and not all of it was justified. Much of that violence is not discussed here. However I was able to use it to analyse the framing of violent encounters, the social and cultural meanings tagged on to them and wider issues involving violence, bouncers and the night-time economy. These incidents were never pleasant, but were always useful to my endeavours. Seeing someone knocked unconscious has a way of putting any ethical dilemmas into perspective.

Other Issues

Ethnographic research of this nature has a number of practical difficulties over and above those already discussed, and it is usually necessary to overcome a range of unforeseen problems (see, for example, Hobbs 1988; Ditton 1977; Williams 1990). From a personal point of view it was necessary to place limits upon the deviancy in which I would be prepared to take part. I will not describe exactly what I was prepared to do and what I was not, but suffice to say that I do not believe my activities would overly disturb the average reader. I have already pointed out the usefulness of some peripheral market engagement for this study, and buying and selling everyday consumer items did not offend my personal sensibilities.

Some initial minor problems grew in scale during the time that the particular research was being carried out. For example, when I attempted to get a job as a bouncer I found it necessary to apply for a licence. It was also necessary to procure introductions to the bosses of a private security company in order to find work in an area well outside of the North East where I knew few people. These may seem minor matters, but the actuality was that neither was easy and both required a good deal of time and effort. Having gained an introduction to the security company bosses in the area, I then found it necessary to prove my abilities and trustworthiness (luckily I was able to cite previous experience in the profession), which was a complex task in itself, and again I encountered numerous stumbling blocks and problems, which, once overcome, simply seemed to generate yet more problems. Such was the multitude of dilemmas and puzzles as I attempted to immerse myself in what is a culture filled with highly intricate and shifting systems of meaning and understanding.

What to include in this book was also another source of perplexity. When the time actually came to put this book into a logical and readable form, it was obvious that a good deal of my research notes would be unusable. The breadth of my initial research interests and the desire to structure this book so that the theoretical arguments were not overwhelmed by such a diverse expanse of ethnography was such that it forced me leave out various notes and arguments. I had hoped to include research findings that would help in portraying my theoretical observations, and leave out those that distracted the reader from the central arguments. This was slightly annoying, given the time and effort I had put into gathering this material, but it also presented the problem of thoroughly explaining my research experiences in this brief methods section.

The research, as it was 'lived', jumped from one topic to another, from one research method to another and from one research group to another. I will not attempt to use a 'chronological lie' regarding the inception and progress of this piece of research (Cohen and Taylor 1972: 32); I had no 'eureka' experience that resulted in a theoretical hypothesis, which I then proceeded to test and concluded to be correct. As my research was haphazard in its progress, so was its theoretical structure, although I am obviously convinced of its validity.

As a consequence of the structure of my research, a number of people who helped me do not appear in any great detail in these pages. Such people have been apparent, however, as I often make reference to a friend or acquaintance who introduced me to this person or that person. None of the men who helped me in this way have been examined in any detail in the final version of this book as discussion of their lives and activities would detract from the central points I try to make.

This Study

> We always wore suits, ties, collars. Today they're walking about with designer stubbles and dirty old shoes and you think – where's the pride gone?
>
> (Bill Gardner, London villain in the 1960s, quoted in Bean 1995: 5)

Male dress codes are not all that has changed in the criminal milieu and its working-class base. This section will offer a brief summary of the main arguments of this thesis, and serves as a general introduction to the economic, social and cultural processes that I examine in detail later.

This book will examine the changing role of violence and masculine identity in the North East of England. This examination focuses mainly on the city of Sunderland and the North East of England, and details how the role of violence and crime in this locality has evolved from the modern to post-modern age. As Tolson said, 'if gender is cultural and social, then it is also historical . . . There is no universal masculinity, but rather a varying masculine experience of each succeeding social epoch' (1977: 13). Indeed, this study exemplifies changing masculinities and the newly developing ways in which they find their expression.

Serving as a backdrop to this study are the widespread changes that have occurred in the North East since the 1970s. Employment patterns have changed considerably alongside a widespread de-industrialization, and the shift to what has been termed 'disorganized capitalism' (Lash and Urry 1987). This has left many with redundant skills and created 'large armies of unemployed, especially among young males' (Lash 1994: 120), who now effectively experience 'both political and cultural exclusion from civil society' (Lash 1994: 133; see also Byrne 1989). As industrial labour continues its gradual decline, we have witnessed the corresponding effect on criminality (see Hobbs 1994) and how traditional male roles involving hard work, physicality, 'shop floor masculinity' (Willis 1977), and providing for one's family (see Tolson 1977; Morgan 1992) have become of limited relevance to a new generation of North-Eastern males (see Murray 1990).

The working-class male in the North East of England is changing, and while many traditional social structures decline in importance and the meta-narratives of sociology's founding fathers carry less weight, those masculine concerns that maintain their influence begin to change in form, and in their use and understanding; the old, reliable means of masculine expression that are still within reach are redefined and moulded to fit the new social, cultural and economic environment. Violence is one such mode of masculine expression on which I focus, detailing its changing character and uses in the post-modern North East. As Daly and Wilson have claimed, and as will become apparent, 'poor young men with dismal prospects for the future have good reason to escalate their tactics of social competition and become violent' (1988: 287).

The modern era in the North East was characterized by industrial and extractive production, and just as the economic base influences social structures, so masculinity fitted in with industrial male roles, especially with regard to physicality. As criminal practices mirror opportunity (Hobbs 1993; see also Bottoms 1994), cultural inheritance and the prevailing masculine ideal (see Cloward and Ohlin 1960), so criminality centred on fighting ability, the readiness to fight, fate and autonomy, as well as the well-documented search for excitement (see Miller 1958), which Miller believes causes youths who adhere to such 'cultural practices [to] automatically violate legal norms' (Miller 1958: 166).

As the modern era failed to throw up any stories of professional criminal success, at least in terms of contemporary standards of criminal attainment (see especially Chapter 4), young delinquent lower class males were denied these deviant role models to aspire to, and as a criminal hierarchy did not exist on anything like the scale it does today, a conflict-orientated subculture (Cloward and Ohlin 1960) developed. In this cultural environment violence was highly prized as a means whereby men could obtain renown within their peer group and wider community. Criminality and deviancy were most commonly expressed through drunkenness and petty thievery (see Chapter 1).

Other locales in the modern era witnessed a more entrepreneurial masculine ethic (see, for example, Hobbs 1988), and it was in these areas that a more financially focused criminality developed. It would appear the most an aspiring criminal in Sunderland and the rest of the industrial North East could hope for, was to 'look after' pubs and the occasional business in their neighbourhood, and thus reap the modest rewards of free drinks and the respect given to those recognized as being adept at physical confrontation (for an example and discussion see Chapter 1). There were seemingly very few exceptions to this pattern, and almost no literature exists on professional criminality in the North East during this period.

Professional and organized crime would appear not to have existed in the North East in the modern era, given that I have been unable to uncover any historical record of anything approaching contemporary definitions of these activities. Certainly that which did exist in no way paralleled professional crime in other areas of Britain during the same period (see, for example, Kelland 1987; Cater and Tullett 1988; Hobbs 1988; Morton 1992, 1994; Murphy 1993) and was minor, small scale, and certainly escaped the notice of a wider public, and was therefore in keeping with the points I make above (see below for further discussion on the motivations to criminal action during the modern industrial era).

Post-industrial Sunderland has arguably changed disproportionately to the amount of time that has past between the modern (roughly 1880–1980) and post-modern (roughly 1980 to date) eras, and criminality has metamorphosed into a marketplace, a 'supportive interchange' (Goffman 1971) where skills as well as goods are offered for consumers in a parody of the legitimate industrial age. As cultural and economic structures have changed, so has associated criminality and enterprise (see Hobbs 1994) and working-class entrepreneurship has arisen in an area previously stoic in this regard. As Bauman has said, the market is the enemy of conformity (1992) and working-class young men are adapting to the growth of the criminal marketplace and the expansion of criminal opportunity.

Cohen (1972) has noted that the post-war era has seen the weakening of histori-cal and cultural continuity in working-class areas, prompting contradictions to arise within young people's cultural inheritance between 'the new hedonism of consumption' and traditional working-class Puritanism; this pattern is perfectly exemplified in a number of North-Eastern working-class communities, where involvement in the hidden economy is becoming a 'cultural interpretation of business' (Ditton 1977: 176) and the desire to acquire material possessions increasingly provides the impetus to criminal activity (see Chapter 2) as the traditional means of acquiring income become increasingly scarce (for example, Byrne 1989).

Linked to this, the pace of change within both legitimate and criminal markets has left many features of the traditional working-class family redundant (Parker 1989; Wilson 1987, 1996). Perhaps most telling is the failure of some working-class parents to socialize their children with 'cultural capital' (Bourdieu and Passeron 1977), which stresses a manual, traditionally working-class work ethic involving skill, workmanship and provision for one's family as this traditional 'gendered life course' (Morgan 1992: 45) becomes increasingly hard to attain.

Masculinity has changed to accommodate the remodelling of cultural structures. Smartness and entrepreneurship, the ability to deal and deal well, has become an admired male characteristic; although, of course, 'within the culture this utilisation of entrepreneurship varies according to the skill and dexterity of individuals' (Giddens 1976: 112). 'Acknowledgement that a deal can be made can be given by gestures and body language as well as in the spoken word. Everything is cagey: A "we rationale" is at work, confirming that those involved know what they are doing and what is involved' (Goffman 1961: 18). Consequently, a sharp verbal style and ready wit have become desirable characteristics, as has the very caginess of illicit business. The masculine protocols and 'gender regime' (Connell 1987: 120) of the past, of physicality, fighting, fighting ability and the readiness to fight, of autonomy, release and skill are not rejected but merge with new influences and take on new meanings in the post-modern age. Physicality need not be expressed by the hardship of manual labour but by the reshaping of the body to accentuate the male image with a larger and more defined musculature; fighting ability need not be restricted to personal displays of toughness to win the respect of one's peers, but can become a viable commercial asset, a career option or a means of defending one's market share.

Violent potential has long been a 'cultural expectation' of working-class men (for example, Wolfgang 1959) and in the post-modern North East has become a means of seeking financial rewards. 'Bouncing' has become one career option in a labour market bereft of opportunity for those who fail to gain significant formal qualifications or decline to train or retrain to fit in with the gradual shift away from industrial labour and towards predominantly service-sector employment. One route for the traditional 'hard' man has been a transformation into a bouncer or an inhabitant of the bouncing, business, leisure and night-time milieu in a seemingly natural progression parallel with a developing marketplace and the corresponding leisure culture.

Where once the fact of being a local celebrity would meet the desires of most 'hard' men, market opportunities have now arisen and economic and cultural changes allow those with violent potential to adapt their male role actively to seek financial reward, to engage and dominate the illicit marketplace, and to occupy the moral vacuum beyond utilitarianism and instrumentality (Hobbs and Robbins 1991: 571).

Violent North-Eastern men now represent a 'cultural authority' and thus, so Bauman argues, have the ability to 'turn themselves into market forces, become commodities, compete with other commodities and legitimise their value through the selling capacity they attain' (1992: 452).

History, Modernity and Masculinities

A Short History of Sunderland and the Surrounding Area

> Sunderland, as a town, has a distinct character. It is geographically set off by its position on the river and the coast. Centred visibly and closely on its productive work, it is the antithesis of suburbia: housing is an annex to the workplace and the community is a working community. It is, in a double sense, a working-class town. Sunderland also has a social distinctiveness, which in part reflection and part cause of its physical isolation. There is a shared dialect and accent of the Wearsider, local patriotism for the town's football team, the community and neighbourhood pubs and social clubs, and the housing in Sunderland.
>
> A. H. Halsey

The observations of A. H. Halsey presented above seem very dated in 1998. The industrial, working-class town with such strong community ties is now a post-industrial city. However these changes are not necessarily recent phenomena. I offer the following passage from a work first published in 1969, as a useful and succinct introduction to the social and economic background of the area:

> Sunderland is a town which is living on the dwindling fat of its Victorian expansion. The legacy of the industrial revolution is apparent in its appearance, its physical structure, it's population growth and in a host of social and economic characteristics. Even attitudes are coloured by its past heritage. The depression years, the final death spasm of the 19th century, are still a real memory amongst much of the town's population and impinge upon the attitudes of the working population. This imprint of the past, rooted in a continuing dependence on heavy industry, is found to a much greater degree than in the towns of the Midlands or even Lancashire, since the spread of light manufacturing has had only marginal effects in the North East.
>
> (Robson 1969: 75)

Much of the research presented here has its foundations in the city of Sunderland. By this I mean that some, although certainly not all, of the respondents quoted were born and reside there, although their activities were far from restricted to that locale. As they were free to move in space, so was I, and my research took me to all the main conurbations in the North East of England. A large amount of time was spent in Newcastle, Washington, County Durham, Middlesbrough and as far south as Leeds, Bradford and Hull, but aside from issues of access and methodology, Sunderland in particular seemed to possess all of the theoretical characteristics that underlie this study. Aside from this, it was the city of my birth and the area I knew best, thus making it the most obvious locale to focus my study and frame my theoretical points. Since cultural inheritance is central to this text and much is made of the nature of masculinity and socio-cultural change in the area, and as few readers – other than those who live in the North East – will have visited the city or know of its urban landscape beyond the generalizations and stereotypical images, then a brief history of the city of Sunderland seems appropriate at this point. I therefore offer this chapter as a means of laying the foundations for later discussions of changing masculinities and criminal practice in the modern industrial and post-modern eras.

History

Settlements around the mouth of the River Wear have been traced back to the Neolithic age (see Mitchell 1919: 3). However, it was not until the first half of the nineteenth century that Sunderland developed into a major concentration of population and a commercial centre, although the port at the mouth of the Wear had achieved a measure of success before this date (Mitchell 1919; Corfe 1973). The bridge that spans the mouth of the River Wear joining the two major urban centres opened in 1796 and achieved some renown by being only the second iron bridge in the world.

The city also has an interesting religious history, being closely connected with the lives of Benedict Biscop and St Bede in Saxon times. Biscop erected a monastery and church dedicated to St Peter as early as 674, which remains a local landmark. Glass was installed in the church and Sunderland consequently became the first place in England where glass was made, beginning a close association between glass making and the city (Corfe 1973).

St Bede was born in Sunderland and was admitted to Biscop's monastery where he proceeded to spend much of his life, becoming the most noted scholar of his time, writing fifty books including *The Ecclesiastical History of England* and other works that provide much of our information on the ancient history of England until AD 731 (Mitchell 1919).

Despite these facts, it is shipbuilding that is most commonly associated with Sunderland and its history, especially in the nineteenth and early twentieth centuries. As Benson has pointed out, it is difficult to overestimate the importance of work to a working-class life, especially during this period. It was the way in which workers spent many – if not most – of their waking hours and work determined how much money they had at their disposal (Benson 1989: 9). This in turn would often determine health, housing, social standing and, in some cases, the political beliefs and other associated values that workers possessed (see, for example, Joyce 1982). As Becker and Carper (1956) noted, one's occupation and commitment to work greatly influence self-identity, and in this respect it is also difficult to communicate fully the importance of Sunderland's dominant and defining industry to the surrounding community. Roberts (1993, especially: 1–10) offers an insightful discussion of the importance of shipbuilding to Sunderland and the surrounding community:

> Sunderland . . . was by no means a one industry town, but the fortunes of shipbuilding had for so long been the major indicator of economic and social conditions on Wearside . . . The rope making and pottery industries did not employ a great number, and coal mining was not as prevalent in the Borough as in the rest of the county. This separated Sunderland from the county town of Durham City, the focal point for miners within the Durham coalfield. Lacking the communications, prestige and diversity of Newcastle, only twelve miles away, Sunderland was a closed community, forever in the shadow of these two centres. Shipbuilding was at the heart of the industrial and everyday life at the mouth of the Wear.
>
> (J.A. Brown 'The General Strike, 1926: Sunderland', undated and unpublished BA dissertation quoted in Roberts 1993: 18)

In 1834 the *Lloyds Register of Shipping* regarded Sunderland as 'the most important centre in the country', its output equalling that of all other ports put together (Corfe 1973: 75). An author who visited the town in this period commented on the 'increasing manufactories which vomit forth their black, broad and long extended columns of trailing smoke' (Dibdin 1838: 314). In the later years of the nineteenth century, Sunderland embraced the shift towards building large steel ocean-going vessels, abandoning its speciality of small coastal vessels, and continued to thrive (Dibdin 1838). A *Daily Telegraph* reporter in 1882 thought the area a 'wonderful picture of thriving industry . . . every acre of land . . . the basis for some great commercial undertaking' (Dibdin 1838: 78). The spectacular advance of shipbuilding was the most distinctive feature of Sunderland's nineteenth-century development. At the same time, the town's importance as a port was increasing. Its growth was based almost entirely on the shipments of coal coming from mines on the outskirts of Sunderland, and these in turn were affected by the emergence of railway networks linking the collieries to the harbour and the general improvement of facilities at the port itself (Mitchell 1919; Bowling 1958).

Shipbuilding, seafaring and the coal trade dominated the town's economy to such an extent that half of all employed men were working in these industries. Pottery, glassmaking, limestone, cement and brick works had also been significant sources of employment in the area, but by the mid-nineteenth century all these industries were in severe decline and 'had either disappeared completely or were on the point of extinction' by the time of the First World War (Sinclair 1988: 31). The population grew rapidly in the nineteenth century, however, as people flocked to the booming town, causing social conditions to deteriorate with the entrepreneurial middle classes, who had cashed in on the expanding marketplace, moving to the outlying areas. Their houses were split into tenements and brothels and taverns sprung up to cater for industrial workers and the influx of seamen. On average, houses in the parish held ten inhabitants and less than 7 per cent had privies (Corfe 1973: 57). Sewerage was far from adequate and dung heaps formed, prompting a cholera outbreak in 1831, the first in Britain, and again in 1866 (Corfe 1973), which focused national attention on the town's distressing situation. Charles Grenville, Clerk of the Privy Council, reflected on the town's 'state of human misery and moral degradation' (Corfe 1973: 58).

A B. Granville, like many other visitors at the time, commented on the wonder of the Wear bridge ('the stupendous structure . . . one of those projections which show the power of man so strikingly' (1841: 266), but also made note of passing though 'a long dirty street . . . inhabited by the lowest class of people . . . and from which branched off, to the right and to the left, many very narrow passages or alleys . . . all presenting . . . the very stink of gloom and filth – an apt nest or rendezvous for typhus and cholera' (1841: 268). Murray commented similarly, describing Sunderland as:

> black and gloomy in the extreme, and the atmosphere is so filled with smoke that blue sky is seldom seen, especially in the lower part of the town, which consists for the most part of a maze of small dingy houses crowded together, intersected by lanes rather than streets: dirt is the distinctive feature; earth, air and water are alike black and filthy.

> (1864: 124)

During this period, slum areas were subject to market forces, which were allowed to run wild producing a 'cellular and promiscuous' residential style of inward-looking, dead-end alleys, courts and blindbacks, a 'perfect wilderness of foulness' (Daunton 1983). The area Murray seems to be referring to as 'the lower part of the town' is the East End of Sunderland, an area that then, as now, housed low-income families. The area became increasingly overcrowded due to the influx of industrial workers, some of whom were Irish labourers (see Belchem 1990 for an overview of Irish immigrant experience in industrial England) who came seeking work at the time of the great famine. In 1851, 5.7 per cent of East Enders were Irish (Census Enumerators Returns 1851). Although most writers portray the bleaker aspects of life in the East End in the industrial age, Corfe believes that 'poverty and squalor, depravity and ignorance didn't necessarily mean that the East End was an unhappy place. On the contrary, outsiders and residents alike felt its inhabitants for the most part enjoyed life; there was a strong sense of group loyalty and good neigh-bourliness; they worked hard and played hard' (in Milburn and Miller 1988: 79).

Many male inhabitants of Sunderland's' East End were seamen, a group described by shipping owners as an 'ignorant, disloyal, drunken rabble' (Plimsol 1873, republished 1980). It would seem that anyone employed as a seaman at this time had good reason to drown their sorrows, given the descriptions of their working conditions: 'The majority of merchant seamen . . . are broken down in health soon after the early age of 35 years, and the expectation of life of seamen (. . . at about 20 years of age) does not extend beyond the forty fifth or perhaps even fortieth year' (1867 'Report of the Society for Improving the Conditions of the Merchant Seamen'). The seamen 'worked harder and longer than the hardest working navvy ashore for wages less than those of the most common labourers, and in every port pimps, prostitutes and publicans waited to strip him of the wages he had' (Patterson 1988: 49).

It appears that seamen were not the only working group to work long and hard in poor working conditions and consequently seek some release in the little leisure time afforded them. Patterson (1988) describes the lot of miners in and around Sunderland as 'long hours of hard and dangerous toil' and comments: 'one master, who even owned the house the miner lived in', created 'particular types of community. On the positive side can be cited village solidarity . . . on the other, overcrowded and unsanitary living conditions, over-large families, huge infant mortality and premature death rates' (Patterson 1988: 47). Commenting on Monkwearmouth coal mine, Patterson points out that the moral elite of the mid nineteenth century believed the pits' close proximity to Sunderland proper could prove costly, quoting one George Eliot as believing that 'generally the neighbourhood of a town corrupts the colliery people. Fairs, dances, theatres, etc. seduce them. Drunkenness is prevalent here. The police prevent at present many disorders' (Patterson 1988: 47).

Although the general picture of Sunderland during the industrial eighteenth and nineteenth centuries is one of a thriving industrial town, albeit with a number of social problems, 'cycles of depression and boom and serious unemployment were always features of the economy of Sunderland and indeed the whole North East' (Dougan 1968: 221). An example of this can be seen in the serious slump in ship-building output in the 1880s (Smith and Holden 1946; Bowling 1958), which caused unemployment and poverty for many. *Shipping World* commented that the trade was never before in 'such a wretched state' and added: 'The present suffering is among a class of highly respectable artisans, self reliant, proud workmen, who will endure long rather than disclose their poverty and want' (cited in Clarke 1988) Some in the town were so impoverished that the food was taken from pigs' troughs and the Medical Officer of Health reported, 'their homes are bare of furniture, their clothes scanty, the season promises cold and fires are a luxury which they cannot afford'

(Clarke 1988: 39). This slump coincided with the general decline of Sunderland's other industries, and when the town emerged from it, shipbuilding was of even more importance to the region.

The collapse of the world economy in the 1930s also greatly affected the town (see Pickard 1989; Roberts 1993). Unemployment in shipbuilding shot up to 74.9 per cent, comprising of a variety of skilled and highly skilled trades. Overall, the level of unemployment in 1931 was 36.6 per cent (Miller 1989: 95), and the plight of the poor was made worse with the introduction of the Means Test in 1931, which promptly entered lower class folklore (Miller 1989). To those who lived through it, it must have seemed that the Means Test was designed to torment and humiliate. National as well as local narratives exist of people being told to sell the sideboard before qualifying for benefit, of parish boots with holes punched in the back to prevent them being pawned, of children having to support their parents with their meagre earnings, as well as of the pleasure to be gained from evading the authorities by creating fictional addresses for young people, thus avoiding their wages being taken into account when their father applied for benefit, or of passing possessions via the back door to neighbours when the 'Means Test Man' was at the front (Patterson 1988: 169).

The War Years

Preparations for the Second World War restored full employment after policies of appeasement towards Hitler reached their limits and war seemed inevitable. Rearming was well under way by 1938 and the arrival of war the following year guaranteed a busy industrial period for Wearside and the North East (Corfe 1973; Miller 1989). Coal was essential for the country's industrial production and was consequently in great demand; armament factories on Tyneside were creating maximum output and two Royal Ordnance factories were established in Spennymoor and Aycliffe (Bowling 1958). In shipbuilding, all the North Eastern yards were at full production levels as war losses needed to be replaced, passenger liners were converted in readiness for military duties and oil tankers needed for the domestic war effort. An influx of work was not immediate, however, as some production was shifted to the west coast for strategic reasons during the early war years before being transferred back and increasing in quantity following the heavy bombing of London and Liverpool (Mearns 1998: 124). As Bowling (1958: 289) records, 'the war record of Sunderland is never likely to be surpassed, for one quarter of the merchant tonnage built in Britain between 1939 and 1945 came from the eight Wear shipyards.'

Other factories opened to satisfy the need for armaments and other industrial manufacturing, and also relieved growing social problems and unemployment.

Jarrow, for instance, which had suffered greatly during the slump in industrial production during the late 1920s and 1930s, and became conspicuous after its 'March for Jobs' to London, saw three out of every four men unemployed after the closure of Palmer's shipyard (Bowling 1958: 283). However, 1938 brought a new steel works, which was in full production throughout the war years. Chemical works on Teesside were kept equally busy. Such was the need for industrial labour that for the first time women and girls were employed in the Royal Ordnance factories (Bowling 1958: 289; Blair 1988).

Sunderland and the North East's experience of war was not entirely restricted to industrial production, however, for as Mearns (1998: 124) points out: 'During the Second World War, Sunderland suffered gravely at the hands of the Luftwaffe, its civilian population and civil defence personnel bearing the brunt with almost three hundred fatalities being caused among them. It is said that the town was the most heavily bombed in the country, north of Hull.' The bombing occurred as industrial production was targeted. 'In spite of being attacked on many occasions, the port itself escaped remarkably lightly, especially when its importance as a shipbuilding centre is taken into account. Nevertheless, some serious damage was caused to shipbuilding and repair yards' (Mearns 1998).

The war was obviously a very important period in terms of changing gender roles (see Marwick 1974; Mallier and Rosser 1987). Women began to take on employment previously occupied solely by men and, although the return of men from war meant the reallocation of jobs, gender relations were altered (see Williams 1989), society, and the role of women within it, began to modernize. Moreover, men's experience of war also had an influence upon images and self-images of maleness, though their return to the workplace did not guarantee continued boom for the regions' major industries.

The Industrial Post-war Period in Brief

In 1960, coal mining in the Sunderland area employed 18,000 workers. By the 1980s this had reduced to 2,000 at Wearmouth colliery, which has now also closed. Today, on the site of the old Wearmouth colliery, stands the 'Stadium of Light', Sunderland AFC's new (1997) football ground.

In shipbuilding around 20,000 workers were also employed in the 1960s, but this figure had gradually whittled down to 2,000 in 1988, when shipbuilding on the River Wear was extinguished completely (Miller 1989: 104; see Roberts 1993 for a thorough discussion and analysis of post-war shipbuilding on the Wear). All in all, over 34,000 jobs were lost between 1971 and 1981 alone (Stone, Stevens and Morris 1986). As early as 1969, the urban ecologist Brian Robson (1969: 75) described Sunderland as 'a town which is living on the dwindling fat of its Victorian expansion', a description which proved remarkably apt. David Byrne of Durham University, who studied three north-eastern areas, analogously noted the 'industrial emaciation' of Sunderland, and gives detailed statistical evidence of this trend (Byrne 1993).

By January 1986 unemployment stood at 22.7 per cent in Sunderland, compared to 13.9 per cent nationally. The high rate of unemployment among young males was particularly disturbing, as was the tendency towards long-term joblessness (Stone et al. 1986: 105) and unemployment blackspots. For example when Sunderland's Ryhope coal mine closed in 1966, 69 per cent of the village's males had been employed there and were left without work. The dismay and depression that swept the area were considerable (HMSO 1970). Byrne has also noted the development of significant 'clusters' of unemployment, and their social and economic impact right through this period (1993).

The physical appearance of the city has also changed considerably. Most towns adopt a particular working-class housing style: tenements in Glasgow, tunnel backs in the East Midlands, and flats on Tyneside. However, in Sunderland this was never really the case, as single storey terraces were often used to house industrial workers and especially the miners (Muthesius 1982: 104). Slums developed and were subsequently cleared away from the centre of the town, while large new council estates were created on the periphery, and these brought their own problems (Byrne 1989). The 1960s saw the creation of Town End Farm, Downhill, Witherwack, Gilley Law, Mill Hill and others as the numbers of people living in the centre of town plummeted. By 1980, 56 per cent of all housing in Sunderland was council owned and only 38 per cent owner occupied. (See Commission on Urban Priority Areas 1984, which points out that in non-London conurbations, the grimmest social conditions are found in local authority 'outer estates'. See also Centre for Environmental Studies 1983; Byrne 1989).

In 1963, out of a total labour force of 85,000, 41 per cent was in manufacturing with only 5,000 female employees. By 1985 nearly half of the labour force was female, reflecting the switch from manufacturing to service industries as well as the changing role of women in society (Blair 1988: 203).

The decline of Sunderland's shipyards was paralleled by the nation's decline in world shipping. In 1963 Britain still occupied second place in world tonnage, yet by 1983 it had sunk to sixth place (Blair 1988: 202). Despite an atmosphere of impending doom an energetic campaign was mounted to 'save our shipyards', amid questions as to whether or not the town could survive without the industry that had supported it for so long (see *Sunderland Echo*, 11 October 1984). The close relationship between the river, employment, the home and community life, noted by Hopkins (1954), was threatened.

Attempts were made to replace Sunderland's dying industries at a number of new sites away from the river and the town's former industrial centre. Television components, radio and electrical equipment, clothing and mail order firms had been attracted in the post-war period, but all tended to employ part-time female labour, the implications of which I shall not attempt of summarize at this point (see, for example, Walby 1986; Beechey 1987; Beechey and Whitelegg 1986).

Thanks to massive subsidies, and with hopes boosted for a resurrection of industry in the area, the Nissan car plant arrived in Sunderland in 1984. This brought with it a different work ethos, however, for those who wished to work would have to do so the 'Nissan Way' (Garrahan and Stewart 1992; see also Garrahan 1986). Other related industries have also come to the area, yet unemployment still remains a problem and government initiatives to create jobs and redevelop the area do not appear to have been greatly effective (see, for example, Robinson, Lawrence and Shaw 1993). Stone et al. (1986: 2–3) sum up Sunderland's economic status as follows:

> All the underlying structural features which disadvantage the region's economy – over-representation of the slow growing industries, lack of local control, R and D activity, poorly developed business services and a weaker small firms sector- apply to the Wearside economy . . . [It] suffers from low incomes and an above average dependence on welfare benefits which adversely affect the demand for local services, overshadowing by the regional capital, and diminishing local advantages relative to the other parts of the region.

In 1998 the region once again began a period of de-industrialization. New manufacturing firms that had been attracted to the area at considerable cost have closed. Highly skilled workmen have been made redundant, for instance, at Fujitsu and Seimens; and numerous other plants have closed, apparently because of the strength of the pound in a competitive world marketplace and the supposed collapse of the Asian economy, where many of these companies find their main base. Perhaps most typical of this spate of closures is the 1998 collapse of Grove Cranes in Sunderland, an American company that had taken over a crane-manufacturing plant that has existed at its Wearside site for over seventy years. Traditional trades such as fabricating, welding and boilermaking have been lost, along with over 670 jobs and, with the average age of the redundant employees standing at 47, their job prospects, given their trades and ages, are bleak.

Sunderland, therefore, certainly does not represent a thrilling roller-coaster ride through the annals of history. It has not been a great seat of democracy or government; no battles of great significance have occurred here; it is not and never has been a centre of culture or art or significant intellectual thought. It has not been subject to great waves of immigrants who have added to and helped shape its current culture. Sunderland is a perfect example of a locality firmly rooted in the industrial modern age, and which is currently transforming economically, socially and culturally to cope with the advent of post-industrial and post-modern society.

Working-class Masculinity in Sunderland in the Modern Industrial Age

> Economic circumstance and organizational structure enter into the making of masculinity at the most intimate level.
>
> (Connell 1995: 36)

Introduction: Masculinity

Not surprisingly, the rapidly growing literature on men and masculinities offers a multitude of definitions of masculinity. However, there appears to be a fair degree of consensus on just what the word means. By way of introduction, it is perhaps useful to look at Brannon's anecdotal ideas on the basic rules of manhood:

> 'No sissy stuff' – only behaviour with no hint of femininity is allowed.
> 'Be a big wheel' – be powerful and successful.
> 'Be a sturdy oak' – show no emotions; be dependable.
> 'Give 'em hell' – take chances, be daring etc.
>
> (Brannon 1976: 5)

Brannon's summary of the basic characteristics of manhood in the modern age comprises a number of basic images of masculinity, which have been added to and analysed by a number of authors. The vast majority of contemporary works on masculinity indicate how it is vital to begin with the understanding that there is no universal masculinity; rather there are a number of masculinities with similar and extremely different component parts. (See Morgan 1992: 80–98 for an interesting discussion on the functions, formations and characteristics of heavy manual labour masculinities as opposed to those of light, clean labour, and so forth.) It should be remembered I am discussing here a specific working-class masculinity, which is operative in a specific time and space, and I attempt no generalizations. For the purposes of clarity, however, it should be noted that 'masculinity is not . . . the possession or non-possession of certain traits. It is to do with the maintenance of certain kinds of relationships between men and women, and between men' (Morgan 1992: 67). Crucially, Brittan also points out that 'masculinity refers to those aspects of men's behaviour that fluctuate over time. In some cases these fluctuations may last for decades – in others it may be a matter of weeks or months' (Brittan 1989: 3). Strate has similarly argued that 'masculinity is a social construction . . . The foundation may be biological, but the structure is manmade; it is also flexible, subject to change over time and differing significantly from culture to culture' (Strate in Craig 1992: 79). Meanwhile, Gutmann claims that 'gender identities, roles, and relationships do not remain frozen in place, either for individuals or for groups.

There is continuous contest and confusion over what constitutes male identity; it means different things to different people at different times. And sometimes different things to the same person at the same time' (1996: 27).

Other definitions indicate that what it means to be a man changes over time, and this scholarly structure is central to the understanding of this book. Below, I offer an introduction to North Eastern working-class masculinity during the modern industrial period, and this should be compared to my depiction of North Eastern working-class masculinity in the contemporary post-industrial and post-modern urban landscape. As will be shown, economic and cultural change has significantly re-shaped masculinity in this environment.

Industrial Masculinities

It is impossible to understand the shaping of working-class masculinities without giving full weight to their class as well as their gender politics

(Connell 1995: 75)

Sunderland and the surrounding areas relied heavily on shipbuilding and coal mining to employ their menfolk during the modern age (for example, Bowling 1958; Mitchell 1919). Although periods of recession and unemployment did occur, notably in the 1930s, working-class men could usually find work in one of these occupations, or in some connected field. Shipyard workers worked a six-day week, twelve hours a day up until 1871. Much of their work was considered highly skilled, comprising trades in which men would take pride in their ability to compete, and wages often reflected this (Corfe 1973: 78–9). In 1882 shipwrights in the port of Sunderland were reputed to have wages three or four shillings higher than men in the same trade in Newcastle. The men who worked in the shipyards around this time were 'skilled and of a hardy breed . . . [with] considerable strength . . . [needed] to carry out their activities' (Mitchell 1919: 142). The keelmen, whose trade was a common one at the time involving the transportation of coal from the colliery to the port were described by Mitchell (1919: 144) as a 'brave and hardy class . . . as a race they were generally strong, thick set, many of them tall heavy men'. It was by such men that the area became inhabited, especially as considerable strength, stamina and skill were also needed in coal mining at the number of local collieries that existed in outlying areas. The entrepreneurial classes profiting from Sunderland's growth, distanced themselves from the coarser element that now inhabited the centre of town. Although most working men possessed considerable skill in the application of their trades, they must still be considered to have formed the very basis of the working class, and in the modern age, Sunderland must be considered as having been overwhelmingly a working class town.

Men born in this and many other working-class areas in the early twentieth century were socialized to believe that hard physical labour was a manly pursuit, not only by Victorian (see Grint 1991) and Calvinist (see Weber 1958) ideals, but also according to those of their peers and family (for example, Jackson 1968; Rose 1968; Benson 1985; see also Pickard 1989 for some excellent oral histories from shipyard workers). Young boys were keen to enter the world of work as soon as possible and thereby establish their masculinity. Jack Hilton recalls that as a boy of twelve he

> wanted to be like the other men-boys . . . I wanted to be able to wear my cap on one side, to smoke a cigarette, and use language that would become my manhood . . . I'd be a little somebody at home, and mother would give me the deference due to a worker. I'd be able to open my mouth and my younger brothers and sisters would have to give me their lip. Soon I'd be full-time, and then would follow my new suit. I dreamed it all rosily.

(Common 1938: 7)

Newly employed boys proudly described their new status: 'When I started work of course I was the big he-man'; 'I now wanted to tell the world I was now a man'; 'it was not the money which encouraged me to work. I think it gave me a sense of manhood' (all quoted in Bourke 1994).

These young men all express a desire to *prove* their masculinity through physical labour. In this environment, 'a woman becomes a woman by following in her mother's footsteps, whereas . . . for a boy to become an adult, he must prove himself his – masculinity – among his peers. And although all boys may succeed in reaching manhood, cultures treat this development as something that each individual has achieved' (Rosaldo: 28). As is clear, many of the attributes required to claim the status of a man are linked with work.

The importance of work to the industrial working man cannot be overemphasized. As Morgan (1992: 76) points out, 'work, in both a general and specific sense, is assumed to be a major basis of identity, and of what it means to be a man'. Nevertheless 'men's relationship with work is complex. They need it in order to survive and yet it can destroy them' (Hodson 1984). Men could not easily neglect the social, cultural and economic pressures to provide for their families and adopt the role of breadwinner. Literature on other working-class masculine forms in the North East during this period is hard to locate (for instance, we know little of homosexual masculinities and communities), and it is likely that all forms of working-class masculinities relate in some way to the economic order.

As the above oral histories seem to confirm, work was the primary place in which men attempted to prove themselves and legitimate their image and self-image as men (Ford 1985). Rose (1992) has argued that working class self-respect and concepts of manliness were constructed in response to class deprivation and the paternalism of capitalism, and at the same time was defined against working-class women. Rose also argues that the strategy of the 'family wage', which long depressed women's wages in the twentieth century, grew out of this interplay (Rose 1992). This may be so, but it should also be noted that, for a man, 'the pressure to be a successful breadwinner was a source of strain and conflict, not pride and motivation' (Kimmel 1996: 265).

Being able to keep a wife and family was often seen as a form of working-class responsibility and respectability (see, for example, Lewis 1986; Pickard 1989; McClelland 1991) and failure to do so was seen as indicating the opposite. As McClelland found, the strong link between work and masculinity meant that periods of unemployment were experienced 'not only as economic but also as psychic depression' (1991: 78).

The failure to find masculinity-affirming work 'carried much greater hardships, materially during the 1930s depression, than it does in the recession today. However, comparative studies have shown that the psychological effects are very much the same, with the unemployed going through various stages of reaction to redundancy, ranging from initial shock and disbelief to ultimate fatalism and depression' (Ingham 1984; see also Humphries 1981). Not only did the failure to work remove the ability to support one's family, but also attacked masculine self-identities by dislodging the 'fundamental importance of independence' (Ingham 1984). Being a man in this time and space meant working; while the failure to do so meant the virtual removal of that identity (see Morgan 1992: Chapter 5 for a thorough discussion of unemployment as a challenge to masculinity).

In the heavy industries that dominated the North East, simply working was not an end in itself as regards this particular working-class masculinity; a complex system of negotiation and confirmation operated within the workplace, which ultimately formed significant structures on which this masculinity came to rely. The workplace represented an environment where masculinity could be re-examined, reinterpreted and reaffirmed. These workplaces were almost completely male environments where the basic elements of masculinity were accentuated, and where behaviour was tested and categorized and took on both specific and changing meanings. For example, Donaldson (1991) claims that hard labour in factories and mines literally used up workers' bodies, and that undergoing this destruction, as proof of the toughness of the work and the worker, can be a method of demonstrating masculinity.

While hard, physical work is an obvious expression of this masculinity, a positive male image could also be attained by the development of levels of skill in particular trades (see, for example, Pickard 1989; Roberts 1993). This is perhaps particularly pertinent in the shipbuilding industry; here we see men building what were often huge, steel ocean going ships. The product of their skill and physical exertion was a 'manly' construction in which the workers could invest a certain sense of worth and accomplishment; workers could point out the huge construction to their sons, and say 'your dad built that' (see Roberts 1993). The symbolism was usually completed by the ships crashing into the River Wear in front of thousands of amassed workers and townspeople.

The heavy industrial workplace was an environment in which friendships were formed and one's sense of self negotiated. As Kimmel (1996: 7) points out, 'in large part, it is other men who are important to . . . men; . . . men define their masculinity, not as much in relation to women, but in relation to each other.' Consequently, the workplace as a male preserve took on considerable importance in terms of the construction of masculinities. It was a place in which a wide range of social relationships helped to shape working men's images of the world around them and confirmed the separation of work and home life. 'Men's friendships are marked by shared activities. Their talk usually centers [sic] around work, sports, and sharing expertise. Men also trade complaints and concerns about women along with talk of exploits, but most of the time their interactions are emotionally contained and controlled' (Spangler 1992: 95).

Men not only expressed their maleness in a form of 'shop floor masculinity' (Willis 1977; 1979; see also Joyce 1982) involving strength, skill, autonomy, camaraderie and the ability to provide for his family, but also incorporated other working-class male traits. A lack of respect towards authority and having a 'laff' (Willis 1977) existed alongside the desire to be released from the bonds of responsibility. At that time, this was often linked to alcohol consumption (which can act and be used as a means of expressing masculinity, especially if an individual can drink and 'hold' more than his peers – see also Vigil and Long 1990) and by disappearing down to the pub. A young boy recalls his father used to call

> at the ale house on Saturday night, and spend half his money before he came home; my mother would sit crying, not knowing how the shop bill would be paid. About twelve o'clock my father would come home drunk as a pig.
>
> (Quoted in Anderson 1980.)

Pubs have traditionally been the domain of male working-class culture (Harrison 1943; Gorman and Dunnett 1950; Dennis, Henriques and Slaughter 1956), and for the working man in Sunderland, and elsewhere, the pub provided a welcome escape from the problems of everyday life (see, for example, Harrison 1943; Cavan 1966: 205; Gill 1977) as well as a habitat in which maleness could be fully explored. Crucially, working-class male culture in modern Sunderland also incorporated violence and an 'immediate aggressive style of behaviour' that Tolson (1977) believes was born out of 'memories of poverty, and physical insecurity, rather than a [middle class] nostalgia for Victorian provincial life' or a 'vision of personal achievement'. History reveals that the mixture of these two masculinity-enhancing activities, drinking and violence, was common (Conlin 1969; Mearns 1998;

Thompson 1998). Although 'men are not simply the passive embodiments of the masculine ideology' (Brittan 1989: 68), it is fair to say that the 'hegemonic' masculine image (see Connell 1987) – if it is possible to conceive of such a notion (Hall et al. forthcoming) – fitted alongside the more obvious North Eastern working-class male image, especially in this period.

Nichols and Beynon's study, *Living with Capitalism* (1977), revealed characters who held the belief that 'northernness' had particular connotations of masculinity. Their influential character, 'Tommy Robson', celebrated a supposed 'northern' strength as opposed to 'southern' weakness, and Nichols and Beynon portray him as the archetypal working man. A number of interviews carried out by the author would seem to confirm this belief, with a number of respondents in the North East reaffirming their male identity by deriding southerners' lack of an industrial past and the fact they have not suffered and managed the trials of heavy labour as North Easterners have. While evidence for this pattern of North Eastern working-class masculinity remains anecdotal, we can see an attempt on the part of such men to positively differentiate themselves from 'otherness' and consequently justify their particular 'male epistemological stance' (MacKinnon 1982).

The above is a brief introduction to the most obvious structures of working class masculinity in the modern, industrial North East of England. Before proceeding to examine less mainstream aspects of this masculinity, I offer the following statement by Tolson (1977: 13) as a useful summation of the central issues of industry and manhood during this period and in this locale:

> In Western, industrialised, capitalist societies, definitions of masculinity are bound up with definitions of work. Whether it is in terms of physical strength or mechanical expertise, or in terms of ambitions and competitiveness the qualities needed by the successful worker are closely related to those of successful man. As individuals, men are brought up to value work, as an end in itself, and to fix their personal identities around particular occupations.

Masculinity, Crime and Working-class Culture in the Modern Era

> Even as small boys, males are trained for a world of independent aggressive action . . . males are groomed to take the universe by storm, to confront the environment directly. Males learn that society's goals are best met by aggression, by actively wrestling their accomplishments from the environment. Force, power, competition and aggression are the means . . . In the Western world, the importance of self reliant, individual action is systematically inculcated in males. To be masculine requires not only self reliance and self control, but control over other people and resources.
>
> (Lipman-Blumen 1984: 55)

Crime throughout the modern era in Sunderland and the North East must be seen in the light of *opportunity* (Cloward 1959: 164–76; Cloward and Ohlin 1960). Working-class males in the area were far from free to become any kind of criminal they liked. Criminal roles were learned through cultural transmission, which in the legitimate world of work included robust physicality, an 'immediate, aggressive style of behaviour' (Tolson 1977), in group loyalty (commonly seen in union membership: see Corfe 1973 for local view; Hyman 1984, and so forth), in traditional masculine displays of drinking and toughness, and a present-time orientation as well as the more virtuous occupations of hard toil and providing for one's family, which of course were more important to some than to others. These legitimate male role protocols can tentatively be said to be mirrored in the illegitimate world.

Sunderland and its surrounding areas were without a thriving entrepreneurial ethic, a community characteristic that can be found elsewhere in the modern age (Hobbs 1988). As Sunderland should be considered a working-class town throughout this era, it is safe to say that most working-class males accepted the existing male role of finding an income by selling their labour, and as working-class males often fought against the school system (Willis 1977; Corrigan 1979) or were denied access to it and therefore failed to gain any significant educational qualifications. This usually resulted in then being ultimately involved in manual employment (see, for example, Robins and Cohen 1978; Belcham 1990). Gaining an income in the field of business, any kind of business, was rarely considered by males, as there were few cases of people in their communities who had done this successfully, or had even tried and failed.

Criminality in Sunderland followed a similar path. Working-class males were restricted in the ways in which they could express their desire to acquire a higher status than their peers. Lower class youths used the adult male cultural precedents as a basis for their delinquency, 'a set of ready-made definitions of the situation that each individual only slightly re-tailors in his own way' (Downes 1966: 4). Denied access to criminal hierarchies, organized criminal apprenticeships and recognizable successful criminal role models, the youths of Sunderland's lowest income areas were also denied the possibility of fashioning a criminal career and were therefore pushed towards a delinquency, which was not wholly different from the dominant adult male culture. Daly and Wilson claim 'men's violence towards men involves a masculinity of status competition and bravado among peers' (1988; see also Polk and Ranson 1991), and indeed violence can be seen as a common means by which they could rise above the throng of working-class youths who also inhabited their neighbourhoods and others like it across the town (see Cloward and Ohlin 1960 on conflict-orientated subcultures). Violence was also a crucial signifier of self-image, a reflection upon a culture that favourably judged those who maintained a credible threat of violence.

Other forms of delinquency would rarely yield great financial returns and would often be linked to a lower class youthful desire to engage in delinquency 'for the hell of it'; acts that might often be contemptuous of authority and might seem irrational to conventional citizens (Cohen 1955: 25). Along with Merton (1938) and Cohen (1955), Cloward and Ohlin (1960: 86) claim 'the disparity between what lower class youths are led to want and what is actually available to them is the source of adjustment', which causes 'intense frustration' so that 'exploration of nonconformist alternatives may be the result'. These writers focused on America, but the same may be true of Sunderland as the end of the modern era arrived and industrialism along the banks of the Wear greatly diminished. Certainly it seems to be the case in the post-modern post-industrial age. During periods of full employment in the early to mid industrial modern age, however, there was no disparity between what working-class male youths were led to desire and what they could actually achieve. From c.1850 to c.1940 working class males youths were not raised with the expectation of achieving 'the American dream' or its English equivalent; rather they were socialized in accordance with a fatalism that led them to believe their lot was basically to follow their father into one of the dominant local industries (see Willis 1977; Liebow 1967: 223).

It must be noted that delinquent lower class male activities in the area were not entirely divorced from wider male culture. Tolson (1977: 43) notes that a kind of performance is at work in working-class males, when 'aggression is the basis of "style", of feeling physical, of showing feelings and protecting oneself' and in this context 'performance' means exhibiting a measure of the general lower class masculine role, as well as that which Cloward and Ohlin have termed the 'conflict orientated sub-culture' (1960). Matza (1966: 28) has claimed 'the delinquent transiently exists in a limbo between convention and crime . . . postponing commitment, evading decision', and as a result many males would become involved in what we can term 'delinquency' without ever completely rejecting the wider social conventions of behaviour in this working-class environment. Indeed, much 'conflict' orientated delinquency (Cloward and Ohlin 1960) can be 'neutralized', with individuals being able to view their behaviour as being no more than normative for the environment in which they live (see Sykes and Matza 1957).

Although crime and delinquency in and around Sunderland in the modern era were not restricted to conflict-orientated action, much delinquency followed this course (see Conlin 1969; Mearns 1998) and a great deal of the literature on crime in the North East during this period is restricted to tales of grisly murders and extreme violence. Little else is mentioned (see, for example, Conlin 1969; Thompson 1998), however, and celebrated cases of murder were rarely the result of financial imperatives (Thompson 1998). Authors occasionally have recounted details of petty theft, pilfering and the like. Mearns, for example, points out:

The River Wear Commissioners [in Sunderland 1900–13] expressed their concern over the amount of theft and pilfering which was taking place in the docks and on the river. It appeared that, on many occasions, the police were experiencing difficulties in persuading anyone to prosecute the offenders. There were always loafers about the docks, but the police had no powers to prevent them from being there, the docks being a public thoroughfare.

(Mearns 1998: 91)

Where notable criminals did exist in the North East, their activities were usually limited to petty theft and violence (see Mearns 1998: 70–1 on 'a river pirate named Thompson' c.1870–1900) and, as I will go on to describe, were occasionally involved in offering protection.

As I mentioned above, crime as a means of making money was not often a course open to lower class males in the area, though criminality did exist, and this may lead us to believe a measure of entrepreneurship did exist in industrial Sunderland. As Henry and Mars have noted (1978), most industries provide an opportunity for illegal activity (see, for example, Faberman 1975; Ditton 1977; Henry 1978; Denzin 1978), and shipbuilding and coalmining in and around Sunderland were no exception. For example, Humphries (1981: 163–4) notes: 'Picking coal from pit heads and slag heaps was so deeply ingrained . . . that it formed part of the daily domestic routine for many children, who were expected to salvage coal both before and after school' (Roberts uses the term 'yackers' to describe people engaged in this practice (1993: 8); see also Hitchin 1962).

Over the course of my research I heard numerous tales of petty pilfering and profit-making schemes from Sunderland's industrial past, most describing activities on a similar scale to the example above. Many were on a small scale and may simply involve the smuggling of tools, raw materials or other equipment from the place of work. Often a transient trading network would arise, for example, when a friend required a metal bracket of specific dimensions he would ask a friend who worked at a shipyard to construct it at work, smuggle it out of work and forward it to him. The person requiring the bracket would often not provide payment – indeed the object would be of minimal value. He might, instead, provide a similar service – perhaps a quantity of fish if he worked at the docks, a new pair of work boots if he worked in a store room of a factory, free labour if it was needed, especially if they were in a useful trade. As Henry points out, business is not always assessed in financial terms and can involve a system of 'reciprocal favours' (1978: 33–4) similar to that described above. The importance of reciprocal favours is not their 'material worth' but their role in 'fulfilling the expectations and moral obligation of the friendly relationship' (Henry 1978: 99). Mars (1982: 174) is perceptive in arguing that 'if money is the medium of exchange in material dealings, drink is often the medium of exchange in personal dealings.' Of course goods might also be taken from work by employees for their own use: tools to complete a job around the house, a new bracket, or some other object.

Mars defines the 'fiddle' as:

> The movement of resources to individual private use that do not appear in official account . . . or that appear in official accounts under different headings and which are acquired by individuals through their relationship to a job. These resources may derive directly from the job itself or be allocated from outside sources that relate to the job.
>
> (Mars 1982)

Mars (1982: 164–5) uses the word 'fiddle' to describe these activities, as he believes it is relatively neutral, but allows us to feel some empathy with the fiddler. By contrast, using the word 'theft' would force us outside the fiddler's view of his own actions. It is unlikely that those engaged in these practices, both past and present, see their activities as any more than a fairly harmless manipulation of their employers' time and equipment, a means of extracting their true worth from the company for which they worked. Such fiddles, commonplace throughout the modern era and throughout history as a whole (Ditton, 1977b; Henry, 1978), seem to be a very basic form of entrepreneurial activity. In the social context discussed here, however, fiddles in the workplace seem to be linked with employees' desire to extract the industrial version of 'perks', a means of reducing the perceived difference between their weekly wage and what they feel they are actually worth – of reducing the 'surplus value' (Marx 1972) claimed by the employer. Many involved in these activities will not see themselves as entrepreneurial, but we may judge them to be so, even though they may not act in a businesslike way, engage in a marketplace, or make money. What we can deduce, however, is that although some illegal entrepreneuriality did exist in industrial Sunderland, it was rarely seen as illegal by those who took part in it and generally was not propelled by the desire to make money but by other social concerns mentioned elsewhere in this book. Deviant entrepreneuriality of this kind should therefore be seen as being present in industrial Sunderland; importantly, however, unlike other deviant pursuits it was not seen as an activity worthy of cultural recognition by working-class males.

As I noted above, one major deviant activity that was worthy of cultural recognition by working-class males in the modern industrial era was the conspicuous use of violence. The ideal of maintaining face (see Goffman 1967, 1971) by controlling and expanding personal space was a vital concern, both culturally and personally. For many working-class males, the fact of not letting another invade your personal domain or bodily space, either in a pub or elsewhere, was crucial, as was a willingness to defend that domain irrespective of the odds of a successful defence. As Daly and Wilson (1988) point out:

A seemingly minor affront is not merely a stimulus to action, isolated in time and space. It must be understood within a larger social context of reputation, face, relative social status, and enduring relationships. Men are known by their fellows as 'the sort who can be pushed around' or 'the sort who won't take any shit', as guys whose girlfriends you can chat up with impunity or guys you don't want to mess with. In most social milieus, a man's reputation depends in part upon the maintenance of a credible threat of violence.

To be dominated by another, or to let an affront go, was and is a process that can strip many working-class males of their image of themselves, and change their image in the eyes of others. Modifications are made, and just how much a person will take and from whom will be noted and stored for later reference. Katz (1988: 332) points out that 'A physical fight can be nothing more than a show of toughness, while a stare-down can accomplish a consummate act of meanness.' A subliminal hierarchy is formed in which individuals place themselves, using their knowledge of others and themselves, as a yardstick. The hierarchy is more overtly seen in actual confrontation and in the willingness to participate in it. It is overt in that one person's pre-eminence over another may be obvious to all observers and participants, though much is left unsaid. Moreover, non-violent confrontations are also taken as indicators, and odds of success are mentally calculated; much as a bookmaker may decide the favourite in a forthcoming football match by computing that *a* defeated *b*, *b* defeated *c*, *c* defeated *d* but *d* defeated *a,* so who is the favourite in a confrontation between *a* and *c*? Opinions vary, and an abundance of factors are taken into consideration and act as indicators. Some observers and participants may be in possession of more indicators than others, although no one is sure as to how many indicators other players are in possession of; some will dismiss some indicators as being unimportant, and, as happens in betting, some may just have a 'feeling'. The hierarchy is never clear and positions in it are only generalizations; for nobody is quite sure who ranks higher than whom, and supposed ranks are constantly adjusted as new indicators arise. Some individuals may rise rapidly, others may remain in what may generally be called 'near the top' for a long time without having to defend their position. Everything is fluid and the hierarchy is never referred to as such. Although observers and participants will often discuss it, they never refer to it, and simply establish positions (which are also not referred to) on the basis of individual confrontations and their imagined consequences.

Perceptions of honour and shame (see Armstrong 1998: 233–61) are of course integral to ideas of self. Friedrichs (1977: 284) has argued that honour provides a structure for a 'system of symbols, values, and definitions' as well as 'categories, rules, and processes . . . which may be specific to the given culture'. Violence and the act of negotiating a route through life that maintains honour and avoids cultural definitions of shame are a central concern of the masculinities in this domain. As Bourdieu (1979: 115) has written, perceptions of honour are strongest in those who see themselves through the eyes of others, and the cultural importance of violence, reputation and violent reputation are exceptionally strong among active criminals and 'hard' men alike.

In some instances the maintenance of honour supplants all other concerns, and as I carried out the ethnography on the character I call Michael in Chapter 3, I witnessed one such example, when a customer in a pub received a severe beating when he would not give up a stool previously occupied by his aggressor. This man knew the reputation of the aggressor and knew what was about to take place, yet he sacrificed his safety, and indeed put his life on the line, to maintain his honour and not appear to observers to be subject to the will of the aggressor (see Pitt-Rivers 1966: 77 on verbal challenges to honour). In attempting to defend himself, he failed, and was beaten up, but maintained face and honour, and indeed among some observers he amplified his status. Taking the beating was undoubtedly a terrible experience, but was worthwhile to the man in terms of honour maintenance; and was understood and empathized with by the observing male culture. There were many other instances of this kind, while other episodes allowed me to witness these same processes operating in terms of negotiation. Faced with a similar situation one man successfully defused the situation with humour, and, in another case I know of, the combatants avoided the crucial determining factor of a pub audience by retreating to a toilet resolved a dispute. As I have said, violence need not always be the result.

To continue the earlier betting analogy, the mental acknowledgement of the hierarchy and its actual playing out contain a 'sensual' aspect (Hobbs and Robbins 1991, speak of 'a euphoric, hyped up sensation') which few males can ignore. Some like to participate and some to observe, but most acknowledge the excitement. Combining this sensual dynamic with the cultural importance of violence leads some to simply observe the hierarchy, to admire its participants and to envy the status they receive, or exist on the lower slopes of it, which merge with virtually the entire working class male population of the area. Some acknowledge the status and the various privileges accorded to those in the upper echelons of the hierarchy and define their personality partly in terms of reaping some of the benefits of serious engagement in the hierarchy; all the while attempting to steer a course to avoid the less appealing aspects of serious engagement, which can range from wounded pride to death. Some avoid engagement completely and attempt to define an aspect of their personality in terms of non-violence (especially those who are able to improve their class position). Nevertheless they will acknowledge the appeal of violent capability, of not being subject to the will of others, and thus display at least a dilution of their working-class cultural inheritance. Some who are aware of the status and privileges accorded to those who are adept at violence will define themselves solely in those terms; amplifying their violence in an attempt to spread the word to all observers and participants that they will meet any challenge, overt or covert, and that they are the embodiment of the local masculine form and are to be feared. In the modern industrial era such individuals were 'hard' men; in the post-industrial era many have been transformed into bouncers.

All participants in the culture must negotiate some contact and engagement with violence and its cultural values and signals. Even females are forced to recognize the cultural importance of violent men and in some locations define their femininity in relation to the dominant men in the environment. Some females clearly set out to ensnare a dominant male, though this will be for cultural rather than genetic reasons, for they receive the minimal perks of being a 'hard' man's women. Occasionally however they have to tolerate a downside in the form of court appearances, a violently fluctuating income, and the attentions of the police. In this context of cultural attraction I have witnessed women actively seek out the company of bouncers, a collective occasionally known as 'bouncer groupies' (see Chapter 3).

As this study pays particular attention to the changing role of 'hard' men and bouncers in the North East, I will now give a brief summary of meetings with a bouncer and 'hard' man I have called 'Tommy'. It is included at this point to help illustrate the implications of the social and cultural shift from the industrial modern era to the post-industrial, post-modern era in the lives of those who choose to follow this path. Tommy's career should be contrasted with the careers of those who were to follow him into this line of work in the post-modern era, and who appear later on in this book.

Violence, Opportunity and 'Hard' Men in the Modern Era

Tommy: A Brief Case Study

> 'Who loves not women, wine, and song,
> Remains a fool his whole life long.'
>
> (Martin Luther)

Tommy is 58 years old and looks like many men of his age who seem to be perennially attached to the same stool in the same pub. He has been present in the *Dog and Duck* public house on almost every occasion in the past two years when I have entered its trapped-in-time ambiance. Continue your observation of Tommy, however, and you might become aware that this man is slightly different from his peers at the *Dog and Duck*. He stands around five feet five or six and, although reasonably athletic for his age, his build is no more than average. His nose has been broken – not that this is especially unusual, but its shape (with a huge dint right in the middle) is quite something to behold. He has scar tissue around both eyebrows and his hands look gnarled, leading you to perhaps wonder if he was a boxer in his younger days. Pale blue tattoos peak out on to his forearms, but appear so old or are so poorly applied that it is difficult to make out what they are saying. His hair is almost completely gone and his clothes are such that, if after having spoken to him, you were asked what he was wearing, you might well struggle to find an answer. He seems friendly enough and will share a joke with those younger men who are beginning to become regulars at the pub. The older clientele always seem pleased to see him, and again if you watch carefully you may see some of the better dressed patrons slide him a pint of beer over the bar, not making a big deal of it.

The *Dog and Duck* is situated in an outlying, low-income estate in Sunderland. I had been there to drink socially on several occasions, but became more of a regular as a number of contacts who helped me during the period of my research used the pub as a starter, before making their way on to the pubs and wine bars of Sunderland's city centre. Tommy always said 'hello'. Well, he'd say:

> One o' these days I'm gonna take the bastard lotta yez outside an' fuckin' kick the shite outta yez! Me an' Billy 'ere! [Billy, Tommy's diminutive friend of around seventy, would laugh so much he would usually break into a huge coughing fit that made his whole body shake.] I dinnit care how fuckin' big yez are! Yez'll fuckin' get it, am tellin' ye!

He was joking. If you'd walk away, he'd say you were a soft tart, and if you came back to the bar on another occasion he'd say, 'Oh, come to 'ave a go 'ave ya!' and off he'd go again. No one minded, and all the older men in the bar thought it was hilarious. He wouldn't always do this, and the more you went into the bar the less he'd do it, though sometimes he'd greet you with 'Alreet, ya big useless bastard!' If he didn't know your name and you were young, you were a 'big bastard', and if you were young and he did know your name you were 'Jimmy', or 'Tony' or 'Philly', but always with 'ya big useless bastard!' as a verbal appendage. Indeed, compared to him and the older men who sat around the bar the younger men did seem very big, perhaps signifying advances in nutrition, the greater stress on body shape in the post-modern age, or a general shrinkage because of advancing years.

It was not until much later that it became apparent to me that Tommy could be a potential source of information. An acquaintance mentioned that Tommy used to look after a number of pubs in his younger days in the same neighbourhood as the *Dog and Duck*. This naturally sparked my interest, and fuelled my efforts to get Tommy's story.

It was surprisingly easy to get Tommy to speak of times past. I arrived at the *Dog and Duck* in the afternoon, to avoid crowds and Tommy's desire to please them. He was seated on his usual stool and seemed quieter than normal, which I took as a good sign. Some of the other older regulars were seated nearby, playing dominoes. I chatted to Tommy for a short while about nothing in particular and led him into my desired area of conversation by mentioning mutual acquaintances, and that someone had told me he 'used to have the door' at the *King's Arms*. Tommy launched into the story in the way that many people do when they meet someone who wishes to listen to their reminiscences of times when they were younger and held a higher status than the one they presently occupy. I sat and listened to Tommy for around two hours on that occasion and, after revealing I was researching this kind of thing, every time I saw him from then on he would have thought of something else to tell me.

For some time in his youth Tommy had been a young tearaway in his neighbourhood. In this era the police rarely had hampered his appetite for violence, and in the outlying districts of Sunderland his reputation was allowed to flourish unchecked by the forces of law and order. Violent, and hard-drinking men and boys were not hard to find in Sunderland and Tommy was forced to distinguish himself to gain the notoriety he would receive. Although Tommy's size was an obvious hindrance, he overcame it by a sheer willingness to fight and use weapons in an era when foreheads, fists and boots were the standard tools of combat. He led groups of friends from his neighbourhood into combat against rival groups in local woods, so as not to alert the police, and took on men twice his size and often twice his age in the local pubs. If he could not win, he said, he'd fight them every day until he did. This of course is not an unusual tale of scaling the hierarchy of violence, but is a necessary backdrop to the events that led him into minding pubs. For publicans did not employ him for his size or menacing looks, but for his name and his role in the community.

SW: Which doors did you have?

Tommy: Well, diff'rent ones from time to time. 'Round 'ere I had *The King's* [*Arms*], *The Robin*, which is called *O'Donnell's* these days, The *Travellers Rest, The Red Lion* and sometimes the [working men's] club at the bottom there. I also worked at *The Palladium* which was an old Dance Hall in the sixties. But, y'knar I'd work wherever, but mainly them ones like.

SW: What did you do at these pubs?

Tommy: Well, what do you think? I was just there to stop any bother really, but a lot of the time there wouldn't be that much. The odd argument here and there, sometimes someone who wasn't from around here shouting his mouth off, but not much.

SW: How did you get the job?

Tommy: Well, it's hard to really explain. Things was very different then. It's not like it is now with everybody going into town for a drink. People would just gan to a local or maybes on a route round some pubs where they live and that. 'Course the younger ones would gan to the dance halls and that in the town centre, but nowhere near like it is now.

Tommy explained how a local publican had asked him if he would mind staying around in the local pub, instead of making his way to the dance halls on a Friday night with his friends. His first offer came when he was around sixteen. At first he was proud to be asked and did it for free, but found that when he went to the bar he would rarely be charged for his beer. This prompted Tommy's fledgling entre-preneuriality:

> *Tommy:*   I decided that if I can get me beers for nowt, I can get me mates to give ez the money and I'd get the beers in, like. This was all right for a bit, but he soon cottoned on.

The landlord limited Tommy to ten pints of Scotch ale every night of the week-end. Still, this enabled Tommy to get drunk for free on three nights a week, which he was more than willing to do. Later he asked the publican to spread the thirty free pints over the course of the week, which the publican was more than willing to do as this would mean Tommy would be less likely to be inebriated in the event of trouble. This also worked for Tommy, as he was beginning to take on similar functions at other pubs in the neighbourhood, and this would basically allow him to drink free all week:

> *Tommy:*   I didn't really keep count of beers or anything and neither did the landlords. They were happy as long as I didn't like take the piss out of them or nowt, you know. It sounds daft now, but getting beers for nowt loses its attraction after a bit and I'd not get as pissed after a while as a did at first . . . in case there was bother as well you know, but that wasn't really a worry.

Tommy would tour the local pubs, having a drink and a chat in each:

> *Tommy:*   'The most important thing was just to get your face seen like, let people know you're around.

Tommy would quickly deal with any trouble in his neighbourhood, but in re-stricting himself to the one locale he began to grow bored. He was still a young man and wanted to be around people of his own age and go to the dance halls, meet girls and get into fights. He apparently went through a stage of constantly drinking as much as possible in the three or four pubs he regularly visited, in the belief that it might all come to an end tomorrow. As time passed, however, his confidence in his status grew and he visited the pubs less but could always count on a free drink.

> *Tommy:*   I think that thirty pints a week stuff was just something to start me off like because the number was never really mentioned. Later I just knew I'd get a drink in like, four or five pubs. I knew as soon as I was in they was never gonna say 'right, you'll 'ave to pay for that, Tom'. It wasn't said, I just knew.

Tommy had been working in the local shipyards since leaving school, and apparently enjoyed it, but was forced to give it up owing to the pressures of his nightly socializing:

> *Tommy*: I was a welder. Loved it. No, really I did. I always liked getting up early of a morning. I'd walk there, about two miles. Canny money as well, and I was never scared of a bit of hard graft like . . . One day I got a flash, off the fucking flame you know, had a day off and just never went back. Jobs was so easy to get I didn't worry about it. I thought I'd be able to get another job no bother. I didn't give a fuck them days.

Tommy began to visit the clubs and dance halls of Sunderland and sometimes Newcastle. The Palladium was apparently the place to be seen in the early to mid sixties, and Tommy talks of it with great affection:

> *Tommy*: 'It was fucking great. You'd get all taffied up [dressed up], suit and tie, no jeans like you scruffy cunts, hair slicked back. A good band on, lasses all done up . . . A bunch of us would go down, and lads and lasses would be there from all over the fucking town. There was like a dance floor in the middle of the place and like people would do laps off the fucker – you know, shoulders swinging in front of the lasses like. If you was really hard like, you'd walk the wrong way round, like against the flow, bumping into people and that! [Laughs loudly] [see Katz 1988: 107 on the 'accidental' bump, used either to begin a fight or to force a humiliating show of deference]. Oh, it was fuckin' great man! Fights? Oh I could tell you some stories . . . The doormen would sometimes check you for knives before you went in, but what I'd do was get one of them metal combs that was popular in them days. Everyone had them in their pockets anyway, so the bouncers never said nowt. Nasty down the side of your face like . . . people would spill out of there on a Friday and the bus station was just opposite like, and it'd be like fucking Beirut or something, no shit.

It was into this world that Tommy plunged himself, fighting his way to notoriety throughout the town. Apparently he was not considered the best fighter, and never really entered local folklore the way other local fighters from this period did. Still, he was well known and a great many people knew not to cross combs with him. During the period when he was without a job at the shipyards he was given a job in the Palladium as a doorman. Tommy can't quite remember how he got the job, but thinks it may have been to stop him and his friends walking round the dance floor the wrong way and turning what was considered to be the smartest nightclub in the town into a scene from a Western bar brawl. Tommy recalls that the doormen then were never really much bigger or much harder than many of the club's patrons, and remembers they used to call you 'sir' when you went in. Tommy was reasonably well paid, but claims the money was unimportant as he got the most pleasure from just being able to flirt with the girls and scare the shit out of the men and generally do anything he liked. During the week he would still drop into the local pubs on his estate, and claims that even though he usually got his drinks for free, people would insist on buying them for him. This was the height of his career as a doorman and 'hard' man. Girls, claims Tommy, were helpless in the force of his powers, especially after his appointment as a doorman at the Palladium. If he wanted to drink he would never have to put his hand in his pocket. Men feared and respected him.

Tommy was eventually sacked from the Palladium after failing to turn up, for being drunk and generally for starting more fights than he prevented. He claims not to have been bothered too much by this, but also claims to have beaten the manager to a pulp over the incident. He continued to watch over the pubs on his estates, but according to other sources I consulted he began to drink too much and would often start fights for no apparent reason and became more of a self-appointed minder of the pubs, rather than by invitation, although the publicans said nothing. He carried on in this capacity for some years, going through bouts of heavy drinking and abstinence, but always remaining a recognizable fixture in the community. He returned to the shipyards for around two years in the early 1970s, but again gave up the job, and later became a full-time barman in the local working-men's club for a short time, as well as working more regularly as a day labourer. He now exists mostly on income support and occasional fiddle work for local builders, and is the doorman at the working men's club, where his talents are more likely to be used for collecting tickets for wedding and engagement parties in the function room upstairs than for ejecting troublemakers on to the pavement. The tales of his time as a troublemaker now seem a long way off.

So what did Tommy get out of his lifestyle?

Tommy: Well, I wasn't bothered about life then. I was young and people sort of look up to you and that. That's what I liked: Big blokes being scared a you, everyone being nice to you and that. Nobody would fuck with me when a was a young 'un. It's a good feeling, hard to talk about, you know? Like always being ready, you know, on your toes, I don't know. You know that feeling, just before a fight? Like that. Part of being young. It's a good feeling, plus everyone looked up to you, women flocked to men like me in them days, because I had a good name and that, I really put myself about with the woman, and this was back when women didn't fuck. I could go out and get a women, get pissed without putting me hand in me pocket. That's all it was, a bit of a flash – you know? It was like, boom boom boom, everything was fast, you know? Time seemed to fly . . . What else was I going to do, work in the shipyards all me life? I liked the work but being told what to do wasn't for me when I was young and daft. I had some good laughs and people still want to buy me drinks.

Tommy never married but has three children by two different women and has never really been part of any of their lives. He lives in a flat paid for by the social security system not far from where he was born.

Tommy exemplifies just what the role of bouncer and 'hard' men meant in Sunderland in the modern period. He took his violent potential to its limits within the confines of time and space. Tommy would be considered by many to have achieved little through his violent career. He has little money and little chance of getting any, and even in his heyday earned a minimal wage, which could have been bettered if he had remained in the shipyards. He has been left without a pension, a permanent job, security in his old age and the companionship of a family. At the age of 58, he still often does hard physical labour in order to earn some money. He has no possessions that would be considered to be of any real worth, and his lifestyle is poor by the standards of much of society.

What is vital to the understanding of this model is that Tommy is subject to the values in which he was socialized. Violence was not a last option to which he could resort. It was the first option, an activity that represented a masculine currency and that was recognized by all he encountered – an activity in which participation was no shame. Indeed the opposite was the case, for violence and its skilful deployment was revered by his peers and not only offered a means of obtaining status in an area and time in which a universal masculine image applied, but a means with which he could define his image of himself in terms of those characteristics that were prized by the people that mattered to him. Tommy took the prevailing masculine characteristic of violence and accentuated it in an effort to differentiate himself from those around him. Katz (1988: 80) ably describes Tommy's concerns: 'someone who is "real bad" must be tough, not easily influenced, highly impressionable or anxious about the opinions that others hold of him; in a phrase, he must not be "morally malleable".'

If being a man means not to be subject to the will of others, Tommy and many of those mentioned in this study, recognized their male image could be boosted by sucking the manliness out of other men by imposing their will; by diminishing the masculinity of others, Tommy could increase his masculine image in the environment he inhabited, for as Katz says: 'Bad asses manifest the transcendent superiority of their being, specifically by insisting on the dominance of their will' (1988: 81). Essentially, Tommy is recognizing the working-class masculine ideals of the area in that period of history, and though being subject to them, accentuates them to fit his subconscious agenda of status advancement, alienating himself from the normative working class experience. Katz (1988: 80) similarly noted that 'badasses':

> construct alien aspects of the self . . . by developing ways of living that appear hostile to any form of civilization, or by inventing a version of civilization that is not only foreign but incomprehensible to native [read universal middle class] sensibilities . . . The foreigner

may often be charming; the alien is unnerving. Managing the difference between appearing to be interestingly foreign and disturbingly alien is a subtle business . . .

(1988: 80)

Just as it is wrong to judge Tommy and people like him by liberal sensibilities of acceptable behaviour, it is wrong to judge him by contemporary standards of success or attainment. We should not underestimate the importance of the status bestowed upon Tommy in recognition of his violent potential as a factor motivating him to action. That status transcended most other aspects of his life, it was that which he desired most; and once attained it was that which he would fight hardest, literally, to maintain. The possibility of using his status to secure financial reward did not occur to Tommy and others like him *at this time and in this area*. It was not the money that spurred him to act as he did. The cultural surroundings that I have described are crucial to understanding why this was the case, and it should be noted that the leisure industry was still to expand fully, that mass consumption was still in its infancy by contemporary standards (see Bocock 1993), that mass production and mass advertising (see Chaney 1996) were still to create the plethora of commodities necessary to satisfy contemporary man with his 'unlimited hunger for more and more goods' (Fromm 1964: 179) and would eventually create a situation in which 'when one want is fulfilled, several more usually pop up to take its place' (Markin 1974: 195).

'Lifestyles' and consumption are now of vital importance (Chaney 1996), yet in Tommy's day the need to acquire money to afford that essential mobile phone, fax machine, wide-screen television, or new three-piece suite was simply not there. Artifacts such as these were yet to take on a meaning over and above their manifest identity and come to represent the currency of 'lifestyles' (Chaney 1996: 43). Consumerism obviously existed at the time, although an actual consumer culture did not arise until Tommy's high life was in steep decline (Chaney 1996: 17). It has been argued that the hedonism of contemporary consumerism can be understood as an unending search for the interdependence of pleasure and meaning, and that fashion in all its various forms should be understood as a search for individuality and distinction in a highly secular society rather than the exploitation of gullible consumers by a unfeeling marketplace (Campbell 1987). Tommy was therefore denied the hedonism of consumption, although we can tentatively assume that if today's sprawling marketplace had been accessible in his youth, financial gain through his ability to engage in violence would have been more likely to have occurred as conspicuous incentives would have been available (though crucial cultural characteristics would still be missing). As they were not, however, other social indicators of status were central to his life. Tommy was far more interested in pursuing the ideal masculine image of himself than getting the money to buy that 'must-have' new pair of shoes or kitchen implement. Tommy simply had the money to maintain his lifestyle and that was enough, for it was the lifestyle and all that this included that Tommy really desired.

This was not his only concern, however, for as Tommy readily admits, he was able to maintain a perpetual adolescence by avoiding any commitment to a career. Free alcohol fuelled his lifestyle and he would go out every night of the week and pursue 'good times', using violence and the mystique and sensuality that surrounds it as a means of 'buying excitement' (Parker 1974). There is much research to suggest that delinquency is in itself exciting: Matza (1964) talks of it being the raw material of excitement, Miller (1958) believes excitement is a 'focal concern' of lower class males, and Corrigan (1979) has argued that delinquency is the by-product of actions that are exciting in themselves. Good times and excitement meant drinking, socializing and chasing women, with perhaps a fight thrown in and that transcendental feeling when you walk in the pub or club that everyone is shit scared of you. Tommy's lifestyle represented the hedonism of the day.

The Cultural Millionaire

As I have mentioned above, Tommy took his violent potential to its limits in time and space, and although he did not measure up to contemporary images of professional gangsterdom he still had much to gain from living his life in the way in which he did. Men in a similar class position to Tommy's envied him then, as he represented an image of maleness they wished they could play – preferably just for a short time so as not to have to deal with the long-term consequences of that behavioural approach to social interaction.

Being envied by others is often highly appealing in any social setting, and even though Tommy failed to achieve lasting financial wellbeing through his violent potential, for a time he lived a life that was exciting compared to other mundane working-class working lives that were devoid of danger and illicit action. Tommy was not constrained by standards of respectable social action, but accentuated forms of social and cultural behaviour that led to a different kind of respect altogether. This life provided a cultural position of a considerable attraction to him. Tommy acted as he pleased and let the consequences unfold without worrying, refusing to be subject to the will of others and reinforcing cultural interpretations of a manhood lived without compromise. Few men can truly manage to do this.

To Tommy, violence was not necessarily something to be feared or avoided; violence could be embraced, manipulated and used to manufacture and reinforce perceptions and self-perceptions. Physical harm mattered less than social or cultural harm. Almost as a way of summing up his approach to life and violence, Tommy pointed out that getting hit in the face hurts a lot, but after a time that pain fades. Backing down from a fight, however, hurts for a lot longer.

Donnie: An Example of Tentative Adaptation

The disruption of the iconography of working-class labourist identity, and in particular the sell-by-date now reached by images of muscular, yet essentially altruistic, artisans, has left us with few contemporary images that have any resonance with past eras; the fighter is one.

(Hobbs 1994: 121)

Donnie is a contemporary of Tommy's, aged around sixty-five in my estimation. He lives in a city and neighbourhood with a slightly different historical lineage than that of Tommy, but his story is similar.

Donnie was also a local 'hard' man who minded pubs. Unlike Tommy he never really attempted to fit into the local industrial employment structures, and although he worked at legitimate jobs fitfully, he never really adapted to the employer–employee relationship. I will not describe his personal history but it should be remarked that he was noted for violence throughout his native city for some time. In Donnie's case, his criminality included forcibly extracting money and drinks from local publicans, petty theft, burglary and robbery.

Like Tommy, Donnie lived his life's prime in the modern industrial North East, and thus found himself subject to the region's non-entrepreneurial criminal sub-cultural structures. Like Tommy, he excelled at violence and, again like Tommy, he failed to gain financially but did succeed in securing an enviable cultural standing. Donnie is bigger than Tommy; not as big as you might tend to imagine when we are talking about a violent criminal. I would estimate he stands just under six feet tall, and possesses an enviably muscular physique for a man of his age. He occasionally attends a council gym, which can be used free by the unemployed on certain mornings of the week, and sports a year-round tan and a goatee beard against a slightly thinning mop of grey hair. More often he not he wears fashionable sports clothes, which clash with the glasses that he wears increasingly regularly, but occasionally he can be seen in a suit. The image tends to communicate a man unkeen to accept encroaching old age.

The reason that a discussion of Donnie is included here is that, at well over sixty, he has reconciled himself, or has at least attempted to reconcile himself, with the region's changing criminal structures. Donnie has not attempted to mastermind a hugely profitable criminal sting, but his activities hint at an adaptive masculinity and a willingness to move with the times.

Donnie occasionally sells £10–£30 lumps of cannabis in or just outside his local pub. This is not the cutting edge of entrepreneurial criminal endeavour in the North East by any means. He has had occasion to dabble in the black economy that thrives in his neighbourhood, selling stolen tins of deodorant, by the box or individually, fake designer watches and dodgy cigarette lighters. The criminal activity he actually engages in is not central to the argument here; here is a man who has embraced, whether grudgingly or wholeheartedly, changing modes of working class masculinities.

Donnie has not meekly accepted the boredom and anonymity of looming old age. He is clearly in better shape than many men half his age, and battles to maintain this image (see the later discussion of changing masculine body images in the post-modern era). Other local faces from Donnie's prime are now clearly old men. Tommy, for example, looks at least ten years his senior. In his old age Donnie seems unwilling to make do with reminiscences of a bygone age of noble combat and the reverence of his peers, for he has recognized the changing criminal practices in the region and has attempted to adapt and engage the market. However, he has not been especially in this regard, and this merely serves to illustrate the point. For why should he be, when what he is attempting is the act of catching up? His problem is that it was never a part of Donnie's cultural inheritance to acknowledge that the market afforded opportunities to those who had developed and honed their violence into a skill? The criminal milieu he inhabited in his youth was simply not tailored to market engagement in the way that it is today, and any money he made in those days from criminal activities was minimal and unstable. Now Donnie finds himself in a competitive market environment with much younger men who have grown up to appreciate the vagaries of the market, to embrace diversity and seek out profit, to understand contemporary cultural references to entrepreneurship and criminal enterprise.

Donnie cannot impose his violence upon the criminal marketplace as he could have done if a similar situation had existed in his youth; for although he is big and skilled in violence, his days are gone. His combatants would be his juniors by an age gap that is too big for even Donnie to make up, and to his credit it would seem he has recognized the Darwinian aspects of the criminal marketplace.

Like Tommy, Donnie still enjoys the cultural capital accrued during his youth. His criminal dalliances are not considered threatening by his competitors, and even the young tough guys afford him a certain respect. If he was not the inheritor of an entrepreneurial criminal culture he has certainly made a small contribution to its establishment, and to the criminal cultural capital that has passed on to the next generation.

Here is a man with one foot planted firmly in a modern industrial era, which is now a world away from contemporary young working-class males, and one foot in the adaptive post-industrial black economy. Donnie straddles a period of huge social change for the region, and in so doing is representative of perennial importance of violence to working-class culture (see Hobbs 1994). Despite de-industrialization, this culture has absorbed its cultural history, emerging global influences and contemporary social realities into an amalgam of behavioural understandings and influences that still values the use of violence in the conduct of working-class lives. Violence may have been used to formulate the emerging means of working-class expression, but the historical uses of violence are not lost, as will be shown in the coming chapters.

As I argue later, the culture I describe, in its present state, has clung to some aspects of modern masculine imagery, has adapted others, and created new means of enacting working-class manhood in contemporary society. Donnie is symbolic of a traditional deviant masculinity that has now been picked clean of meaning and consigned to history. Violence is one of the few forms of masculine expression that still has resonance within contemporary North-Eastern working-class culture, while many non-deviant aspects appear to have been rendered redundant (Wilson 1987; Parker 1989).

Donnie's acceptance of the past and present also serve to detail the adaptive nature of this culture. Changes from industrial to post-industrial and from modern to post-modern are not always jarring, with immediately distinguishable trends. For the fact remains that the populations in the grip of these huge global powers are still forced to negotiate their immediate social environment; adaptation is adopted as a survival strategy by some, a means of maintaining a contemporary engagement with the social. Donnie is one such example. Others simply conduct their lives one day at a time, and in doing so accept a lived reality without being aware of how or why it came to be or what happened to the way things used to be. It would be understandable, even expected, that Donnie would stand on the sidelines with his valued reminiscences, living out his remaining days with his peers in an atmosphere of nostalgia and sentiment, but he has chosen to re-enter the game and adapt to the rule changes. Not only this, but he has chosen to enter a field of criminal business seemingly despised, for whatever reason, by people of his age (Kray and Kray 1988; O'Brien and Kurins 1991; Fraser 1994). Donnie has not relaxed into the 'it wouldn't happen in my day' rose-tinted world view so often expressed by those old enough to witness the before and after of social change (see Berman 1983). It is not for him to express plagiarized arguments about drugs being the root of all social problems and discontent. Drugs for Donnie are a source of income making up the difference between his lifestyle and the next social security cheque.

Donnie's legacy

Donnie led an active romantic life as a younger man. He has at least five children that I have been able to verify, and there are rumours of more. He has had varying degrees of involvement with his children, some of whom carry his surname, some of whom do not. Not all of his children are on speaking terms. Some do not recognize the legitimacy of others, and the family could certainly not be described as cohesive or nuclear. Despite this, Donnie's offspring are worthy of note in this study.

Three of Donnie's sons have established reputations for violence and are now notable characters in their own right in the criminal milieu of their native city.

One is a bouncer, one has established himself in a legitimate business, and others are rumoured to be involved in a variety of criminal activities. I do not wish to rely on rumour, but I can confirm that all have violent reputations and links to other notable faces in their native city.

The adaptive nature of masculine cultural inheritance is displayed within Donnie's family, its patriarchal base and the changing criminal opportunities and practices in the North East of England. As Hobbs has pointed out 'entrepreneurial reproduction, of which crime is an integral component, is bonded to family life and the duplication of traditional roles that are tailored to both negotiate structural arrangements, and exploit ever shifting markets' (Hobbs 1994: 191) and while I do not wish to over-emphasize the influence of Donnie on the criminal leanings of his offspring, as I am given to understand that his role in their upbringing was minor, this short anecdote of criminality in the North East is certainly indicative of wider cultural and criminal changes that have occurred in the region over recent decades. As masculinities and crime have changed from the modern to the post-modern in the North East, Donnie has attempted to reinvented himself and tailor his violent potential and local celebrity to dovetail with contemporary criminality in a personal parody of working-class masculinities' battle with the same.

Donnie now has numerous grandchildren, and although I do not wish to be too deterministic, the likelihood of the males rejecting the cultural importance of violence seems minimal.

–2–

And Then the World Changed . . .

All that is solid melts into air.

M. Berman

The North East of England is a locale that ideally exemplifies the demise of an ordered traditional modernism and the advent of post-modernism. The world described and analysed for much of the previous chapter is now all but gone, and the most obvious facet of this change is in the rapid decline of industrial labour. The influence this has had, coupled with significant global changes in such areas as communication, transport, economics and commerce, has left the people of the North East to redefine and re-tailor their traditional social institutions, along with the social meaning they had sustained with such clarity for so long.

Characteristics of modernism such as 'universality, homogeneity, monotony and clarity' (Bauman 1992: 188) were clearly visible in the social, cultural and economic life of this region throughout the now defunct period of 'organized capitalism' (Lash and Urry 1987) and prior to the destruction of its 'workshop economy' (Rowthorn 1986). As Chapter 1 indicates, the history of Sunderland and the North East of England cannot be fully understood without acknowledging the fundamental importance of industrialization and the region's commitment to heavy industry throughout the nineteenth and much of the twentieth centuries. As Byrne suggests, 'any understanding of the North East has to be grounded in terms of the nature of industrial development and of the class and other social relations which derived from a very particular industrial experience' (Byrne 1989: 42). As might be expected, the centrality of industrial production greatly influenced all social, economic and cultural structures that shaped the lives of all those who resided in this region during its period of industrialism. Perhaps most notably, it created 'one of the oldest and most organised working classes in the world' (Byrne 1989: 40). The world has changed, however. Heavy industry has now all but disappeared from the region (see Byrne 1995), and consequently the nature of the old, taken-for-granted structures has been transformed. The organization that the working classes of this region once knew has been replaced by 'pluralism, variety, contingency and ambivalence' (Bauman 1992: 187), which have infiltrated every aspect of their social experience. Now, as Bauman has pointed out, 'to the individual, culture appears as a pool of constantly moving, unconnected fragments' (Bauman 1992: 31).

As Berman (1983) has suggested, those who experienced an extended period of cultural modernity and all that that period of history entailed have met its passing with feelings of loss and regret. In the North East there still exists a propensity, especially in the media, to view the region's history of industrial production through rose-tinted spectacles, and to view contemporary developments negatively in relation to that history. What the North East has regrettably lost is the certainty and stability that could be found in employment, labour markets, politics, welfare provision, the class structure, gender roles, cultural inheritance, the public sphere, values, personal expectations and even criminal practice. Much of that which could be relied upon has been transformed, and there now exists 'a culture of excess . . . [which is] characterised by the overabundance of meanings, coupled with (or made all the more salient by) the scarcity of adjudicating authorities' (Bauman 1992: 31). North Eastern working-class males (like all others) now find their cultural habitat in a state of 'constant change, yet devoid of a distinctive line of development' (Bauman 1992), and the consequences of this will be examined in this and the following chapters (see also 'introduction').

It is not my intention to offer a description of the profound impact of global forces on the North East of England. However, I will now discuss the effect those forces have had upon the region's once-stable cultural continuity. A great deal of cultural adaptation has occurred because of the resultant changes in employment and the labour market, notably the re-shaping of an embattled masculinity. I will take it for granted that the reader has some understanding of the global trends of which I speak. The demise of mass production as the engine of growth and capital accumulation (Piore and Sabel 1984), the decline of regional economies organized around single industries (Soja 1989; Hall and Jacques 1990), and the general move from organized to disorganized capitalism (Lash and Urry 1987) should be viewed as a background to this analysis, as should the advent of post-modernism within our social and cultural world (see, for example, Harvey 1990, Bauman 1992).

While 'most students of contemporary culture agree on the unique role of the media as the principal vehicle of culture production and distribution' (Bauman 1992: 31), I will not address this and other global influences directly as it is my intention to concentrate on what the working-class North Eastern cultural milieu is at the time of writing, rather than to explore what made it that way. Issues surrounding the decline of traditional modern North Eastern working-class culture and its replacement by a complex mixture of global and local influences are discussed elsewhere in this book.

As the world has changed, so has Sunderland. Since 1971, a year in which 'Sunderland was probably as prosperous as it had been . . . since its late Victorian heyday' (Byrne 1993: 243), the city has changed in a multitude of ways. At the base of these changes is of course de-industrialization, the effect of which can be seen in Table 1.

Table 1 Changes in Sunderland's Labour Market, 1971–89

	1971	*1981*	*1989*
Male full-time industrial	48,000 (44%)	31,000 (31%)	23,000 (25%)
Male full-time services	18,000 (16%)	20,000 (20%)	20,000 (22%)
Male part-time total	2,000 (2%)	2,000 (2%)	3,000 (3%)
Total male employed	67,000 (61%)	53,000 (53%)	46,000 (50%)
Female full-time industrial	11,000 (10%)	6,000 (6%)	7,000 (7%)
Female part-time industrial	2 (2%)	2 (2%)	2 (2%)
Female full-time services	17 (16%)	20 (20%)	17 (19%)
Female part-time services	12 (11%)	19 (19%)	21 (22%)
Total females employed	43 (39%)	47 (47%)	46 (50%)
Total employed	110	100	92

Source: Byrne (1993): 211

As can be seen from Table 1, Sunderland's labour market has been transformed, with the city losing more than half of all its industrial jobs between 1971 and 1989, and although the table itself is now out of date, it is reasonable to conclude that those patterns that Byrne identified have continued (see Callinicos and Harman 1987 for a discussion on the changing structures of social class in the light of these issues).

As Urry states, 'when we consider de-industrialisation of the UK economy, this implies both the growth, relatively and absolutely, in service employment, and enormous increases in unemployment and under employment' (Urry 1983: 35); although Sunderland has seemingly failed to replace its lost industrial jobs with service-sector employment, it has certainly witnessed the creation of 'large armies of unemployed, especially among young males' (Lash 1994: 133), the consequences of which I will discuss shortly.

Those jobs that have been created in the service sector contrast sharply with the North East's previous employment history, with the region witnessing a movement from skilled or heavy manual work carried out by men working shifts, to semi-skilled or unskilled routine assembly work done by married women (Hudson 1986; see Wheelock 1990 for detailed analysis of the social consequences of this change in the North East). Much of this female employment may be part time (see, for example, Byrne 1986; Wheelock 1990), yet despite this, this fundamental change in gender roles has wide implications for the social structure of de-industrialized society. As Henwood and Wyatt point out, 'in this situation of high male unemployment, this increasing participation of women in the labour market, if only on a part time basis, threatens patriarchal structures and it is by no means clear how this conflict will be resolved' (Henwood and Wyatt 1986: 109).

As the above suggests, 'the process of industrial restructuring has involved a process of social recomposition and class restructuring' (Marshall 1987: 218; see also Massey and Meegan 1982). Over and above the more obvious effects of a serious decline in full-time male employment, it should also be noted that

> service sector employment growth seems to have simply reinforced social divisions by offering, in the main, part-time female employment which is primarily attractive to married women, who are members of households already connected with employment. Such full-time jobs as are created in the service industry offer very low wages. Members of benefit-dependent households gain minimum advantages by taking up such job opportunities, which simply create working poor. At the same time, male and female employment has declined dramatically.
>
> (Byrne 1989: 139)

Wheelock's research in Sunderland has also revealed what would seem to be a serious decline in opportunities for the traditional working classes of the city, acknowledging that male full-time skilled and reasonably paid industrial employment has declined dramatically and has only in part been replaced by female, part-time service-sector work. Wheelock points out 'it is almost impossible for low-paid wives to use their earnings as a cushion against their husbands' unemployment' (Wheelock 1990: 48–9; see also Callaghan 1996).

The decline of full-time industrial employment and the failure of the service sector to compensate for this has had considerable implications for the social organization of the city of Sunderland and similarly affected areas, one of which is the creation of a situation 'where working class fathers breed underclass sons' (Lash 1994). As Wilson (1996: xiii) has argued, 'many of today's problems in the inner-city ghetto neighbourhoods – crime, family dissolution, welfare, low levels of social organization and so on – are fundamentally a consequence of the disappearance of work' and, as I hinted above, these trends lead inevitably to discussions on the development of a permanently disadvantaged underclass.

Even though I should discuss some issues involved in the underclass debate, I will not attempt a definition of that underclass. As Mann (1992) has pointed out, authors have used terms such as 'excluded groups, marginalised groups, underclass, residuum, the poor, reserve army of labour, housing and social security classes, stagnant reserve army, relative surplus population and the lumpen-proletariat . . . to describe a layer within, or beneath the working class'. Other terms could also be added to this list (see, for example, Byrne and Parsons 1983 who use the term 'reserve armies of benefit dependants'), but most authors appear to accept that a permanently socially disadvantaged group does exist, and it certainly exists on Wearside (see, for example, Wilkinson 1995).

Social Change and Changing Gender Roles in the Contemporary North East

On the underclass:

> the lack of relevant skills amongst such a group and their consequent long-term exclusion from the production process means that they are the first exclusively consumption class of post-industrial society. That is, what differentiates this group is both their dependence upon and marginalisation from the markets of advertising, fashions and other leisure industries. The underclass in this view lack the autonomy to sustain a way of life but are at the same time permanently excluded from recruitment to any lifestyle fractions.
>
> (Chaney 1996: 97)

On the setting:

> the older industrial cities of the North of England . . . are plagued by previously unknown levels of theft and burglary, car stealing, interpersonal violence, and a crippling sense of fear and insecurity, which cuts thousands of their residents off from the pleasures of the broader consumer society and also from the compensations of friendship and neighbourhood; and it is also worth pointing out that they are plagued by quite extraordinary levels of personal and family poverty, by poor physical health resulting from bad diet, and also by the increasing levels of suicide and early death associated with loss of a personal sense of morale and self-regard.
>
> (Taylor in Maguire et al. 1994: 488–9)

The purpose of the brief discussion of the underclass below is to shed further light on changing masculinities in the North East of England. For although the material available on the development and existence of an English underclass does not focus on criminality and masculinity directly, much of the research that has been completed can deepen our understanding of the central issues addressed by this book.

The structures of North-Eastern working-class masculinity have, of course, been profoundly shaken by the decline of industrial labour. Working-class men have been denied the possibility of expressing a measure of their masculinity through hard manual labour and a considerable number have had their image and self-image further attacked by the relative and absolute rise in unemployment and their inability to find any sort of paid employment. If we add to this the increase in female involvement in the labour market, it becomes apparent that we have witnessed a process of change that 'undermines the traditional view of the husband as the economic provider for the family, the breadwinner, or less emotively, the worker-earner' (Wheelock 1990: 49). Research by Jane Wheelock (1990) and by Gillian Callaghan (1996), carried out in Sunderland, indicate that the structures of working-class and lower working-class families are undergoing a degree of change. The transformations they note within working-class home life, the domestic economy and gender roles within these begin to suggest a disturbing decline in social organization within certain areas in the city.

As long-term unemployment becomes intergenerational unemployment, young males become fatalistic about their chances of prolonged employment and their ability to provide for their offspring. As a result, males become undesirable marriage partners, and this creates welfare-dependent female-headed households (the rise of which is noted by Peterson and Jencks 1991: 621; see also Anderson 1991 on teenage pregnancy). Paralleling this, middle-class and working-class families move out of the decaying neighbourhoods inhabited by the developing 'underclass' (see Wilson 1996, 1987; and Friedman 1977: 137–8 who noted this trend in the UK), thus isolating the increasingly downwardly mobile unemployed and denying working role models to the children of the underclass (Wilson 1987). Wilson's research in the US ably portrays the cyclical nature of poverty in these increasingly isolated and introspective neighbourhoods (Wilson 1992; 1996), as dysfunctional and antisocial behaviour becomes contagious, and leads to sexual promiscuity, crime, violence and drug and alcohol abuse (1987). The neighbourhood increasingly offers an 'excess of definitions favourable to the violations of laws' (Sutherland 1949), and this lifestyle becomes self-perpetuating. The young people of the neighbourhood become less and less adjusted to the world of work and increasingly value dysfunctional behaviour, which offers a release from boredom and the situational constraints of the neighbourhood and can offer an accessible route of status. As Parker's research reveals, the low-income neighbourhood can become a '"condoning community", as regards its general attitudes towards most kinds of delinquency . . . The hatred of "Authority" is implanted at all age levels. In their own way parents and sons feel the same way and protect each other against officialdom' (Parker 1974: 190).

As Peterson (1992: 625–6) points out, street life in these run-down, low-income communities can be exhilarating, especially for the young: 'In a world where jobs are dull, arduous or difficult to obtain and hold, it is more fun to hang out, make love, listen to and tell exaggerated stories of love and danger, plan parties and escapades, and exhibit one's latest purchases or conquests.' In this world, 'gangs provide young people's thrills, protection, mutual support, friendship, prestige, and enough income to allow them to buy fashionable clothes, alcohol and drugs' (Peterson 1992). Although Peterson's research refers to American society, it is relevant to developing cultural forms in the North East of England as the world becomes increasingly subject to global trends and changes. Wilkinson (1995), for instance, found similar characteristics among the poor in Sunderland itself, noting that some young people living on socially disadvantaged estates in the city have effectively 'dropped out' of conventional society. His study reports that these young people from low-income families often leave school with little or no educational qualifications, cannot find work and do not wish to take up educational or youth training schemes. Wilkinson vividly portrays a section of society made up of people whose lives are aimlessly drifting and devoid of meaning and who face ever-diminishing employment prospects. These young people have effectively dropped out of official society because they are not in work, not in training, not in education and not on official registers. As he also points out many of those researched felt disassociated from school and the workplace and often came from a home environment involving poverty, parental unemployment and domestic turmoil and violence. This 'tangle of pathologies' (Coffield's introduction to Wilkinson 1995) has produced for them a sense that the world of work has no connection to their daily lives and never will do. Homelessness is apparently increasing among this section of society, and Wilkinson indicates that many of those studied were heavily involved in criminality, or at least were on the fringes of it (Wilkinson 1995; see also below).

This discussion of de-industrialization, the development of an underclass and the social and cultural transformation of the North East suggests changing gender roles and images of what it means to be a man. Murray (1990) has talked of the 'unreconstructed masculinity' of unemployed working-class youths and argued that 'when large numbers of young men don't work, the communities around them break down . . . Men who do not support families find other ways to prove that they are men, which tend to take various destructive forms.' These 'destructive forms' lead us to criminality, the form of behaviour I have primarily chosen to indicate the transformation of working-class masculinity in the North East.

Chapter 1 of this book indicated that criminality was, in the North East's modern industrial era, inextricably linked to that masculinity of the time and locality. While

North East males were subtly and subconsciously moulded to the world of the industrial workplace, entrepreneuriality in criminal enterprise was slow to develop as concerns more in keeping with the industrial milieu (conflict, aggression, violence and status) maintained supremacy.

As I have already mentioned, industry and the social forms closely associated with it have collapsed. Employment has long been acknowledged as a key component of identity and self-identity (see Becker and Carper 1956) and as the service sector has failed to replace lost industrial jobs, the working-class masculinity of the region has been plunged into a state of flux. Families have changed in form and function (see, for example, Parker 1989) and, from the late 1980s to the present day (see Ogburn 1950 on a 'cultural lag' between economic changes and their translation into culture), masculinity has adapted to its new setting.

Research indicates that the development and entrenchment of a continually disadvantaged underclass have slowly eroded the desire of some actively to seek employment and have promoted favourable attitudes to delinquency, especially as a means of getting money – the desire for which has not diminished, despite such people's disadvantaged social position. We thus begin to see the slow advent of criminality, not just as a means of obtaining status (although this function has endured with various modifications), or of injecting some excitement into an otherwise dull social situation (Foster 1990), but as a entrepreneurial concern: a means of getting money. One should not be wholly deterministic about this transition because, as Foucault has observed, 'the world we know isn't this ultimately simple configuration where events are reduced to accentuate their essential traits, their final meaning, or their initial and final value. On the contrary, it is a profusion of entangled events' (Foucault 1986: 89). However it is clear that the shift from an industrial economy to a post-industrial economy has greatly affected masculinity and criminal practice in the region, and that crime and violence are now careers in themselves. Money can now be made from violent ability and repute both legitimately and illegitimately (see the study of Michael later in this chapter and that of contemporary bouncers in Chapter 3), and the anatomy of crime in the region has shifted to allow a hierarchical criminal pathway to emerge. It is hard, if not impossible, to maintain that illegitimate careers have arisen to replace lost industrial labour, but it is clear that de-industrialization has massively affected the region and greatly contributed to the creation of circumstances that have led to this situation.

The rise of post-modernity is also a factor in an increasingly global environment. I have attempted above to indicate the size and nature of the changes that have occurred within the working-classes in the region and some of the reasons for and the effects of the development of an underclass. As I have pointed out, the male role in low and very low-income families has mutated considerably, but young lower working-class and underclass males have other influences through which to shape and form their fragile yet potent masculinity. I have briefly touched on the growing seductivity of criminals and criminality, but perhaps the most notable input into the men's lives comes from the worldwide media. The role of the television as a socializing and educating force and as an influence on behaviour has yet to be fully explored, despite repeated postulation on the effects of prolonged exposure to on-screen violence. However the debate is perhaps particularly relevant to the young males discussed in this chapter, because it appears that, without work and access to more fruitful leisure pursuits, watching television becomes for them the day's focal point. Campbell (1993: 323) insightfully recognizes that 'the alleged absence of role models . . . came not from the absence of men and masculinities in their lives – the lads were surrounded by a macho propaganda more potent in its penetration of young men's hearts and minds than at any other time in history – they were soaked in globally transmitted images and ideologies of butch and brutal solutions to life's difficulties.' Campbell's comments accord with the behavioural characteristics that I witnessed over the course of this research. The effects of gangster films, for example, upon things such as speech codes, verbal style and vocabulary, and obviously criminal goals, practices and expectations were palpable (see especially Chapters 3 and 4).

As the traditional structures have disappeared and as others lose their solidity, young men – particularly those from lower class backgrounds – find their identities as men changing rapidly and influences upon those masculine identities arriving from a variety of new directions. Those elements of traditional male identity structures still available then merge with the new to create a fluid mixture of influences from which certain individuals and groups draw a variety of identity indicators. As Giddens (1991: 32–4) has pointed out, 'in the context of a post-traditional order, the self becomes a reflexive project . . . In [these] settings . . . the altered self has to be explored and constructed as part of connecting personal and social change.'

That said, the new working-class masculinities are not completely devoid of any established foundation, so that even as it appears that in a new post-modern environment the North East's working and underclass masculinities are propelling a completely new identity and ideology out of the methods of expression they encounter along the way, some of the old structural yardsticks of masculinity are still present. As Huyssen (1990) has written, post-modernity 'operates in a field of tension between tradition, conservation and renewal', and following generations of working-class males have clung to those aspects of maleness to which they still have access.

As a shop-floor masculinity is now out of reach, its component parts are sifted, sorted and evaluated and those that can be moulded to fit in with the new post-industrial and post-modern cultural habitat are translated and made to work in this new environment. (In Chapter 3 I use bodybuilding as an example of the expression of male physicality to illustrate this point. See also Rose (1962: 14), who points out that an individual can 'within the limits permitted by the culture, define for himself somewhat new patterns [of behaviour] suggested by the variations among the old ones'.)

Violence, of course, is certainly not out of reach, and as a means of gaining status remains a constant. However, it has now taken on new uses, meanings and interpretations and can be used as a tool with which one can fashion a criminal career, as an 'instrument of commercial control' (Hobbs 1995), as well as a means of manufacturing a degree of cultural authority (Hobbs 1994: 120). Violence has therefore become a valued skill in an increasingly diverse illegal marketplace, a means of obtaining an income and cultural status, the gateway to the new hierarchical criminal milieu.

Immediate gratification has long been acknowledged as a feature of working-class life (see Goldthorpe and Lockwood 1964), but its importance among some sections of the working and lower working classes becomes amplified, distorted and infected with a culture of consumerism and consumption influencing lifestyle and identity (see Shover and Honaker 1992 and the following section on 'Artie').

It could reasonably be argued that a pride in and commitment to a particular skill or job, along with other industrial male concerns, are moulded, embued with the global capitalist imperatives of self-interest and financial independence, and, in the new post-modern setting, transformed into pride in the ability to get money. As Currie (1997) has pointed out, the dog-eat-dog ethos of the global marketplace has invaded every aspect of the social world, and this, he argues, encourages the use of violence to attain self-interested ends. Contemporary North Eastern working-class masculinities have 'appropriated many of modernism's aesthetic strategies and techniques, inserting them and making them work in new constellations' (Huyssen 1990).

The remainder of this chapter is devoted to the discussion of the lives and careers of two criminal entrepreneurs. In many ways they are unremarkable, contemporary urban lives – two young men encountering reality in an environment of changing male imagery, business, leisure and pleasure. In a sense they are starting afresh, creating around them an ethic of criminal business competency that relates far more to media images than to the world of their fathers. Even though they are not the only criminals in the North East motivated by money and its trappings and by a complex and changing system of values and desires, their stories are included as a means of portraying the new field of criminal ideology and practice in which they move.

Michael and Charlie

[I]n a world of complex organisation the hustler defines himself as an entrepreneur, and indeed, he is the last of the competitive entrepreneurs . . . The political conservative should applaud all that individual initiative.

(Horton 1977: 67)

Michael is twenty-four years old at the time of writing and has already realized the dream of many criminals. He is co-owner of a medium sized and reasonably successful car repairs garage (see Akerstrom, 1985, who has found that many prison inmates possess a common dream of owning a small firm). His story to date is characteristic of the rapidly developing hidden economy and the mutating cultural habitat in which he moves. Michael displays the adaptive nature of the capitalist entrepreneur and the contemporary professional criminal (see, for example, Hobbs 1995), and indeed is happy to move from legitimate to illegitimate marketplaces as money-making situations arise. He is also happy to blur this boundary if he determines he will benefit by doing so.

It would be easy to label Michael as an entrepreneur, but he is uneasy with the description. It does not fit in with his image of himself; he does not have a mobile phone, a beeper, or a broker, and he never wears a suit. He doesn't believe the business he conducts merits the lofty title of entrepreneurship, with its 1980s imagery. He can't think of a title for what he does, but gets on with it. It's just work. Michael's work, however, incorporates a good deal of criminal activity, some of which I have included in this piece, some of which I am aware of but have not included, and some of which I am not aware of and which Michael is not willing to disclose.

Michael was greatly surprised by my desire to include him and his activities in this study. He considers himself to be nothing out of the ordinary, though he acknowledges that in terms of his more vocational illegal dealings, he could be considered to be 'doing alright at the moment'. He likes money, but is far from flamboyant with the money he earns. He sees a career and life mapped out for himself, he takes much of what he does seriously. His life is not a party (Shover and Honaker 1991) and he mixes deferred gratification with a good measure of hedonism to achieve as many of his goals as possible. To him much of his life is mundane, his working day is too energy sapping, and it took some time to convince Michael that I really would be interested in what he had to say.

The following piece is the result of a number of interviews I welded together. It was difficult to get Michael to talk in front of a tape recorder – not because he didn't want to be recorded, but rather because the presence of the tape recorder stifled conversation. It became easier, however, the more bottled beer he had to drink or the more cannabis he had to smoke. Although other methodological problems arose, the words attributed to Michael are his, or are a very close representation. I have modified some of the actual words slightly to facilitate the complex dialect Michael speaks.

I met Michael through an acquaintance who had known him since his early teens, and was therefore able to check biographical data before starting the series of interviews. Slowly but surely we built up a friendship, which greatly aided the collection of the data presented here. Our mutual acquaintance, and eventually Michael himself, told me of his background and business dealings, and the first exploratory conversations eventually turned into a series of interviews and many hours of fieldwork.

Since childhood, Michael has apparently always seemed to be the boy most likely to 'achieve good the wrong way'. His interests always seemed to lie away from usual childhood and adolescent concerns, and this, coupled with his obvious yet unusual charisma, kept him slightly aloof yet strangely appealing to the circle of friends and acquaintances who were forever keen to seek out his company and bask in his reflected glow. In retrospect, however, it can be seen that Michael had a significant leg-up in his chosen career path. He was certainly not a rung above any of those in the lower working-class landscape into which he was born, nor did he have a solid education (he left school as soon as the law would allow). However, his stepbrother had already become established in the fledgling criminal enterprise culture. Michael's stepbrother, Charlie, is his most obvious male role model, and although Michael is loath to admit it he has had a considerable influence upon him. Although Michael and Charlie have different fathers, which neither has seen for years, they were both raised by their mother and her third husband, Ronald, who worked in the local shipyards. Eleven years separate the stepbrothers, and despite the fact that they have different fathers, they seem remarkably close. Their childhood years were far from easy, characterized, as they were, by considerable family discord and turbulence, but these mutual experiences seem to have bonded the two men together, although their relationship does not always run smoothly. The age gap between the two men seems to have developed a kind of father-son relationship between Charlie and his younger sibling, Michael, although I never mentioned this. They have a third stepbrother, Ronald's son, Stephen, who attends a local comprehensive school in the area. Michael and Charlie's relationship with Stephen seems to be amicable enough, but doesn't approach the closeness to the relationship between the two adult stepbrothers. During interviews Michael was always happy to talk about his older stepbrother, and often displayed an element of pride in his achievements.

> *Michael*: Charlie was never really a fighter, but even at school he was getting known for certain things. He was always well in with the local hard cases even when he was still a young lad. He hung around with the older lads all the time, didn't play about with kids his own age . . . It wasn't like he was always in trouble or anything, because he always had a brain on his shoulders, you know, always selling this or that, all kind of stuff in his bedroom, although I didn't know what was happening at the time. He moved out of the house when he was seventeen, got his own place and left me to put up with my stepdad's shit on my own.

As Becker (1964: 52) has noted, the experimentations, experiences and influences of youth are often sifted and sorted, and crucial issues located and brought to bear in adult life and this is clearly the case with Michael. Michael admired Charlie's standing in the community and the rising respect now accorded to somebody who is adept at getting money. Michael was known by many not by his given name, but as 'Charlie's boy' or 'Charlie's brother'. Other influences are of course crucial in the formation of Michael's chosen career goals, but his brother's character and standing are obvious to observers.

Initially, Michael did not follow in his brother's footsteps. The traditional working-class, industrial male work ethic was undergoing significant change as Michael left school, but still carried some weight, and Michael eagerly grasped the possibility of a full-time job in an area of very high unemployment. He obtained a job at a local factory that produces heavy machinery. A friend of Charlie's had a slight influence in procuring the job for him, though Michael gave little or no allowance to this (he says he would have got the job anyway). Nevertheless, the job did allow him to work in the preferred masculine environment of manufacturing, which had all but disappeared from the region (Byrne 1993), but which so many young working-class boys still favoured over employment in the slowly rising service sector (see Winlow 1996).

Around this time Michael began to emerge from his brother's shadow and forge his own identity in the eyes of the ever-vigilant masculine habitus they both occupied. Michael's chosen stepping stone to local celebrity was somewhat different from that of his brother however. His route did not possess the new and slightly seductive allure of deviant business, but did possess a long tradition of working-class status advancement: Michael began to establish himself as a fighter. Skinny during adolescence, he began to fill out and grow taller, and correspondingly developed the self-confidence that size and a fighting ability brings. These physical and psychological changes seemed to dovetail with a fight-anyone attitude he had always possessed. He now stands around six feet and three inches tall and weighs around seventeen stones (around 240 pounds), but has never lifted a weight in his life (unless he then proceeded to throw it at someone). His body lacks definition, and he comes across as a tall, skinny bloke who just happens to have put some weight on. Narrow across the shoulders, wide at the waist, not skinny, not fat, Michael seems undaunted by the post-modern stress on body shape. However, in addition to his talent for violence he has the air of someone who is supremely confident in his own physicality and his ability to vanquish all foes; and this influences other areas of his personality, for he says exactly what he thinks and looks people directly in the eye, which can have an intimidating effect even when this is not his desired goal. Charlie on the other hand could not be more different: He stands no more than 5 feet and 8 inches in height, but is exceptionally broad across the shoulders and chest. He weighs around 15 stones (around 210 pounds), some of which is fat, and is now completely bald, contrasting with Michael's full head of closely cropped fair hair.

Michael's reputation as a fighter grew slowly but surely. He did not figure in the league tables of violence that young men tend to compile at school, but fought a lot, and, as in most fields of endeavour, practice brought great improvements.

Fighting a lot engenders a knowledge of how best to conduct a violent encounter and of what can be expected, and has a fundamental desensitizing effect in relation to the fear and foreboding that most feel when violence seems about to enter into any social interaction. Those who fight often recognize the signs that violence will ultimately be the result of a confrontational encounter at a much earlier stage than those who do not; and, recognizing the inevitability, they may often seek to act first to secure the upper hand. They understand the futility of arguing, pushing or attempting reconciliation or pacification, and therefore cut straight to the chase. In this, they are exhibiting an intricate knowledge of their social environment, which may well be very different from a middle-class (or different working-class) setting, where a heated disagreement need not end in extreme violence. Simmel (1971) talks of a non-serious feeling that can descend in the midst of great adventure, and this can be the case in a violent encounter, a situation that can be construed as 'adventurous' (see, for example, Taylor 1985: 74 on calmness during an armed robbery). Adrenaline is a vital component in the sensual dynamics of violence, but the non-seriousness that Simmel mentions can represent a sense of inevitability in this context.

Michael defeated a large number of opponents, rather than opponents with recognized fighting ability, and thus 'subtly manipulated . . . everyday life rather than in the dramatic or revolutionary gesture' (Cohen and Taylor 1976). He built up his fledgling fighting reputation by the established fast-track route of football hooliganism, an activity which Hobbs and Robbins (1991: 368–9) have noted 'can be sensible, even sensually compelling' and can lead to 'some becoming local personalities'. Michael began to get noticed. Football hooligans fight for 'honour, reputation and above all pride' (Hobbs and Robins 1991), and in this masculine mix Michael became one who went that little bit further in upholding these three values, and subsequently received the near-veneration of his football supporting peers. As Michael's stock rose amongst those who mattered to him, it apparently began to dawn upon him that his violent potential and the fear it could generate could be a means of imposing his will upon others, and that this could establish his status as 'cultural authority' in the illegal marketplace. Entrepreneuriality thus became an option that was open to him, a field in which his cultivated fighting ability would offer him a head start. It was also an alternative to his mundane working life, and he began to see gaps in the market. Michael slowly came to 'commodify reality' (Hobbs 1988).

Michael takes up the story:

> *Michael:* After about a year and a half I think it was, they [his employers] let me go. Said it was a numbers thing, last in first out. I remember nobody wanted to tell me. There was some decent blokes there and they felt bad, but it'd been coming for a while. I was gutted at first, didn't know what I was gonna do, but I

didn't really like it anyway. They had me doing really boring stuff and I didn't like the apprenticeship I was doing. I wanted to be a mechanic . . . I worked hard though. Never missed a day. Hated it but stuck with it, you know. It's better than nothing, and me stepfather was always on me back about how I was lucky to have a job and all that shite that people his age come out with . . . Well after a while I wasn't bothered. I didn't worry about it, money and that, and as the song goes 'things . . . can only get better!' [sings].

Losing his job brought about a period of 'bumming around on the dole', to which Michael was not at all averse at this stage of his life, although his mother and stepfather quickly tired of Michael's diminishing work ethic. Michael's stepfather, Ronald, had worked in various shipyards since he was a boy, and had been made redundant when the shipyards finally closed. He was still in his mid-fifties and found it impossible to find a new job. He apparently pushed his stepson very hard to get another job, but Michael wasn't interested, and this and other family problems appeared to be part of a growing rift between the two as Michael slipped sullenly into adulthood. Michael told me he lost all desire to get another legitimate job after discovering his stepfather still woke up automatically at six every morning, a hold over from his days in the shipyards. By the time Michael got out of bed at eleven his stepfather had been to the job centre, been to get the newspapers and walked a daily constitutional of around three miles. Even as Michael was eating his cornflakes his father would already be getting on his nerves by telling him of the advertised jobs he should apply for and nagging him about not being a burden to his mother, sponging off the state and the responsibilities of adulthood and man-hood. Michael considered his stepfather to be institutionalized, and unable to adapt now to his empty days. Their growing mutual animosity obviously related to more complex issues than their difference of opinion about paid employment, and it is apparent that Michael never accepted Ronald as a true father figure, even though Ronald supported the family for much of Michael's adolescence. Michael's un-employment and unwillingness to search for a job appears to be merely one of a series of familial battles, but nonetheless it proved to be a major one in the lives of both men and served to accentuate the personal and generational differences considerably. On one occasion Michael apparently got up at five in the morning to go to an away match, and discovered his stepfather sitting in his chair in his slippers, vest and cap reading the freshly printed newspapers. He had apparently been unable to sleep because his body clock still told him that it was time to be at work, and Michael tells me he did not want to end up like this even if he could find a job. Other avenues would have to be explored.

Michael and his parents argued more and more. He now dwarfed his stepfather and their clashes became more severe as Michael would come in drunk at all hours and openly smoke cannabis in the living room. Michael's stepfather continued to try and discipline his young charge, provoking confrontations in which he could no longer physically prevail. Charlie would be called to calm Michael down, but Charlie's relationship with his stepfather was also far from harmonious.

Charlie had moved out to live with his girlfriend and newly born daughter some years previously and advised Michael to do the same. He even went as far as to offer his stepbrother a job. Michael left the family home shortly after and will not return unless he knows his stepfather will not be present.

Charlie had capitalized on his early entrepreneurial promise and at the age of thirty-four owned three businesses, all in or close to the neighbourhood in which he and Michael were born and raised. He had set up his first legitimate business at twenty-four, a newsagents, and since then had also opened a popular sandwich shop and a car-parts store. Alongside these endeavours Charlie had purchased two small terraced houses, which he refurbished, cut up into individual flats and rented to students and people on welfare benefit. He had financed his legitimate businesses partly through illegal business and an intricate understanding of the government welfare and benefits system. I was aware of some of Charlie's illegal activities, and Michael helped fill in *some* of the gaps. He continues the story in his own words:

Michael: Well, I suppose I wasn't that easy to live with. My Mam wasn't well either. I'd been getting in a bit of trouble with the law as well. Just silly stuff, assault, public order stuff, drunk and disorderly. Just fines. Charlie had the parts place and said I could work for him, just to get me out of the house away from the old man.

I knew he [Charlie] must be doing well. Nobody I knew had their own business and stuff, houses. You know better than me, but anyone who ever made a few quid 'round 'ere pissed it away. He [Charlie] wasn't like that really, wasn't flash with his money. He'd save, pay off the debt as quickly as possible on all of his places. All the rent he got, he paid off the mortgage, didn't take any money out. He'd say he was skint and people would say, bollocks, call him a tight bastard, but nobody ever really knew what he was earning or anything.

SW: How did he make his money?

Michael: Apart from the legit stuff? All sorts. How far back do you want me to go? He always bought stuff he thought he could make money on. When he lived at home he always had a load of gear in his bedroom and that. He'd buy stuff off kids who'd go out burgling, thieves who'd do over vans, ram raiders when that was the thing to do. I've seen like, hundreds of bottles of perfume and that around at his place. He didn't tell me about everything. He'd buy gear off sad cases and drug heads who'd run up their credit just to get a couple of quid, hire purchase stuff just like that. He'd have car stereos, CD players, videos,

TVs . . . He got into cards [credit cards], that type of thing, store cards as well as bank cards. Silly stuff at first. He'd go out and start blagging [using illegally] the card on electricals [electrical goods], easy to sell. I know for a fact he knew a lad who worked in a clothes shop in York who knew the cards were dodgy, but he'd let them buy till the card was reported stolen. You know, when the card's stolen, been reported, they've got this machine that 'phones as soon as you try to use it. Well, the lad would pick it up, or whatever way it worked, and give Charlie time to get out. This is a while ago. If they find a stolen credit card and keep it they used to get a reward or something as well, but obviously he can't be claiming that all the time, and you can't be using the same shop over and over. Most of the time he just used the lad in the clothes store just to check the cards, see if they were reported stolen. It was much easier back then, no cameras and that; it still takes bottle, but it was much easier. Sometimes he'd use a card in the corner shop just to get the groceries in. The bloke who owned the shop would know the score, but he always gets his money anyway, and Charlie would let him ring up loads of other shit on the till that he hadn't really taken. It wasn't an easy thing to do, because it's so easy to get caught, even back then. After that he started to distance himself a bit. He'd buy cards off the actual owners who'd give him the cards on a Friday and, say, report it stolen on the Monday. Give him the weekend to make whatever he could. The best is absolutely brand spanking cards, because then you can just write a really easy signature on the back so you don't fuck it up in the shop. People would give him [Charlie] the cards as soon as they get them through the post then just say they'd never got them . . . Also you can just nick them straight from the post, especially in like, big buildings that have mail boxes in the hallway, student places; they all open bank accounts at the same time and are probably too stupid to notice they haven't got their cards anyway. You can earn money doing stuff like that, but it's a serious charge if you get caught, you know. Still, you get a really good video, CD player or something your looking at three, four hundred quid aren't you? You might have to split a bit of that to the guy you take with you to watch your back, or give the bloke who gave you the card a few quid, but it's all right. Back then you could keep using them when they were reported stolen, by keeping under a shop floor limit; they won't check up on stuff less than say forty quid or something. Maybe sell them on, buy loads of kettles, toasters or something, but that was really dangerous then and it must be impossible now. Banks have really clamped down.

In the end Charlie was getting cards from all over. He'd have people go out and bladder them for him [actually go out and use the cards to buy as much as possible] just for a small cut. No risk to him then is there? He'd have burglars and TWOCers [car thieves or joy riders, from 'Taking Without the Owners Consent'] coming around who'd turned up cards from houses or cars. Even usually straight people were queuing up to sell him their cards [so they could report them stolen after a period].

The one [scam] I liked best, he'd just started to get into property. That's a straight scam right there. Most of the property owners, landlords and that around here are a bit shady or at least used to be. He'd have Giro drops, you know, empty flats, but get someone to claim they're living there when they aren't so they get an extra Giro [a social security check] to pay the rent. He even had Sue [Charlie's girlfriend] go down the job centre and say she'd moved into one of his flats. Sounds daft, but it's like an extra fifty quid a week, maybe more depending. Regular as clockwork. With money like that coming in plus his legit rents, the money from the shop, and other bits and pieces, he can go down to the bank, get another mortgage for another house and just keep going like that. He's got like five houses now, is it? I don't want to make it sound easy, because you've got to figure out the ways they can catch you and then block them off; that's the hard bit, that's the work of it. Going out and doing it's easy, it's not getting caught that's hard.

It's not like we talk about this stuff all the time. Some stuff he has to tell me, other stuff he'll tell me if he's pleased with himself and we're getting on OK. Like to his way of thinking, it's not just beer tokens he's doing it for, he's got to be serious. It's like growing up and not being a kid anymore, being sensible and that. He might be doing well, but to him there's got to be another way, there's got to be another angle he can earn some extra money from. One scam's not enough; he's got to bleed some extra money out of it. In one of his Giro drops, he had a lad who used the place to run up credit. Again it was easier then. If he's got an address he can get a catalogue, he can get a bunch of catalogues, send away for stuff, pay on the drip, but he's never going to pay. He can get store cards, he can walk in off the street to Curry's or Dixons or anywhere and walk out with a four hundred quid CD player without handing over a bin lid [quid/pound]. You've got to be careful with cameras, but you might drive across to the Lake District or something where they're less likely to have them and aren't as sharp to it. People fall over themselves to give you credit. You've just got to suck up as much of it as you can. I don't know how much he made but it must have been a bit because I made a nice chunk selling the stuff on. All sorts of gear. In the end they [creditors, police] . . . [were] coming around the flat, but then Charlie just claims that he [the man who's name was used to run up the debt] hasn't seen him for weeks, he's skipped, and that's it, isn't it? The best way is to get some fake IDs then you cut the risk down much more. Who do you chase? Again you've obviously got to be careful for the little things, not let them find any way to follow it back to you. He [Charlie] can also smash the electric meter and try and get out of paying the bill. Nick some furniture, TV and that, claim the insurance. It's all down to the bloke who skipped the rent, even makes it sound more convincing. Charlie only did it the once; it's a dangerous thing, you know? Him and his mate did something similar in another landlord's place and split it with him. I don't know much about that time because we weren't talking at the time.

Despite Michael's obvious pride in his brother's daring exploits, their relationship has never run smoothly. Arguments are commonplace, often taking place in public. They are the types of argument that inspire people to stare into their pints, rather than intervene and attempt to defuse the situation. Nevertheless, Charlie reciprocates Michael's brotherly pride. Charlie had never achieved a reputation for violence and Michael's growing status in that field has caused pangs of quiet admiration for his younger sibling, although he tries to hide this with the quiet reticence many older brothers display towards their younger brothers' achievements. Michael's success has been in an area in which his working-class peers can acquire high status; and though his brother has attained a measure of success in the legitimate and illegitimate marketplace – a relatively new means of status advancement – Charlie still recognizes the vital importance of violence in the cultural environment they both inhabit. Some may be forgiven for thinking that despite his relative wealth and success, Charlie still secretly yearns for a little of what Michael has, for violence and its intimidatory and seductive effects still seem to pull at the very core of Charlie's masculinity. Meanwhile, Michael possesses a similar appreciation of, and perhaps envy for, Charlie's obvious business acumen.

The brothers often go weeks without speaking, which is difficult when they work together almost every day, forcing them to communicate with grunts and shrugs. Despite this the bond between them is obvious, and their brotherly partnership became a business partnership after Michael had worked at the parts store for around a year.

Michael: Well, as soon as I started with Charlie I could see the potential of the place. I'd always messed about with cars and stuff and I knew the score. I'd be about nineteen, twenty at the time. Business was pretty steady. He gave me a hundred quid a week at first . . .

I suppose I first made some extra money off one of the lads, Donnie. Someone had run into the side of him at a roundabout, bit of a bump on the wing, that was all. Well, the other guy's insurance was gonna pay, so he brings in the car and says, stick in a high bill, fix it up and we'll split the profit. I was a bit silly back then, didn't know an insurance company could look for a better quote . . . I claimed for everything. I needed the money at the time, holidays coming up and that. Put in a bill for about eight hundred quid and change when the job only came to around a hundred and fifty tops. Made about four hundred quid on that alone. Charlie goes off it when he found out, about the risk and that, but so fuck, it's four hundred quid isn't it?

After this escapade, Michael began to realize he could make money out of stolen car parts:

Michael: I got to know this kid, Paul. He'd been stealing cars since he could crawl, so I put it in his mind that maybe he should drop by and let me have the doors before he burns out the cars [laughs]. He couldn't bring the car around the garage – too risky – so for a while he'd bring the stuff in the next day. His brother brought him down in a van . . . I just gave him pennies . . . Still a lot of work to do from there though . . . After a while I learned how to get stamp numbers and shit like that off all the gear so they couldn't be traced. Sometimes I'd go up to meet him [Paul] and take the gear off the car myself so he didn't fuck anything up. Mostly I'd get wings, bumpers and stuff like that. Easy to get rid of and nice and quick . . . I didn't like to fuck about up there (Paul's neighbourhood) – coppers all over the place. I'd get skirts and spoilers for the boy racer element. Some people I'd tell, if I knew them, you know, I've got some stuff out the back I'll give you a couple of quid cheaper. They'd always go for it.

It got so I was buying so much, the legit business was getting a bit worse. I didn't tell Charlie about any of this. I was making good money but I was shitting myself. It's a serious offence you know? . . . Some weeks I would get three hundred quid on top of my wages, but I was fucking working for it. I got to thinking that it only takes one of the little car thieves to grass me up and I'm in a world of shit, so I sold all the dodgy parts I had to a friend of Charlie's who was a proper car ringer and that's how [Charlie] he found out.

Michael was greatly surprised that Charlie wasn't furious. In fact from these humble begins blossomed a fully fledged car-ringing operation. Charlie took over the buying of stolen cars and parts, mocking Michael's youthful contacts. Michael and a family friend who worked for the stepbrothers would actually do the cutting up of the stolen cars and the assembling of new cars with false identities. Charlie would see to it that the cars were sold on. Business blossomed for a period until Charlie decided that the business was becoming more and more risky and likely to end in prison terms for the stepbrothers. A couple of friends and business acquaintances were arrested, and Charlie urged that they retire from the business, at least for a while. Charlie bought a new house. Michael was now a prosperous young man. He bought two window-cleaning rounds and had unemployed friends do the work, while he just collected the money.

As the car ringing operation came to an end, other money-making schemes quickly homed into view for Michael. Michael now mimics Charlie's approach to illegal business and is far more circumspect about money-making opportunities. He believes a good deal of his past exploits were merely childish recreation and considers himself lucky to have avoided arrest on a serious charge. He is now of the opinion that his deviant business is safe and well organized.

Michael: Look, the way I see it, nobody is just gonna give me money, not the kind of money I want. You might be able to get a job some place, making what looks like good money, but the way I think is, if they're willing to pay me this, what is the bloke who owns the place making? That's where you want to be.

I don't want to just get by and stuff. My stepdad, Ronnie, was right about one thing; he used to say, this isn't a dress rehearsal, you only get one chance, so, you know, I want what other people have got. I want some real money . . .

Michael has also had a positive effect on his brother's legitimate business interests; at his urging the garage now employs a tyre fitter who has increased business, and he is thinking about setting up a car-valeting shop close to the garage. He also urged Charlie to consider a establishing a delivery service for the sandwich business, run by Sue, Charlie's girlfriend, to local office buildings and businesses, which increased business substantially. This has not led to him neglecting more guileful business opportunities:

Michael: I started to earn a little more from the garage but not that much. It's not like a gold mine or nothing . . . I still go to the match every week, still enjoy it. On away games people always wanted some whiz [speed, amphetamine]. We meet about eight in the morning to get the coach wherever we're going, sometimes earlier if it's down south or we're expecting trouble. A few times I saw that some of the lads would bring some whiz and everyone would try and greed it off them. So that's how it happened. I knew this lad who could get me a nice bag of speed and wouldn't dare rip me off, so the night before the match I'd cut it up into little bags. Sell about ten, fifteen to get your money back, then everything's a profit. It was very much in demand; it's a long day, an away match. Sell some at home matches too, you know?

I don't really make that much out of it. It depends. Charge a fiver a bag, maybe make seventy quid profit in one day. It's not much, but it's worth having if there's no risk. It's a free day out isn't it? That's the way I see it anyway . . . I started to buy a bit more of the stuff and sell it on a Friday and Saturday, maybe a Sunday to people out for a night out or the out-all-day Sunday crowd. I'd only sell to people I knew, no risk. Sometimes I'd get a load of bags cut up and give it to a mate to sell on the coaches going over to Manchester or Liverpool, to the big nightclubs, the dance nights. I'd sometimes sell it to mates in *The Lion* [Michael's local pub]. Sometimes I'd buy five ounces or something and just sell it on like that; less profit but it cuts down on all the fucking about. I had a good run of making about a hundred, two hundred, sometimes three hundred quid a week over and above the other stuff I was doing. Easy.

Michael has also made money directly from his reputation for violence. A friend of Michael became embroiled in a dispute with a drug dealer from another area of the city, which was based – almost traditionally – on the affections of a female. Michael's friend had had paint stripper poured over his car, was suffering nuisance telephone calls at all hours of the day and night and on one occasion narrowly escaped a serious beating by outrunning his foes. Michael's friend mentioned the incidents over a drink, not directly seeking help but seemingly dropping a hint. Michael, under the influence of alcohol, said he half knew the man involved, and if the problems continued his friend was to tell him that Michael would offer support if he did not desist. The problems continued, and Michael's friend returned to seek advice. Michael told me that he wished he had not become involved, but events seemed to have cut off any retreat. Michael visited the man and asked him to stop:

Michael: It was a pain but I had to do it. I went up where he hangs about, went in a few pubs. He wasn't there, but I asked about for him and word must have gotten back. I went up again, he wasn't there. And again. Now I'm getting a bit pissed with this fucker. People are starting to whisper about this, you know? I eventually caught up with him in this pub before the match. He saw me before I saw him, and he comes up next to me at the bar. People are starting to move away now. He starts off with 'alright, I haven't seen you in ages', all that shit. I told him to get outside. You can feel the eyes. One of his mates starts following us out, and I just fucking let loose on this cocky fucker, swearing my head off at him, telling him to go back inside or I'll murder him. He goes. Now I'm really pissed off. Now he's not in front of his mates, he really wants to be best friends. I say he's been dodging me and I fucking hate that. He says he didn't know what I wanted, if I was looking for trouble. By now I've won. He's shitting himself and I wasn't sure if I should give him a beating for spoiling my match day. Anyway, he gives it, 'I didn't know he was your friend' and all the shit's coming out. I just told him, you know, I don't joke with this shit, I'll kill him, like fucking dead, you know? He doesn't want any bother, says he doesn't know how all this shit started. I've won. I send him in the pub to buy me a pint, just so everyone knows I've won and didn't even have to slap the fucker. Made him walk from one side of the pub to the other to give me the pint . . . He was a drug dealer and wanted to be a gangster, but in the end he bottled it.

Michael's friend was extremely grateful, especially given how close the incident came to violence. His car had been broken into three times inside of two weeks and he felt his foe was responsible. Michael was unable to buy his own beer in the presence of the said friend for months.

A similar situation arose shortly after. This time the victim was no more than an acquaintance – a local builder who was doing quite well – however, he told a tale of woe involving a fight he had had with a bouncer in the city centre. Though he had apparently acquitted himself quite well, when he had gone to the hospital to have his wounds tended, the bouncer and ten friends had turned up and threatened him with decapitation. The victim recounted how he had only got into the fight while trying to calm down a fracas in which the bouncer was involved. Once sober he was consumed with fear, and sought out Michael in *The Lion*, where he holds court on Sundays, to seek his help:

Michael: I don't know how I got involved in this shit! The second time I thought the lad could have sorted it out himself, but he was shitting himself. He was a street-wise type of guy, more of a friend of Charlie's, but it was all getting a bit gangsterish for him; there was talk of people coming through from Leeds and stuff. I wanted to help the lad out, and the bouncer he had the bother with was Nigel, who works all over the city on the doors. He's big, but not up to much and I knew him quite well. Anyway, I say to the lad why should I help, and he says he'll sort me out. OK. I go to see Nige when he's at work and tell him. He says he's not really bothered but he still wants to fight the lad. He's says, fair fight and we'll leave it at that. I tell the lad and he's still shitting himself; he doesn't want to fight him. I tell him it's his only way out. I didn't want to get myself involved any more than that.

It was arranged for the fight to take place in a pub car park on a Sunday afternoon, but in actuality it took place in a nearby park area, cut off from prying eyes. Around a hundred men gathered to watch the spectacle, one sporting a video camera to record the unfolding events for posterity.

Michael: It was a good fight, and I thought the boy did quite well. Nigel was bigger but this lad put up a good performance. He just got his mad up and went nuts. Nigel and his fucking huge mates weren't happy, they wanted to tear this lad apart, but they let it go. The lad sort of knew that was because I was there. He came around the pub the next week and dropped me a hundred quid, which was very nice of him. He's all right actually. I saw Nigel and he let it go and I'm still all right with him; just had to tell him how he easy won the fight and he was happy . . . I helped out this other kid who asked. The lad he had the bother with, which was only Eric [a close friend of Michael], so I said I'd sort it out for a hundred. I phoned Eric up and we had a laugh about it; I gave him twenty quid for a few drinks.

Michael continued to expand upon his business interests and violent reputation. His entrepreneurship has, at the time of writing, still to attract the attentions of the law, although his capacity for violence certainly has. Michael is mostly quite business-like in his criminal dealings, but on occasion he is prone to violence at the slightest provocation, especially when drunk. Violent escapades in his younger days brought minor convictions for petty public order offences, and at the age of twenty he received 140 hours' community service after breaking someone's jaw on a night out. At the age of twenty-three he narrowly missed his first custodial sentence for a serious assault. This close brush with prison failed to dampen Michael's commitment to illegality, and indeed he stepped up his criminal enterprises even as he was awaiting his final court date at which he would receive his sentence. Michael had met a man from Leeds who was also in the car business, and who would offer him the opportunity to get a foothold in the newly emerging market of fake bank notes.

Michael: Right at first I knew it was gonna be good. This was three, four years ago and fake tenners were nowhere near as common as they are now . . . the quality was good but not great and I bought a grand's worth at two quid each. This is when I'm doing well off the speed as well. It was all new back then and you could get rid of them anywhere. It was like buying real money at a big discount. Charlie started putting a few in the business takings. The bank didn't notice and would put the real money in your account. If they do spot one, it's like, oh, a customer must have passed it. It wasn't risky back then. Pubs were easiest; very dark, the barmaid's in a hurry. Two quid a bottle of Budweiser and eight quid change! I get excited just thinking about it. Eight quid profit every pub, and a beer. Then, you know, taxis, backwards and forwards. Two quid journeys, give them three quid to keep them happy, seven quid change. Nice, isn't it? Over and over again. I drove all over the Yorkshire in taxis, different taxi firms so word doesn't get around, just backwards and forwards. Even better, at first, newsagents, buy a paper for thirty pence, nine pounds seventy change . . . After a while it started to get in the papers and stuff, and shops started getting special pens and lights and shit to check the notes, but by then I'd made a fortune and went back to this bloke to get some more. I wanted fifteen grand's worth of dodgy tenners off him. He said that he'd let me have them for three thousand nine hundred; I told him to piss off, I'd give him three grand. He took it, but in the end I only ended up giving him two grand six hundred. He was lucky to get that.

   . . . Of course you use as many as you can yourself, then your making more money, you know? But it was harder to get rid of them. Most times in a shop or a pub or something they'll just give you the tenner back if they think it's dodgy anyway. I started to sell a couple, maybe five quid for a single, maybe three fifty if they bought a few and I knew them, but after a while I just thought I was robbing myself for that, it was a profit but not as much as I could be getting. In the end I got a couple mates of mine who worked in pubs to use them. You couldn't just go in and give them to your mate behind the bar anymore, they'd find out and dock their wages or something, so I'd give them a little bundle and they'd give them out in change every time someone paid for drinks with a twenty. Most of the time they can't tell because they're pissed, and anyway, the chances are they just hand it back in at the next pub they go in to. I had four people doing this for me at one time. I said I'd paid five quid for each note and I'd split the profit with them, two fifty each. They were happy with the money and liked the buzz. One of the lads who was doing this for me went along all three tills in the pub and took out all the real tenners and put the dodgy ones in instead at the start of the night. The pub was trading on dodgy tenners all night, all the staff were changing them and didn't know it. It worked; the coppers came around the pub at closing time but they just thought the pub had been targeted by a gang of people changing dodgy tenners. The staff got a bollocking off the licensee, told them to keep an eye out, check the notes carefully and all that. Things like that were rare though. It was mostly just steady and slow, just get rid of them and make your profit.

Earning and Burning Money

Michael went back and got a third consignment of fake ten pound notes. His contact also gave him five hundred pounds' worth of fake fifty pound notes free of charge as a bonus for his good custom. Even though their quality was variable, Michael felt that they were such a rarity in the circles in which he moved that he could get rid of them in some way.

Michael: We went down to London to try and get rid of some, just spend the weekend on the piss really. The best memory I have of all this is of going into the Savoy and the Hilton and stuff, suited up and that, all the best places with that bloke outside who holds the door open for you and gets a taxi and stuff; tip him a dodgy tenner just to hold the door, tip the barman, go to the bog and there's this bloke asking if you want some aftershave and stuff. Finish me piss, and I'm just shaking off and he comes up behind me and starts dustin' down the back of me jacket! Fucking comical. Get mucked in to all the after-shave, wash me hands and he's got the hot towels ready. Unbelievable. I see a tray of ten bobs [fifty pence pieces] . . . He's a decent old bloke, and you've got to feel sorry for the cunt having to work like that, so I slip a dodgy twenty in his palm – 'there you go son, get something nice for your lass'. His jaw drops, 'thank you very much sir, I will'. Fucking sir, he calls me now I'm dropping notes. I could turn up any other day and they wouldn't let me in the place, now it's fucking sir . . . Dropped the bloke at the door a tenner and off we go clubbing. Went to this flash place, couldn't get in at first, no member-ships. A tenner apiece sorts it out. Great night, everyone trying to be a bit flash in front of the birds and that. What a laugh. Sid [Michael's friend] gets caught with a dodgy tenner and gets chucked out by this fucking ape while we [Michael and his remaining three friends] piss ourselves laughing! . . .

Next day we was walking around this market, forget the name, hangovers all over the place, but we're making up for all the dodgy tenners we wasted the night before, we're doing quite well. This tart comes up to Sid and gives it; I know you from somewhere, don't I? She's a good looking bird, no shit, and Sid is a right ugly little fucker, so I start to get the picture, but Sid's fallen in love. Can't get his words out and he's just mumbling on about nothing and looking at his shoes, so I spelt it out, you know, 'have you got any mates about?' She says, 'yeah, I'll be back in ten minutes, meet you in that pub over there'. It was funny as fuck, honestly. We went for a pint, we knew what they were, that they'd seen us with money and pegged us for tourists. Anyway, I bottled it, Gav bottles it, Wayne bottles it but Sid and Dennis [all Michael's friends and companions on the trip] are all for it and wait for the lasses to come back. We'd been using my dodgy tenners, and I was sort of paying for the train and hotel and that. Sid was skint, and he and Mark are begging for me to lend them some so they can get laid. I wind them up and say no chance, but I give in and give them two hundred quids' worth. The birds turn and they're all supermodels. I'm not fucking you about, really they are. We leave them and meet them later on. The bastards got the works, and these birds get stuck with a bunch of dodgy bank notes. Sid still owes me for that, the little bastard!

The thing is, if I'd took it serious, worked the tenners hard down in London, I could have made a lot of money. I'm talking thousands. In the end I think I just about broke even, if that. We had a good drink though, food and stuff included. We got caught about ten, fifteen times. Nearly every time they gave the dodgy note back. Only one time it got a bit heavy and we had to had drag Sid away from this big fucker on one of the markets. That was their job though, that's why they were there. Back home I was kicking myself, thinking of all the money I could have made. It was a laugh though, like a holiday really . . . The lads were grateful as well, and now I know I can ask a favour of them and they'll do it, which counts for a lot, you know? You've got to have a few boys about and it all adds up. Do a favour to get a favour.

Michael went on to describe other ways to squeeze the maximum profit out of fake currency. He'd managed to get some fake pesetas and travellers cheques and did a roaring trade as friends and acquaintances booked up for summer holidays. He has recently taken some of the money earned from his various nefarious activities and bought a share in a local business he'd prefer me not to describe. It was a proud moment for him, and it briefly brought about a reconciliation with his mother, if not his stepfather. Michael's arrival as partner coincided with an increase in business, which he puts down to his influence. He is keen to expand and has an eye on the vacant lot next door.

Charlie has branched out into industrial carpet cleaning with the help of his long-term girlfriend Sue and some of her friends. Michael apparently helped secure the trade of a number of publicans, and although this is just a sideline for Charlie, run mainly by Sue, they are apparently doing quite well, legitimately.

Michael continues to keep his eyes open. He still sells amphetamine and has branched out into the cannabis trade, a hobby that he decided he should be making money. He restricts his trade to a strictly vetted clientele to avoid contact with the police, and has no plans to expand in this field. He now offers a delivery service which he argues is good business as it stops a steady stream of customers turning up at his door or at his local, thus camouflaging his trade, and is also appealing to dope smokers as they never want to leave the house. He makes his deliveries in a new four-wheel-drive jeep on which he has a monthly payment plan. Michael still goes to the match every week, and is trying to stay out of trouble there, despite his virtual folklore status among a certain segment of the crowd. He still gets drunk and hangs around with his mates, and has even been known to become emotional when he hears *Two Little Boys* by Rolf Harris after the match, with its poignant lament to true manhood and friendship. Michael's goals in life are changing however. Recognition of his fighting ability just doesn't cut it any more:

Michael: I tell you, MONEY! . . . that's what I want! Who sang that? Can't remember, but anyway it's true. I love it, love to have it, you know, in my hands. Whip out a fat role and stuff, people looking over and stuff, nudging their mates, 'Look at that flash cunt.' I get butterflies in my stomach . . . Just got to keep grafting and I'll get it. Keep looking over my shoulder. Everyone wants money, the difference is I'm not waiting for the lottery.

Few would doubt Michael's ability to earn money. He is no longer reckless in his quest for money, his skills have increased and he possesses the power of violence to back up his moves. What's more, time is on his side. At twenty-five he still has time to realize the multitude of money-making schemes that whirl around in his mind. His criminal and legitimate connections are expanding and he has the ability and charisma to use and abuse them in just the right way. As Bauman (1989) points out the marketplace thrives on diversification and both Michael and Charlie are adept at this.

Michael Revisited

Carolyn Rothstein, wife of the famed American racketeer Arnold Rothstein, on her husband's attitude to money:

> Until the end of the war he had money, but it was not too much for him to be able to count it. Afterwards there was so much of it he could not keep track of it. When we married, it was his ambition to have $100,000. Then he raised the limit, first to a quarter of a million, then half a million, and finally to a million. When he had his limit, he took off the limit. All he wanted was more.
>
> (Quoted in Bean 1995: 247.)

I saw Michael not too long ago and his life remains much the same. His status in his native city and particularly in his neighbourhood continues to grow steadily, as does his involvement in the marketplace. He has three window-cleaning rounds in which he has little involvement other than collecting his money, and has a burger and hot-dog van that pleases him greatly. His Auntie Janice serves up tea, coffee and assorted fast food to crowds going to football matches and to those coming out of pubs and nightclubs. Michael brags about his profit margins and recently bought shares in the football club on whose terraces he first forged his reputation.

All of this would seem to be a case in point of meritocratic advancement into the middle classes, albeit with a slight twist. Despite the indications of a fat roll of cash, a nice car, a variety of incomes and a growing interest in *The Times* financial section, Michael remains irrevocably working-class; his personality, voice, mannerisms, and dirty hands portray an individual, who, despite his entrepreneurial status, is still rooted to the neighbourhood in which he was born and the varied socializing influences to which he was subject. He still holds court in his local pub on Sunday afternoons and would still sell you a tenner bit of dope if he knew your face. Other services may or may not be available upon request. He may be able to recover the goods taken in a burglary if the right person is asking, which can be especially useful if the insurance company has already been forthcoming with the full value of the goods taken. Michael is your first point of contact with the murky yet seductive netherworld of illegality and profit. Want some fake designer goods? A nice new shirt for Saturday night? A bottle of perfume for the woman in your life? Step outside and he'll see what he can do for you . . .

Michael also seems to have gained a sense of perspective on his entrepreneurship. One afternoon he tells me 'little fires warm you, big fires burn you', in answer to a question about his plans for the future. A decline in ambition? 'No chance, just being sensible. You don't earn any money when you're banged up, do you? Don't bite off more than you can chew and all that.' Seven pints later he's got his arm draped over my shoulder, slurring his Marlon Brando as Vito Corleone impression . . . 'What have I ever done to make you disrespect me? You should know, you come to me, I make it easier . . . '

Artie the One-man Party

The hedonistic strand to serious criminality reflects a division of labour that is rooted firmly in traditional practices and traditional proletarian notions of leisure and pleasure.

(Hobbs 1995: 116)

Artie, in comparison with the other respondents in this study, was easily recruited. He is naturally talkative and in this respect an ideal interviewee. He would tell me anything at all regarding his extensive criminal career, far more than most active criminals would consider prudent. If I hadn't been introduced to Artie by one of his closest friends who verified a good deal of the material our interviews produced, I would have been forced to question the validity of his tales as at times he carries the air of someone who will say anything just to keep talking and remain the centre of attention. However, I am sure that all of what is included here is true, and indeed this has been confirmed by numerous sources (see Douglas 1976). Artie is a 'master communicator' (Williams 1990), a born showman who thrives on an audience, holding their attention with a complex lexicon of drug phrases, rhyming slang, dialectical terms, wild gesticulation and imaginative vernacular. The hardest part of the series of interviews was not the usual ethnographic problem of coaxing out the most desired information from a circumspect criminal, but trying to keep Artie on track and restrict him to the topics I wished to cover. He would start to describe one criminal situation and move onto another without offering a conclusion to the first; and a result of this I carried out nine interviews instead of the two or three I had foreseen. After a period of trial and error I found the most effective way to conduct the interview was simply to let him talk. At times I would throw in a pertinent question to help drag him back on track, but this was not always successful. As with Michael, the piece below is a composite of a number of interviews.

Artie is an all-purpose drug dealer who sums up the fluidity and adaptability of his trade and wider drug economy, the characteristics of which have been widely detailed (see, for example, Adler and Adler 1983; Mugford and O'Malley 1991; Collison 1996). At twenty-six, Artie has seen and done just about everything in the drugs market, and has recently been released from a fifteen-month prison sentence for a variety of drug-related offences. He remains on probation and is currently unemployed.

SW: When did you start selling drugs?

Artie: About fifteen I suppose. That's when I started proper . . . I was just that way inclined, I think. I could have ended up doing anything, you know. Some do this, some do that, I got into drugs, but fuck it, you know? That's the way it goes. A lot of people, lads I know too, think, oh, drugs, all junkies, dirt, grime and crime. Drugs screw you up and stuff, needles, stuff like that, seen the adverts and shit. Even a lot of thieves I know, real wrong 'uns, would never get involved in drugs. They think if you have an E you'll be addicted, fall down dead. Someone told them that's what happens and they just swallow it up without even thinking about it. Well that was never me. I was never one to knock something I knew nothing about or haven't even tried. I mean drugs are powerful things, and I suppose I had a natural aptitude for it [drugs]. That was just my thing really. It was the music, raves and stuff when I started taking gear. Before everyone started jumping on the bandwagon. House music now, garage, whatever. It was the music and everything around the music, around 1989, 1990, 91. It became the most important thing in my life, I'm not kidding. The atmosphere back then was just amazing . . . they called it the second summer of love, 1989. It's not like it is now, with all these big super clubs, people thinking more about their clothes than the music. We were the originators. I sound like a kid about it, don't I? But that's the way it was. It was really . . . [pauses] meaningful [laughs]. No really, I had some great times and that's the way I saw it you know?

 As soon as I got into house music that was it for me. I had to go to clubs and raves, those big warehouse jobs, remember those? It wasn't should I go, because I just had to go, I had to be there in case I missed anything. You know what it's like, you have a night in, the next day someone's telling a story about who did what and all that and everyone's laughing except for you because you don't know what the fuck they're talking about, and you're thinking, bastard, I should have gone out. I just loved being on the spot, being part of the excitement and stuff. I was just meant to be there. We'd travel all over the country, all the top places, and that's how I got into dealing. It's an expensive lifestyle and you need to earn some money. If you're out every night people get used to seeing you about and you get to be part of it: drugs, motorways, bouncers, after hours places, more drugs, you just get deeper into it. You need the money to keep up, and once you're that deeply involved it's obvious what you are going to do. It's a natural progression. It wasn't frowned upon or anything like that, it was just expected. One day so-and-so is dealing, the next he's buying gear off the guy he sold it to the week before.

Back then it was different. Today you think about big bad drug dealers, gangsters or people hanging around school yards selling gear to kids. Back then it was like you were doing people a favour, it really was. People would thank you after you sold them an E because they weren't always easy to get and people would search all over for them. I actually enjoyed it. I always tried to get good stuff, and it was like being famous. They'd be pleased to see you, they'd ask how you were doing and I actually wanted all the people I sold to to have a good night, get into the spirit of things. I wanted them to discover something I knew. I'd walk in a place and everybody's saying, 'all right . . . all right . . . how you doing . . . hey, how are you, all right . . . all right', on and on, everyone's shaking hands with me. I really enjoyed it. It's nice especially when you're a young lad. Money was just the tokens back then, just to keep me out and about . . .

Everyone wanted Es and there was a lot of money to be made. The stuff was generally better than the gear you get today and you could sell all the Es you could get your hands on . . .

As criminal opportunities usually present themselves in situations commonly encountered in one's everyday environment (Bottoms 1994), Artie found the act of moving from clubber to drug dealer to be unproblematic; and although he may have started his deviant career as a form of altruism towards his fellow clubbers (see Dorn et al. 1992), the sudden influx of money changed his outlook on his participation in the emerging rave and dance music youth culture (see Redhead et al. 1993 for background and discussion) and its attached drugs market. Drugs were becoming a 'normal aspect of a commodified society' (Mugford and O'Malley 1991: 29) and Artie found himself in a position to exploit the growing market. As many of those who engage in other deviant activities (see, for example, Shover and Honaker 1992; Katz 1988) and legitimate occupations also find, Artie's lifestyle and spending habits expanded to fill his income. This pulled him into further drug dealing to maintain his extravagances, pushing him to amplify his activities to get more money so that he could again feel and exhibit a sense of excess. Artie's spending habits at this time often prompted fond reminiscences from him and his friends. Apparently, whatever he had in his pocket he would spend, then sell more drugs and start again. I include the following anecdote from a close friend of Artie to illustrate the hedonism that Artie had incorporated into his everyday life:

Oh, fucking unbelievable. He just didn't give a fuck [about money]. He recognized it for what it is, I think; dirty bits of paper. It's just stuff that lets you enjoy yourself. The more you've got the more fun you can have. People worry all their lives about money; must pay this bill, must pay that bill – they're missing the point. It's like people say about smoking; you know, I might get run over tomorrow – that's the way he thought. Why worry? I was never like that, and other people who were selling at the time weren't; most people were still greedy . . . He had a lot of money through his hands. A lot, and that's saying something because there were lots of lads who were risking it and getting fuck all . . . One time we were down Manchester shopping. I think he ended up spending over a grand without even really thinking about it, and it's not like he's even into clothes that much. He didn't even try the stuff on most of the time, like he didn't care. Once he'd spent it he'd forgotten about it. We'd go into clubs, he'd go to the bar, and it's like, [mimicking Artie's voice] 'Champagne! And keep it coming until one of us falls over!' He wasn't all business, not back then, not when we were out. Walking around a club with a bottle of champagne in your hand and a straw in the top. People thinking, look at that flash bastard, and that makes it even better. Remember this is going back as far as he was eighteen. Women everywhere, all the best gear, Es, bit of Charlie every now and then when we could get hold of it. He'd be talking to the DJ, the promoters, the bouncers, all the local gangsters; he knew everyone . . . It's not like he was thick or anything, because he wasn't. It's just the way he was, you know?

On closer examination it is hard to maintain the impression that Artie merely viewed money as dirty bits of paper. He often refers to money as 'the chips', the means with which he can pursue his party lifestyle; however, symbolism and the reaffirmation of values (Shover and Honaker 1992) are also involved in Artie's conspicuous consumption.

Even if Artie lived for the day (Shover and Honaker 1992), this did not rule out a degree of forethought as to how he could earn more money in his chosen profession. Money was a means to an end, and the hedonistic lifestyle Artie led meant he required ever increasing amounts of 'dirty bits of paper' to maintain and expand it.

Artie: I just want to say that it's not always like they say in the papers. Not like one guy sells to another guy who sells it to another guy who sells it to another guy and all that. I got gear regularly off a bloke called Joe Montgomery [name changed], but I'd get it from other people too. Sometimes I'd pay up front if I had the money – that way I get a better price – but I got credit mostly. And then what do I do? Do I just go out and sell them? Not always. I've got to think a little bit. I mean, if I've only got a few I sell them myself – that's what I was good at. I was really good at actually selling gear. I just knew how to talk to people who used Es back then, and a lot of lads didn't. I gave it the full pitch; these Es are new to the area, give them a good name and that, or these are very dancy Es, mongy Es whatever. They weren't always stamped with a logo back then. I knew what I was talking about. Es is Es, but people might want dancy Es, which are cut with speed or whatever. I sold speed as well; everyone wanted it and if I could get it I'd sell it. What if I've got a lot of Es? Do I sell them all? Depends again. Is the bloke asking for his money? Can I put him off? Can I get some more? Are they any good? Sometimes I'd give them to some of the lads to sell, let them make a couple of quid an E. Make sure to give them to them on the night so you can get your money off them straight away. But at the same time I might sell a few myself – that way I get all the money. Sometimes you might get someone who wants to buy ten or twenty or whatever, just for themselves and their mates. Think of a price? Who is it? How much can I charge them? Even the lads who sell a few for me are thinking about this. Do they know the person? Do they seem to know what they're talking about? That kind of stuff. It's horses for courses. Maybe I just middle fifty or sometimes more, make a quick profit and start all over again. But then you've got to think, do I keep them to myself, because I might not be able to get any next month. You've just got to make it up as you go along. One day I'm selling one at a time in a club, next I'm selling to a guy who is going to sell them to a guy who's going to sell them in a club . . . It's like that.

Artie was doing well. He was making and spending a lot of money.

Artie: I think back now, and the money I had and blew was unbelievable. But that's what it's for. No point in having it and not spending it. But back then, when I was eighteen, nineteen, twenty years old and you've got five or six hundred quid in your pocket, what are you going to do? It's like winning the lottery, isn't it, a lad of that age? I remember having three hundred quid in my pocket once, when I was about eighteen – I was waiting to meet a mate. He was late and I had nothing to do. I went into this arcade [computer game, gambling machine arcade], thought I'd have a go on the bandits. I ended putting about a hundred and fifty quid in this bandit in about twenty minutes. Absolute truth. My mate turned up, I tell him, and he's like, you've got three hundred quid in your pocket, what do you want to gamble for? Three hundred quid isn't enough or something? I remember him being upset, said if I didn't want it I could have given it to him, that kind of stuff. I wasn't bothered though. Well I was, but I just thought you've got to get on with it. Nothing you can do about it now. At eighteen what do you need? I had all the clothes and that, whatever I needed, but I've got three hundred quid left. What do you do with it at eighteen? I wish I'd saved a bit now, but I'm just saying that because I'm skint at the moment. Should have given some to my Mam, but where do I say I got it?

It's not like I was loaded all the time. You go through spells. What I had going for me was I never stopped; I'd be out every night, not just weekends. Most people weren't. That's the thing; you've got to be on the spot to get the business and thinking back I'd sell to anyone. I wasn't careful at all. In those days you got a lot of people asking around in clubs if anyone knew anyone selling Es, so because I knew a lot of the lads around in the club the business was mine. They'd bring them over and, boom, you sell a couple . . .

If there wasn't a decent dance night on, we'd go to Leeds, Manchester, Liverpool, even as far as London. All over. Someone would always drive. Go up to Edinburgh and Glasgow, give one of the lads another bunch of Es to sell somewhere else. Give someone else a hundred wraps of speed. I did well because Joe [Arties friend and a regular supplier] was getting loads of Es off this bloke from Doncaster, and he'd let me have as many as I could sell. Still I'd be skint some of the time because the profit isn't always that big. Sometimes I'd have to bum drinks off people. Sometimes I got in bother because Joe would want his money and I'd gotten carried away and spent it, or at least some of it. He'd take it off me straight away so I didn't fuck up. He knew what I was like and I tried not to piss him off. But remember the same thing can happen to me on a smaller scale. I'd have to chase daft tenners up and stuff, people thought they could beat me out of small amounts, that I wasn't bothered, and that sort of stuff is really fucking annoying, but generally I got on well with everyone who I gave gear to. There were always times when there was a bit of shit going on, because you can't always be friends when you're dealing with money. I didn't suffer as bad as some because people knew it wasn't just my money they were fucking around with.

One time I was skint and this lad who was a bit older than most of us comes up and says he can get a thousand Es at a nice price. He had the money to put up, fuck knows where he got it from. No matter how cheap he gets the gear from we're talking a lot of money. His problem was he couldn't really sell them. He's a big fucker and doesn't know his way around, doesn't know people, plus he thinks the coppers are on to him and he wants to play the big man. It's not always easy to just come in like that. You might piss people off, plus people like to know who they're dealing with and this guy was new. He says, 'If you think you can sell them, I'll get them, but if you don't I'm going to pass on it.' Remember, he shouldn't really be talking to me. This is a lot of Es, he should have gone to someone like Joe if he had any sense. Anyway, I was skint so I say get the fuckers.

To drastically shorten a long and complex story, Artie managed to sell a great deal of the Es, which he was given in increments of two hundred. Artie maintains he only received six hundred in total. He also managed to swallow quite a few and spend a good deal of the income. The time came and passed for Artie to pay his new supplier.

Artie: I knew right away I wasn't gonna pay him. Well not right away, but I hardly know this lad, you know. Lots of people know him but nobody knew him well. He was quite a big bloke. I wouldn't like to fight him, but I just got the feeling he didn't know what he was doing. He wasn't really part of that whole scene, you know? It's like he thought he could just come in, make a couple of grand and get out. He was a nice enough bloke at first, but then he starts giving it, where's my money? If he saw me when I was out I'd give him a hundred quid or something, but what does he think, I'm gonna walk up to him and say, oh, here's that two grand I owe you? Not in this life. There's other ways to deal with situations like this and I thought I could lie my way out of it or try and get some other people involved so he does give me a beating or anything.

Luckily for Artie, the supplier was arrested on an unconnected charge just as threats started to be issued. Apparently the supplier clung to the belief that given time Artie would get him the money he was owed. It appears that the supplier failed to impart enough fear into Artie, who, in a development tangential to this story, was becoming closer to Joe, his regular supplier, in both a business and a personal sense. Joe Montgomery, a middle-aged man of some repute in the area, seemingly gave Artie the confidence to continue stalling the new supplier. Artie is vague about what Joe had to gain from this alliance, but it seems to be a mixture of business and personal attachment.

Artie is full of business anecdotes such as this. A quick glance over the notes and transcripts from the series of interviews I conducted with Artie confirms that he did indeed make a lot of money from his illegal activities. Artie continued to sell drugs for some time.

His business relationship with Joe Montgomery continued and his social circle began to include a much shadier cast of characters. The music and club culture that had been so crucial in bringing Artie into drug dealing became less and less important as Artie's friends and colleagues began to change from long-haired young men who liked to dance and take drugs, to men with big shoulders and crew cuts who liked to drink lager by the gallon, to fight and wouldn't dance if their lives depended on it. Eventually Artie received a prison sentence, which ended his drug dealing career. The interviews from which the above quotations are taken were conducted around three months after his release, when Artie was at home or spending most of his time in the pub and was not dealing drugs.

Artie Revisited

I know that the only way I could live the style I liked was by being a thief. It was easier than working for a living. The money rolled in. Sometimes it went out faster than I could steal it, but it was a good life. I liked the excitement. There was a kind of a thrill to everything I did . . . It's hard to explain, but there was a feeling of power being on the street with men that were always hustling, outfiguring the straights. It seemed that every-one I knew or grew up with was a thief of one kind or another. We were all living pretty good, spending high, dressing well, hitting all the good spots. It was a helluva life.

(Teresa 1973: 60)

Artie did not stay out of the drugs business for long. Eighteen months after my first series of interviews I again contacted him with a view to getting information on his current activities. The following piece is offered as evidence of Artie's commitment to his deviant lifestyle and the immediate gratification that this incorporates. Although his commitment remains, Artie has refined his operations somewhat, in the hope of avoiding a further prison term and in an attempt to fit in with the present market climate of drug supply. Artie's deviant business is becoming more businesslike and increasingly complex as entrepreneurial crime in the North East of England becomes increasingly embedded in the consciousness of criminally inclined working-class males.

For the last five Friday nights Artie has conducted business from Reggie's flat in a quiet neighbourhood in Leeds. Reggie is an old friend who works in a local factory and supplements his income by occasionally selling cannabis. On this particular Friday we watch Chris Evans on television as Reggie rolls his first joint of the night and Artie sets up his electric scales.

Artie has already told me that he usually likes to deliver his merchandise to protect himself from the prospect of having his parental home raided. He has resided there since his release from prison. Delivering also rules out the prospect of being caught with a large amount of drugs and having a succession of shady-looking characters turning up at the door and upsetting the neighbours. Artie believes Reggie's flat to be safe, as very few people know of their connection; the neighbours never pay any attention, and he will only be dealing with a small and trusted circle of clients.

Tonight is a special occasion. Artie has cocaine, a drug that is growing rapidly in popularity among young, fashion-conscious club goers with a disposable income and a desire to distance themselves from speed – which they seem to consider a dirty drug, with its high content of cut and its excruciating come downs. Artie is pleased; he can sell all the cocaine he can get his hands on at the moment. The bad side to this is having to sit with a ruler and a glossy magazine ripping out strips and then folding them into wraps, into which he will put the cocaine. It is time consuming and boring and consequently he is not in the best of moods. He can't put the cocaine into the little plastic bags he uses for his mainstay, amphetamine, for apparently it slowly turns into a paste in bags. He reminisces about the good old days when all speed used to come in wraps. We talk about now-defunct night-clubs, DJs and nights out. Artie gives me some insider information about speed; evidently dealers would add food colouring to give it a pink tinge so the speed could be sold as 'pink champagne', a supposedly stronger version of the drug.

I ask Artie what happened to the ecstasy tablets he used to sell. He tells me that it's close to impossible to sell them in clubs these days because of increased security and the wariness of clubbers. I'm told that most club goers prefer to buy from a regular dealer to cut down on the risk of buying a dud. He also mentions that setting up a drug-dealing business inside a nightclub usually involves dealing with gangsters, which can be dangerous and cuts profit margins. He still sells them occasionally, but he only 'middles' them to other dealers or users who buy in bulk.

Reggie leaves the room to get a round of beers from the fridge. I can hear him complaining about the smell in the kitchen as Artie tells me he has a large, unspecified amount of speed in his possession, around half of which he will sell tonight. He's also got a couple of stops to make tomorrow. His mood visible brightens at the prospect. He avoids telling me what additive he uses to cut his speed with, and laughs for the first time that night. He likes his job, and likes to talk about it. He wants me to go away with the idea that he never uses additives, in case I should discuss the issue with mutual friends. Later he tells me he does cut his speed sometimes, but I wasn't to tell anyone; he won't tell me what he uses, but launches into the advantages and disadvantages of various substances as additives to speed. He tells me glucose is a bit sweet tasting and that in the old days less scrupulous dealers would add household products like nail varnish to counteract the sweetness. He says he wouldn't do that, of course, and tells me he never has done.

Reggie tells Artie it's his turn to make a joint; he smiles and takes a packet of Silk Cut cigarettes from the top of the fire. Inside are a number of ready-made joints. He throws one at Reggie as we discuss what's on television.

Artie is relaxed now. He tells me to follow him into the kitchen. He hands me a heavy Sainsbury's carrier bag, which oozes an acrid stench that sticks in my throat. Inside are a number of smaller bags containing various amounts of speed. I take one out for a look; it contains what I guess to be about fifty small plastic bags of speed. Artie tells me that's for Brian who prefers to buy his speed already in the bags. Artie calls him lazy, and informs me that he would give Morris a better price if he bought the speed in one big bag. Brian should be first to visit the flat tonight; he is going down to a nightclub in Manchester with friends and will find a ready market on the coach that will be taking them there. He may also want a small number of Es, which Artie will be happy to provide. The Es Artie has tonight are not very good but were all he could get. He has twenty-eight Es in total tonight and considers them to be merely a sideline these days. Artie then asks me to look into the fridge; next to the bottled beers are two Mars bar-size chunks of cannabis. Artie glows with self-satisfaction; he tells me he'll be cutting it up into smaller chunks to sell for ten pounds each later. Some of the people who'll be calling tonight might want some; it's there if they want it, but Artie plans to sell it later in the weekend. The cannabis is another sideline used to accentuate profit margins by keeping the customers happy. They might turn up to buy speed, but if they can buy some Es and a bit of cannabis at the same venue, well, that's a bonus and, to use a cliché, everyone's happy.

We go back into the sparse living room and Artie puts on his *Goodfellas* video. He says he has seen the film at least a hundred times, and with a gleam of content-ment tells me he has also read the book. Soon Artie is singing along with Tony Bennett's *Rags to Riches* and saying the opening lines of the film: 'As far back as I can remember, I always wanted to be a gangster.'

He asks me what I think of his setup and tells me he is doing well at the moment. He is again getting a regular supply, this time of speed, and he is having no trouble getting rid of it. He mentions the names of a number of gangsters and tells me never, ever to repeat those names. He then moves on to discuss his hectic schedule and the need to be careful and avoid the police. He complains he doesn't have time to enjoy himself any more. He talks about the benefits of cocaine, and then turns his attention to the television as Joe Pesci and Robert De Niro finish off the body in the trunk of the car. He smiles to himself and is quiet for the first time in the evening.

But not for long. Artie now has ambitions, a business plan, about which he is keen to inform me:

> I'm going to make some real money this time. All I need is to keep getting this stuff regular. I like, well, I know I've got to concentrate on business more. Don't get me wrong – I've haven't gone all serious about it, it's still just about getting the money, but, I don't know, this is what I do, and I'm good at it, so well, that's the way it's going to be. I still like a laugh, but if I fuck up now it's serious people. So that's the way it's gonna be and I'm gonna make fucking sure I get paid as well. As far as I can as fast as I can, just get a good run.

Brian turns up at a quarter past seven. He makes small talk with Artie about holidays and ignores me completely. Artie gives him his package and they make plans to meet tomorrow. Brian leaves. As the film progresses more customers arrive and leave. Some leave money, some don't. Artie tells me they will all be selling the stuff on, and then again goes into a series of drug-dealing reminiscences.

Six customers call in all. One wore a shell suit, which Artie poked fun at. This man bought one of the chunks of cannabis and eight Es. He sits and watches the film for a while and tells us about a plan to rob a truck, which fell through. He says can get us as many fake designer shirts as we want, and in response to a request from Artie will attempt to get a him a dodgy mobile phone.

The night progresses and I leave at midnight. Artie asks me if I want to accompany him to a local nightclub; I tell him I have no money. He responds that he knows the bouncers and will get us in for free; we won't even have to queue up. He'll take a bag of coke out and we'll go mental. I again decline. Artie tells me to be at a certain pub at a certain time if I want to join him and Tony – one of an increasing number of his muscle-bound cronies – on the rounds as he collects some of the money he's owed. My taxi arrives and I leave as Artie has a line of cocaine and Reggie lights up another joint and prepares to phone for a pizza.

–3–

Bouncing as a Contemporary Urban Career: Post-modernity, De-industrialization, Masculinity and Cultural Adaptation

In the post World War II era, the bureaucratisation and rationalisation of work, along with the decline of the family wage and women's gradual movements into the labour force, further undermined the 'breadwinner role' as a basis for male identity, resulting in a 'defensive insecurity' amongst men

A. Tolson, 'The Limits of Masculinity'

Introduction

The avenues by which one might approach the analysis of bouncing and its social and cultural organization are numerous. Because of the social, cultural and economic trends explored earlier, in this chapter I restrict myself to depicting the advent of bouncing as a career – in many instances a career in being physically intimidating – and issues associated with its social organisation. I have avoided the pertinent topics of location and strategy, ideal markets and drug supply (see, for example, Hobbs 1995: 74–80), the private enforcement of public law, protection rackets (see, for example, *Mixmag* 1998; Hobbs et al., forthcoming), the involvement of private security firms in all of these activities (Morris n.d), and the usefulness and implementation of bouncer registration schemes to weed out undesirables and regulate what is a highly problematic marketplace.

I do not offer this chapter as a journalistic exposé of bouncers and the criminality their occupation may allow, or as a definitive structural analysis of the occupation's social organization. Essentially, I suggest that the changing role of the bouncer/'hard' man is indicative of the social, cultural and economic changes that have so greatly changed the North East, and in continuing to develop my earlier arguments, I will focus on crime. It should be remembered that what follows is not intended to be a thorough regional analysis of bouncing. I focus on the deviancy of individuals who also happen to be bouncers, and do so in order to continue my analysis of changing deviant cultural practice and adaptation. I do not wish to impart criminal motives to an entire profession, but use it and the individuals researched in this chapter as representative of masculine, cultural and criminal change fitting closely with social and economic change in the post-industrial and post-modern North East. I will explore the opportunities bouncers now have to use their position and status to gain financially (criminally), this itself being a huge shift in deviant practice and opportunity in the area (see Chapter1).

Why Bouncers?

> Many [men] still equate a secure sense of themselves as men with the size of their bulges – from bulging wallets to bulging muscles to bulging crotches. And so every arena becomes a masculine testing ground: After a day's work we 'work out' so that in the evening, with our wives or lovers, we can 'get the job done' with our 'tools' and thus calm our 'performance anxiety'.
>
> (Kimmel 1996: 331)

It is my contention that an analysis of contemporary bouncers provides a particularly useful opportunity to depict the post-modernism manifest in a specific form of masculinity. Contemporary bouncers, in their very physicality, if nothing else, represent changing masculinities, and the majority of men employed in this occupation hail from a similar cultural background to that which I describe in these pages. It can be convincingly argued that masculinities within the lower social classes have been forced to change more than most, and it is overwhelmingly from these social groupings that bouncers have emerged. The decline and eventual collapse of traditional industry has transformed those masculinities that were closely linked with the world of work (see, for example, Ford 1985); and the failure of other industries to replace these employment structures has unavoidably led to the central role of breadwinner being lost in some sections of our society (see, for example, Tolson 1977; Ingham 1984). This and other challenges to traditional masculinity are explored elsewhere in the book; suffice it to say here that lower class men in contemporary society find their masculinity in flux and are in essence redefining their masculinity as they go.

The desire for a muscular physique certainly appears to be a growing concern among men of all social classes (although I would contend that those who take body-building seriously in a desire to build size, and in some cases extreme size, are largely from lower class backgrounds), and this has been linked to the acceleration of changes in the structures of male power and identity over recent years (for example, Kimmel 1996; Mishkind et al. 1987). What better way to depict masculinity than by encapsulating it in the body? As Connell (1995: 45) points out 'true masculinity is almost always thought to proceed from men's bodies – to be inherent in a male body or to express something about a male body.' Having large muscles immediately illustrates vibrant maleness; masculinity does not need to be spelled out through complex verbalizing or accepted modes of mutually congratulatory conversation (see, for example, Spangler 1992). You do not need to tell stories that thinly disguise your desire to be considered a man's man among peers; your very physicality is laying claim to the spirit of all that is masculine and accentuating difference from all that is feminine.

Bouncers are, of course, generally large, muscular men, but this is not the only reason for drawing attention to them in relation to post-modernity. Bouncing is now a viable career option for those men who consider themselves up to the job, and that usually means men from lower class backgrounds, and who have a good deal of violent potential, and large, muscular physiques. Their job is unusual in that it incorporates the likelihood (and sanction) of violence, and is often carried out in environments that typify the post-modern condition (see in the coming pages). Skills required for the job, understandably, are seldom articulated but for the most part revolve around violent reputation and a physically intimidating appearance. Experience, as with all jobs, is of course useful. Bouncers bring with them a crude bodily capital (see Wacquant 1992) and are offering themselves, and their bodies, as marketable assets, yet this is not simply a process of use and exchange value (see Baudrillard 1993). Just as important as the physical ability to carry out one's job is the sign value of one's body, speech and body language, facial expression and demeanour; for they signify the danger inherent in contravening the behavioural strictures imposed by various licensed premises. Customers understand the significance of the muscles, the tattoos and the shaved head, and this is also a crucial, if unstated, part of the employer–employee contract.

The arrival of a legitimate occupation based on these understandings has to some extent offered a legal avenue for income gain and expression based on some manifestation of traditional male working-class cultural concerns as described and discussed in the opening chapters of this book. As I have repeatedly stressed, violence remains a culturally valued commodity. The character I call 'Tommy' discussed in Chapter 1, recognized and revelled in the cultural veneration of violent potential, but was unable to capitalize on his hard-won abilities because of the cultural and economic climate in which he found himself. Today, if he were a young man he may well be a bouncer. The character I call 'Michael' in Chapter 2 was able to use his violent ability to gain both financially and culturally, because economic and cultural change allowed him to do so. His violent potential could now open the door to illegal entrepreneuriality and offer a highly valued platform from which to engage with the marketplace.

The bouncers I go on to describe illustrate the societal, cultural and economic changes which I have made central to this work. I feel that bouncers provide a particularly useful focus for the examination of these changes, and since I have framed these changes in the context of masculinities and crime, I consequently look at those bouncers who are involved in crime. As the North East has changed, so too have the boundaries of criminal action and, in consequence, those under discussion find themselves in a position to gain financially, and in a way that, for the most part, their criminal forebears could not. Again I stress that being a bouncer does not necessarily mean being a criminal, though a further reason for this group's inclusion and a recurrent topic of this book, is the link between occupation, economic and cultural change and crime. I am therefore referring to how these individuals use their physical capabilities and standing among their peers, along with their occupation, to benefit themselves criminally and financially. For being a bouncer offers the criminal entrepreneur a number of avenues to exploit, and their role as literal gatekeepers to a thriving night-time economy makes this restricted community an increasingly interesting group for the police and the social researcher alike.

Background: Bouncers as Literal Gatekeepers

> Professional crime has moved from an occupation foundation of neighbourhood orientated extortion and individualistic craft based larcenies towards an entrepreneurial trading culture driven by highly localised interpretations of global markets.
>
> (Hobbs 1994: 114–15)

Doormen, door supervisors, or more commonly bouncers, are literally gatekeepers to a night-time economy, which is symptomatic of the cultural and economic fragmentation of post-modern society. This night-time economy is not immediately apparent to some sections of society as it is not instantly visible during daylight hours; but it is most certainly there. Town and city centres of Britain often reawaken after shopping, business and work crowds have dwindled, to welcome a new clientele, and the dull thud of bass-heavy dance music reverberates to welcome visitors to or ward them off from a subterranean environment of pubs, wine bars, nightclubs and a gamut of associated industries, ranging from illegal drug supply to pizza parlours. Here, in a phantasmagoric (Baudrillard 1975, 1988) world of flashing lights, ear-bursting music, shady characters and like-minded peers, young adults can attach themselves to and become submerged in a 'lifestyle' (see Chaney 1996), which fundamentally shapes self identity and consciousness. In these environments there flourishes a Dionysian ritual of dance and hedonism (Nietzsche 1956), a bacchanalian culture of transitory indulgence diffuse with signs and meanings (see, for example, Bataille 1986, 1989).

It is in this environment that young people bond with mates and seek mates, get drunk, take drugs and seek out fun in a 'hyper-real' world where almost any hedonistic desire seems within reach, and the baggage of ones normative identity can be left safely at the door. Baudrillard (1988) believes the realm of the hyper-real to be 'more real than real, whereby the models, images, and codes of the hyper-real come to control thought and behaviour'. He has also argued that the post-modern world pushes people to flee the 'desert of the real' for the ecstasies of hyper-reality and that the 'narcoticised and mesmerised media-saturated consciousness is in such a state of fascination with image and spectacle that the concept of meaning itself dissolves' (Kellner 1993: 8–9).

Bakhtin's idea of the carnivalesque seems to correspond with the character of this hyper-real habitus (see the work of Bakhtin, esp. 1968, and Stallybrass and White 1986, who claim that 'recent thinking has largely confirmed Bakhtin's insistence on the relation between body-image, social context and collective identity'). In its symbolism and simulation, and the transformations taking place in its patrons' identity and self-identity, this environment is seemingly the very epitome of the post-modern. Use and sign value appear to merge in the consumption of designer beers and designer drugs, even as high fashion is donned by the majority rather than the lucky few and simulation is apparent at every turn.

Anyone who has visited this environment will be aware of a highly visible, but slightly detached yet integral community within it. Bouncers have the vital role of deciding who is admitted to this world, and then of policing those who succeed in gaining admittance. This job can be highly problematic for a number of reasons, the most obvious being that it is the bouncers' remit to deal with any disorder that occurs in an atmosphere often heavy with a potentially dangerous cocktail of strong lager and amphetamine-based drugs. This is not an entirely new problem, but the bouncers employed to keep order in this world are a reflection of changing economic and cultural patterns and a transforming mode of masculinity.

Contemporary Bouncers: Brief Hows and Whys

> The only visible aspect of continuity and of the cumulative effects of self-constitutive efforts is offered by the human body . . . : the material, tangible substatum, container, carrier and executor of all past, present and future identities. The self-constitutive efforts focus on keeping alive (and preferably enhancing) *the capacity* [italics in original] of the body for input of sensuous impressions and producing a constant supply of publicly legible self-definitions. Hence the centrality of *body cultivation* [italics in original] among the self-assembly concerns, and the acute attention devoted to everything 'taken internally' (food, air, drugs etc.) . . . In the post-modern habitat, D.I.Y operations (jogging, dieting, slimming [and bodybuilding] etc.) replace and to a large extent displace the panoptical drill of modern factory, school or the barracks; unlike their predecessors, however, they are not perceived as externally imposed, cumbersome and resented necessities, but as manifestos of agent's freedom. Their heteronomy, once blatant through coercion, now hides behind seduction.
>
> (Bauman 1992: 194)

Although it has been claimed that masculinity itself is an inherently frail identity in need of constant reaffirmation (see, for example, Chodorow 1978; Epstein 1991), it can clearly be seen that the arrival of post-modernism has led to traditional masculinities being attacked from a diversity of angles (for example, Brittan 1989; Connell 1995; Kimmel 1987, 1996), and I have already touched on the various crises bound up with working-class masculinities. Significantly, Giddens (1990: 92) has argued that wholesale social change has affected 'the confidence that most human beings have in the continuity of their self-identity and the constancy of their surrounding social and material environments of action'. As we are talking about contemporary bouncers, this distrust in one's own identity can be linked to the increased desire of men to redefine their masculinity by changing that most instrumental of masculine facets, the body – an 'active, self transforming subject' (Freud 1988). And though the quest for muscle may reveal men locked in a 'passionate battle against their own sense of vulnerability' (Glassner 1989: 315) and bodybuilding may be 'the archetypal expression of male identity insecurity' (Pleck 1982), bodybuilding and analysis of this quest for muscle can also provide added insight into the growth of bouncing as a profession, and criminal and cultural adaptation.

Although bodybuilding is not new it

> forms a unique prism through which to examine [male vulnerability] because muscles are the distinctive symbol of masculinity, the specific armamentarium of an embattled manhood. Their wilful acquisition and exhibition serve to establish or repair a damaged sense of oneself as a properly gendered being, i.e., a virile individual. Surveys have shown time and again that man's self-esteem correlates highly with having a muscular upper body, that males with slight or 'soft' physical makeups have lower levels of life satisfaction than their more athletic peers . . . bodybuilding stands as the prototype of . . . existential angst of masculinity because, by reducing the agonistic engagement of sportive competition to a battle with and against one's body, it strips athletic avocation down to its purely manhood-generating and manhood-affirming functions.
>
> (Wacquant 1998: 171).

As Dubbert (1979) asserts, bodybuilding is a 'primary masculinity-validating experience', though the body is also a tool of 'impression management' (Goffman 1969). Nearly all the bouncers I encountered during this research were engaged in bodybuilding, although commitment to this pastime obviously varied. Any visitor to the pubs and clubs of the North East will be struck by the size of those employed to keep order in these establishments aimed at those young people with a disposable income. In short, bodybuilding has arisen owing to significant economic, social and cultural upheaval, and is paralleled by the expansion of a leisure and lifestyle industry that has boomed in accordance with those same upheavals. The arrival of men made large by the wish to acquire muscles, to display their masculinity in its barest essence, has fitted symbiotically with an industry in which violence and drug dealing are likely to occur and need to be discouraged. In this social environment the body and its symbolism are being used to intimidate potential wrongdoers, dissuading them from acting in a way that the management feels would be detrimental to business. The sign value of large muscles is of course important here, but many bouncers also bring with them the ability to back up the symbolism, creating an efficient marketable package. In this sense the bodies of bouncers are a form of capital and bouncers become entrepreneurs of body capital (Wacquant 1992), able to use 'the natural forces of his body' (Marx republished 1972: 173) to secure employment in an area where this is not always easy.

Even though it is perhaps misguided to suggest that this type of overtly masculine employment has arisen to replace lost industrial labour (which, as I have argued, was also surrounded by a distinctly masculine imagery) it is true that the vast majority of bouncers are from and remain in what we would once have termed the 'working-class'. A few of the older bouncers with whom I spoke had memories of working in the North East's main industries; but in the main, traditional heavy industry is consigned to history, with the vast majority of bouncers being under the age of thirty-five. Some bouncers did have other full-time employment, which, overwhelmingly, tended to be manual and low skilled, whereas others lived solely on their wages from bouncing.

Bouncing and bodybuilding can become an attractive lifestyle for some, in that their night-time occupation allows them to spend the daytime at their leisure, or training in a gym. In this way, both the night and the day can be dedicated to the maintenance and amplification of one's masculine image and self-perception. However, the money earned from a bouncing career is rarely enough to adequately support a young adult male, and this can lead to criminal enterprise as a means of sustaining the lifestyle (see the discussion of 'Jimmy' below). It should also be noted that being a bouncer can be a highly attractive occupation for some men; for at the most obvious level the job allows one to mix with young females, and with friends and acquaintances in the engaging setting of a pub or nightclub. The job also allows an elaborate display of the masculine self, a distinct 'male epistemological stance' (Mackinnon 1982), and the potentially beguiling prospect of subtle status advancement as your peers recognize the violent potential that is encapsulated within the individual, the occupation and the friendship networks which surround it.

In the text below I focus on two specific instances of bouncers using their occupation and status as 'cultural authorities' (Hobbs 1995) as a foundation for entrepreneurial criminal enterprise. Both 'Jimmy' and 'Mark' epitomize changing masculinities and the changing nature of criminal activity in the North East. As 'market information and investment opportunities manifest themselves as part of the social milieu' (Hobbs 1995: 449), they are both able to capitalize on their position and occupation.

Jimmy: Intimidation as a Marketable Asset

Craft skills and traditional trades which have shaped images of masculinity may no longer be available to create viable gendered careers for men. In addition, unskilled employment opportunities have declined, along with the patriarchal base upon which recruitment, work practices, and neighbourhood ecology were grounded. Crime can be seen as a way of rebuilding this patriarchal base on the original site and with many of the traditional ingredients.

(Hobbs 1995: 107)

At the time of my first meeting with Jimmy he was employed as a bouncer in a large nightclub in the North East of England. We were introduced by a mutual friend who had served in the armed forces with Jimmy. The meeting and introduction were completely coincidental, at the time only seeming to be beneficial in that it saved me the eight pounds admittance fee to the nightclub. Jimmy, however, was to become a tremendous source of information and rumour for me throughout my research and provided me with a perfect model of a transformative lower class masculinity.

Jimmy's life and activities encompass a great deal more than will be discussed here. What he had to say opened up numerous avenues for sociological analysis, however the main reason he is included here is that, as a bouncer, he at once used his occupation, his reputation and a masterful use of intimidation to take advantage of 'a market geared to rationalisation and domination by a single commodity: drugs' (Hobbs 1994: 449). As will become clear, Jimmy was in the ideal location, and possessed the necessary knowledge and skills, to benefit financially from the market for amphetamine-based drugs that flourished around 1990.

Jimmy stands around five feet ten inches tall, perhaps a little taller, and as I write this piece has a large, muscular physique. I say 'as I write this piece' because over the course of my acquaintance with him, his size has varied considerably. On our initial meeting he came across as muscular, but in an athletic way. He has also been very muscular, with a 'cut' (exceptionally well-defined) physique, and very muscular with a more bulky appearance, and has drifted between these at various times. He has, however, consistently sported a crew cut, and has a number of tattoos of which he is very proud. Though smaller than many of the bouncers I met, he still exudes a palpable sense of menace; he leans towards you in conversation and stands closer to you than would normally be considered appropriate. His bearing, body language, conversation and style of gesticulation would certainly register as a warning in the minds of many who meet him.

Jimmy grew on a large council estate in one of the larger North Eastern conurbations. After minor brushes with the law he decided to join the Army in an attempt to see some of the world and to inject a measure of excitement into what he saw as a dull and highly predictable lifecourse. He saw no obvious route into full-time employment, was not keen to work anyway and liked sports and the activity that the Army seemed to offer. His parents were glad that he had joined and seemingly found a way of channelling his youthful exuberance.

Jimmy was always keen to talk about the Army, especially in the company of the friend who introduced us (which was often, especially at the start of our acquaintance). He would talk with enthusiasm about past and contemporary military events and activities, and about military hardware, and was especially keen to share his insights into the advantages and disadvantages of a wide variety of guns. He obviously enjoyed the lifestyle and regimentation, and has very little bad to say about his experiences there.

When Jimmy left the Army he had planned to work with a friend as a labourer for a contracting firm. However, the job did not materialize, and Jimmy drifted into working as a bouncer.

Jimmy: I asked someone if they could get me a job. They asked someone, and they said go down to this pub in the town. Big place. I just saw it as a way of getting some money at first, you know. I thought it would be a piece of piss, easy money, most of the time just standing around and that. I knew I could handle it if it went off, and that's all you need . . .

It wasn't like I always wanted to be a bouncer, it just sort of happened and I didn't even think about it. When I was young I always thought bouncers were a bunch of wankers – think they're really hard and that – and I'd had a fair bit of bother with them, especially in the Army – you know this and that – but it was all right. I liked it. Most of the time when I first started it was just throwing out pissheads, no bother at all really . . . The lads that worked there turned out to be good lads, and we had a laugh. Plenty of women about, good music and that, and I started to get into it. I started with the weights pretty seriously, trained every day and started getting into that; something to do during the day. I sort of slowly stopped looking for a proper job, but maybe that was just laziness like, I don't know. I was still claiming dole when I first started and had some money saved from the Army, but that was gone quick enough and the manager [of the pub Jimmy worked] said it was too dodgy, he'd have to put me through the books. I got myself a licence no bother, no convictions still standing. I rented a flat, and it was like a hundred – hundred and odd quid wasn't enough.

It seemed easy at first, but there was always the potential for a bit of serious bother. It would go off occasionally, especially after the match. People were out on the piss all day and you're bound to get that. Drugs were starting to kick off in a big way too, this is like 1990 or something. People would come in trying to get rid of a couple of pills or a couple of wraps of speed, but the pub I was working on was basically a pisshead place at the time; we'd get it but not loads. You're more bothered about frisk [violence] in those places, you know.

I was skint; I was into the weights and wasn't that keen on a day job if I tell you the truth. I ask a mate if he could get me a job at *The Factory* [a large dance music night-club] and he swung it so I could go and do a couple of hours there after I'd been on down the pub. They paid better money, and I was coming out with an extra hundred quid a week or something, three nights a week. Sometimes I'd work four, do a Thursday student night or something for a bit extra. Fucking hard though. You're on your feet all fucking night, get home maybe half three or something. I needed some more fucking money.

People think it's good money, being a bouncer, but it's not. Well, fair enough, there's a lot of times when you're just standing about, but to you it's still work isn't it? You're not there because you want to be. True, it's money for nothing when you're standing about, but you've got to be there. You've got to have some-one on the door. Just being there is work, because people know they can't fuck about; if you're not there they think they can. It pans out though, because you can be working and think, this is all right, but other times it can be one thing after another, and you're like fucking thinking Christ, I'm only getting so and so for this.

SW: So it was the money that pushed you into selling gear? How did you start?

Jimmy: Well I noticed that all the other blokes on the door of *The Factory* had a lot more fucking money than I did. This was when it was all like new, you know. The fucking drugs and the rave music. You'd see gangsters floating about from time to time. I knew it was drugs, but I didn't know fuck all about it back then. The bouncers would let in certain dealers and get a rake-off, but all this was happening before I got there, you know, so it wasn't like obvious to me . . .

This lad who got me the job at the club spelled it out. I turfed this kid out who I knew was dealing, and he's fucking crying on about who he knows and whose gear it is but you've heard it a hundred times before, you know? He saw what was happening and I've had to give this kid a little slap while I'm tossing him out the fire doors because he's fucking not having it like, just a slap. After the door's shut he comes over and thinks I know what's happening and he's like 'no, not him!' and I'm like 'fucking what?' From then on he gave me a few quid; he'd say like 'There's some money for a taxi' or something like that. It's only pennies, but I still never really knew what was happening. Drugs were all over the place at first, but they cleaned it up. Like I say, I'm only working there half the night so I'm never really on the spot. I don't see dealers coming in and that and even if I was you couldn't really tell unless you know what's what.

Some people were earning a lot of money, and only some of the bouncers were getting a share. I'm not getting anything but I see what's happening. I should say that every bouncer wants to work here. It's a smart club, never really any serious bother, no riff-raff, and they gave you a better wage than most places. Nice-looking women all over the place, you got two guests in each so you could get a couple of mates in for nowt, couple of women or you could sell them for an extra tenner or so to some other kids you might know. It was obvious that some of the blokes who worked there were just there for the flash, didn't want to be gangsters or anything, just, you know, decent lads. Get their money and fuck off home . . . A lot of the time it's the bouncers who get a lump for letting in certain dealers but at *The Factory* it was serious people and it just sort of blurred. You had blokes knocking about who weren't bouncers but were there every weekend who'd point out dealers to whoever and get them turfed. You get the fucking idea, but why bother pissing people off? Just give me some fucking money. Pay me my money and you can do whatever the fuck you like 'cause it's none of my fucking business.

I thought, I may as well get myself some gear, see if I could get myself a couple of quid because it's like I'm the one missing out, you know. I mean, at the time, drugs were like all over the place. Everyone wanted them and it seemed like everyone was selling them, so it was just like to earn a bit of money. It seemed like a piece of piss, and if everyone else is doing it, it's like you're daft not to, isn't it? Me and this young kid from the gym split up on a bag of thirty Es, which is nothing really. I get him in the club and watch his back and we half up the profit. This is just on the side; I don't want to step on anyone's toes, but I figure I may as well be earning something if they are, you know? I told him not to sell to anyone he didn't know, not to mention me, that kind of thing. It was slow at first . . . I wasn't getting to the club till around midnight and so he couldn't get in till then. Most people had been sorted out by then, you know?

We got rid of them and did the same again. Then I told him I was packing it in, got myself a bag off the same bloke and got this other kid I knew to get rid of them. More money for me. This is really small scale and it's only earning me about a hundred [pounds, profit] on the bag. The kid always did what he was told and I didn't have any bother. About this time I moved to working at this other pub. It was nearer to the club, which made it easier, and they gave me an extra ten quid a night . . . This is a different type of pub altogether. It's not one of these pubs where you go to get laid and that, it's a blokes pub really. People would say it was a bit rough, I suppose . . . Some lads in there were dealing, and the place was full of dope, you could smell it a mile off.

Jimmy's move to *The Crossed Keys*, the pub he mention's above, is highly significant. The pub was indeed considered rough, and Jimmy had taken on a much harder job, accompanied by only two colleagues, one of whom had worked there for some time. It appears the pub's owners were attempting to reverse the pub's lawless image by hiring two doormen to police the doors in conjunction with another who had been working there informally.

Jimmy: Of course when you go into somewhere like that you've got to make your presence felt, let them know you're not going to take any shit. A mate of mine, Tony, started working there at the same time and he knew some of the locals. Some blokes sat in there all night and people were coming in there to buy gear all the time; they were smoking dope all over the place. You can't just go in and start throwing right handers. You've got to be a little tactical. Make on like you want to be friends and ask them please to stop, because it your job and you don't want to fuck it up and all that. Be polite: 'Sorry but we can't have it anymore.' Some of them were OK. Other times I'm pissed off and you're going to get to fucking know about it. Say I tell you to put a joint out. Ten minutes later you've got another one. It's like you little fucker, I just fucking told you. You're going to lose your rag sometimes, aren't you, and you've got to get fucking rid of them. It not your fucking pub any more. It just gets on your nerves. I told all the dealers nicely to fuck off, and if you do that then a lot of the time it's going to get rough.

SW: How rough?

Jimmy: Sometimes they go just because they don't want to piss you off. Some of them are only boys, sometimes we might know the same people and that. Sometimes it sorts itself out. Sometimes I had to threaten people, let them know [that] if they want to push it a bit you going to fucking push back. You don't want to get rough, because if you give someone a slap then he's going to be pissed off at you the rest of his life. I mean, if people have seen it and that, he's going to feel as if he's got to have a go back. I only had to have one real bit of bother and I did that during the day, outside this gym . . . People get the message. These weren't gangsters, just lads selling a bit of gear, and they may as well swallow it. Why bother with the aggravation?

In the above passage Jimmy fails to mention that he had started selling drugs from *The Crossed Keys* himself. The same friend who had sold Es for him in *The Factory* nightclub moved into the pub. Jimmy also did not clean up the pub totally and there was still a lingering smell of cannabis. Jimmy is keen to stress that his friend's selling of Es could not readily be linked to him, and was subtly constructed so that unsuspecting patrons would be hard pushed to recognize drug transactions. The pub regulars were for the most part friendly towards Jimmy and any customers seeking to buy Es would be sent over to Jimmy's friend, who would then take them outside or into the toilets to complete the purchase. His friend was instructed to tell customers that this was necessary as he wished to avoid the prying eyes of the bouncers. Other regulars would also sell cannabis in a similar way with Jimmy's tacit approval (Jimmy tells me that you can never stop this kind of thing completely.) A further layer of protection was added by the obvious fact that only friends and acquaintances and those unlikely to wish to inform the police knew that drugs could be purchased in *The Crossed Keys*.

Jimmy: The pub was a better place for it. There wasn't like ten, fifteen dealers all operating out of one place. Obviously I didn't know everything that went on. I told the manager to get a DJ in to do a bit of mixing so he could get some of the younger crowd in which was good for business. It was a nicer place and there wasn't much bother . . .

     I was getting rid of a fair few Es back then because it was like everyone wanted them. Some kids would come in literally begging to be sorted out and to me I may as well be making money out of it instead of someone else. It wasn't like I felt like a criminal or anything. I wasn't really dealing; it was just like someone giving me money at the end of the night, even though it was me who's investing the money in the gear, and as long as I could keep getting the gear regular I knew people would buy it. A few times I'd buy some Es and sell them straight on [to another dealer] to make some quick money without all the fucking about. It didn't seem like I was doing anything really wrong because everyone was into Es in '91 and '92 and you don't really stop to think about it much.

Jimmy ceased selling drugs in *The Factory* after a brief period for he believed the risk of arrest or of impinging on someone else's marketplace outweighed the rewards he was reaping. Jimmy was obviously aware that other drug sellers in *The Factory* represented serious criminals and that the penalty for his own activities could be severe. Instead he shifted his entrepreneurial glare to wider and less crowded markets and instructed a growing number of minions to seek out new locations around the city centre. Often these new locations were among the city's many pubs aimed at a young clientele and his dealings in each case relied in no small part on the selling abilities of each particular vendor. One dealer who would sometimes sell drugs on Jimmy's behalf (although the drugs were effectively his as he was given them in advance and would pay later) did particularly well selling from his own flat. For around a year Jimmy continued in this fashion:

Jimmy: It wasn't like I had loads of people working for me. Some lads would only take maybe twenty off me; I'd give him a price and then as far as I'm concern and they're his. I had a couple of kids who would get rid of loads, so you maybe say give me the money later, or maybe you say I'll give you one for every ten you sell, or maybe you give him a number and say anything over that's yours, or maybe you have someone on his shoulder all night and take the money straight off him, or maybe you've got two kids working it: you pay one and he sends you over to the other kid who's gonna give you the gear. You don't want to start doling out gear all over the place because it can get fucking complicated and you don't want the fuck on and that many people knowing your business. I was earning a fair bit of money because I kept getting the gear regularly. That's the main thing. It really isn't that much though, and it still takes a bit of work. Some people do well but then things dry up for them. I was lucky because I did it all slowly, not in one big lump . . . I would sometimes sell gear to other dealers because it was easy and I could always get more . . . You've got to do a lot of fucking work for the money you make. I've got to chase up some of the lads who've got their hands on my gear, because they're always liable to have too many themselves or start playing the big man with a bag full of Es, or try to rip me off, or maybe some doorman's going to tax them and all that shite – you've got other blokes pissed off trying to have a go and it's one fucking headache after another. This, and I'm still doing the door [bouncing] so I can't always be on the spot.

I packed in working at *The Factory* because I was fucking knackered all the time, so I stopped dealing there because it was far too dodgy; I wasn't selling that much gear in there anyway and it's wasn't worth the risk. Less people were buying their Es in the club because you had people going around selling aspirin and that. Plus, all of a sudden coppers are all over the place and the management's trying to clean their clubs up. Cameras started to spring up . . . If you're a young lad going to a club you may as well get sorted out off your regular dealer, neck it in the queue and avoid having to scramble around all night trying to get sorted out and maybe getting ripped off.

Jimmy remains vague about much of what happened over this period, but from time to time he would add another piece to the jigsaw and tell me something noteworthy when I didn't expect it. He hints at the size of his drug-dealing operation and is vague about the amount of money he earned. Sometimes he will imply that he earned a fortune and bought and sold a great deal of Ecstasy, and other times he will play down his involvement in the North East's drug economy. Other sources place Jimmy as being one of the biggest dealers in the city around 1991, and one source believes he worked in conjunction with an infamous large-scale dealer and ran the door at *The Factory* for him. Others are unsure, placing Jimmy lower down the ladder but pointing out that he was, and indeed still is, a figure of considerable repute in the area:

Jimmy: Look, I don't know how much gear I sold. A lot, how's that? . . . I can't say how much money I earned because I don't know. I can remember having maybe two, three grand in my hand at one time, tops. But even that goes because you have to keep going back [and buying more; reinvesting the money]. The truth is that people think you're a drug dealer you must be fucking rich, but the profit isn't always that big. I maybe earned a fiver profit a tablet, absolute tops. Sometimes it was a lot less, maybe only a couple of quid if I'm selling them straight on. But it's like that, you know? I don't know if that's what other people were getting, but that's what I got. I wasn't the biggest dealer in the city, far from it. We had fucking big time gangsters up here and I was fuck all, believe me. You had to deal with these people and I always tried to keep what I was doing quiet, you know? Some people did earn a lot of money, you can see it when you walk around the town now [commenting on the reinvestment of drugs profits in legitimate businesses in the area]. Some people were clever with the money. I did all right but it wasn't like I was rich. I haven't got the timeshares, the flats, the flash cars and the Rolexes and stuff have I? It was just something extra for cash, you know?

Jimmy continued to deal in drugs up until 1994, although he never again earned the kind of money he earned in 1991 and 1992. He also continued to work in *The Crossed Keys* and also worked periodically at a number of other pubs and clubs in the city. In the summer of 1994 he left the North East for a prolonged working holiday in Ibiza:

Jimmy: I took a bag of about three hundred Es over with me, which is quite a fucking bit. Just in my case, inside a jar of instant coffee. If I got caught I was fucked big time but they just treat you like cattle going over on those tourist flights and I had no bother . . . I fucking love it over there, the fucking sun, relaxed atmosphere and all that. I got myself this little pad I shared with a couple of mates I knew who was over there looking for work. The first few weeks I just took it easy because the big tourist rush hadn't hit. One of the lads I was with got a job touting tickets outside this pub and he would send people over to see my other mate to get some Es. I got myself a job on the door of this Spanish owned place, which basically involved doing fuck all. I just sat about and necked the free beers they gave you. The owner didn't say a fucking word. I'd sell a bit of gear but not much. I couldn't be bothered really, and pill heads sometimes don't like to buy gear off someone like me because they think they're going to get robbed or something. When the tourists started coming over I got my mate who was really selling the gear to hang around the Cafe Del Mar and that and try and get rid of as much as he could. He just sat on the fucking corner asking people if they wanted any gear. Fucking great, got rid no bother . . . It was just one long holiday, with a nice bit of spare cash. The Spanish bloke who owned the bar where I worked got me to go next door to talk to this other bloke. He asks me to come in from time to time and, you know, walk about so people know they can't fuck about. I say OK. I work the two of them for two lots of wages and all the beer I can drink. Later these two blokes and another bloke who owns another bar sort it out so they chip in to pay me about a hundred and twenty quid I think it was. That's quite a bit for over there. I get my mate a job and he's on a nice wage as well. It's peanuts really, but OK for over there . . . Basically we're getting paid to fuck about and we had a good laugh. Then Spanish blokes loved us because we're fucking big and let us do whatever we wanted. Our mates got free drinks and that; we got in all the clubs for nowt and we got rid of the last of the Es. I stopped over there till December getting the same money and they would have kept me on all year if I wanted.

Jimmy had dreams of going back the next year with some friends and forming a sort of informal private security firm, but the plans never came to fruition, although he did go back the following year and did much the same thing. In the mean time Jimmy resumed his career as a doorman, but had ceased his drug dealing:

Jimmy: I was glad to get out it. It's a hard business, and fucking full time. I just couldn't be bothered any more. It's all or nothing, you know? It's like you've got to really push and bring in mates and really put yourself about or it's not worth the bother and your scraping around for pennies . . . If you're going to do it you've got to do it big time, and it's getting harder and harder. It's fucking hard to sell in clubs these days because people won't stand for it. People who run clubs are shit scared of losing their licenses and if you take it on you've got to fucking be a gangster, get yourself a fucking gun and that . . . I think the market's drying up a bit as well; people don't want some spotty faced kid coming up and asking if you want any Es. They can sort it for themselves. You've got Leah Betts and all that as well, plus Charlie's [cocaine] fucking everywhere these days. To be honest I just can't be bothered with it . . . I got offered better money on the doors and I've worked a few different places. You can get a living wage out of working the doors but that's it most of the time. I can get by on what I earn now so it's [drug dealing] not worth it anymore really. I go to a mate's gym and I started working there during the day, which is good. He gives me a couple of quid for it. You just stand behind the counter and take the money . . .

People still come to me with deals and that. They think I can get them fucking so many kilos of coke and stuff like that . . . Sometimes I let someone use my name to do whatever, but not drugs any more. Es aren't as popular as they were and I've never sold coke in my life. Maybe I'm getting old, something like that. At thirty four and I don't need it. I've got a car, a decent house and a mortgage and that and I'm out. Never got shot, stabbed, arrested . . .

Jimmy Revisited

It was then some time before I saw Jimmy again. I had expected this as he lived some distance away from me and as I had now, somewhat selfishly, got enough information to put together a viable piece of research there was little need to seek out his company.

Despite this, in the back of my mind I had always planned to make further use of Jimmy in some way and to tap the wealth of detailed information he was able to bestow in some other academic endeavour. Research opportunities and personalities like Jimmy are not easy to find, and I was sure he could provide the basis for a further analysis of criminality in the North East of England.

I put off further cultivation of Jimmy for over a year. I had now moved on to other specific research interests, and a visit to Jimmy was allocated a lower position on my list of priorities for any given day. At the best of times Jimmy could be a frustrating research source; he would swing between what I considered to be full disclosure and a seeming desire not to say anything, however unrelated to my study interests. Uncontactable for weeks on end he would then leave a rash of messages for me at work and at home. And so we would make plans to meet and he would fail to turn up or be excessively late. He would also get up to make phone calls in the middle of taped interviews, backtrack on certain issues and contradict himself on others; yet despite these and many other infuriations, I always tried to remind myself that anything I got was valuable. Moreover, I was crucially aware that he had next to nothing to gain by accepting my presence. Obviously I was using Jimmy in my efforts to further my research, and the careful negotiation of our research relationship was never far from my mind.

I put off continued contact with Jimmy because I felt I had enough to write a viable piece, but also because the strains of continued fieldwork was, to use a colloquial phrase I heard regularly from my respondents, 'doing my head in'. I grew to dread the late-night phone calls and the near scrapes, the complex relationships and the underlying current of potential violence. These things were not alien to me, but I didn't have to be there. Moreover, the interesting facts I did uncover during my research were far outweighed by the amount of time spent in the grips of sheer monotony. For every night spent in a flash nightclub talking about drug deals, gangsters and extreme violence there were two spent in utter boredom; such is the nature of ethnographic research.

When I did eventually see Jimmy again, our meeting was accidental. I was in a nightclub with friends, with no interest in research, when I saw him. This was not his native city and I was surprised to see him there. I went over and said 'all right?' He said 'all right?' and we talked for a minute or two. Our conversation was uncomfortable, and it seemed he did not want to talk to me at this particular time. That was OK. I was used to having to leave myself out of discussions at times because people do have lives and relationships outside of research. Our brief conversation, however, seemed to indicate that too much water had passed under the bridge since our last meeting, and that our once close research relationship would not easily be re-established.

He wasn't rude. He answered my questions and asked his own, but it was clear that the days of our talking for hours would not return without a great deal of pushing on my part. I was slightly disappointed by this. I later arranged a situation in which our paths were likely to cross; they did, and while I did not push for a conversation, the most I got from him was an 'all right, mate?'

I did not wish to push for another meeting and was not disposed to ask him outright if it was OK if I came down to see him with the view to another interview. I didn't want to put him in the position of having to make up an excuse; it just seemed that the opportunity had passed.

Rereading this piece has prompted me to regret lost research opportunities. What would he have said about this? Why didn't I ask him that? And so on. I doubt whether I will ever speak to Jimmy again, outside of an occasional accidental meeting. What Jimmy does for a living now remains a mystery.

Mark: Illegitimate Markets and Cultural Authority

You can't cure a thirst by law . . . They call Al Capone a bootlegger, yes, it's bootleg on the trucks, but when your host at the club, in the locker room, or on the Gold Coast hands it to you on a silver tray, it's hospitality . . . [I] supply a legitimate demand. Some call it bootlegging. Some call it racketeering. I call it business.

(Al Capone, Chicago 1927. Quoted in Schoenberg 1992)

Mark is employed as a bouncer in a large pub that serves a community often associated with economic and cultural retrogression and the most demoralizing aspects of de-industrialization and urban disintegration. In an era of growing surplus populations, this area and the people who live here may increasingly be categorized as segregated from mainstream consumer society; unemployment, poverty and crime are apparently rife here, a trend that shows no sign of abating.

While much of the area does have some of the social problems most often associated with underclass domains, it has not yet lapsed into the post-apocalyptic urban wasteland so often analogous with such territories. Community life still flourishes in parts of this locality, and indeed the area seems to possess a level of vibrancy rarely considered to be the norm with the lower working-classes. Perhaps in this area more than any I have visited over the course of this research, subsections of this community and area clearly exhibit the fledgling North Eastern working-class entrepreneurial zeal of which I have spoken.

A striking aspect is in its colourful night life, with one part of the area possessing a well-trodden 'route' of pubs leading into the city centre, which visitors and locals alike still frequent. What is perhaps startling is that in addition to the traditional public houses that have dominated this very working-class area for so long, a number of larger establishments have sprung up to cater for the younger elements in of the area and its visitors. Now these pubs pump out loud music, simulate atmospheric smoke and present laser displays, all the while standing cheek by jowl next to their traditional neighbours. The clientele of 'the route' is highly diverse, from young men and women in the latest fashions, to elderly couples who have been frequenting their local for decades.

It is on the door of one of these new bars that Mark works. He is well known within the community which possesses a long history of local 'characters'. It seems every customer has at least a greeting for Mark, and a great deal of banter flies back and forth as young men and women enter the pub. Mark is not especially big for a bouncer, but makes up for his lack of intimidatory presence with his knowledge of the local community and his standing within it. Those most likely to cause trouble in this locality are generally known to Mark, and friendship ties and no small measure of respect can defuse a great many potentially dangerous situations. Mark adds a quick wit and amiable manner to this subtle mode of private policing, along with a vast circle of friends, and a good working knowledge of violence and how to employ it to the greatest effect. A boxer in his youth, he gained a reputation for violence during adolescence and early adulthood while frequenting city-centre pubs and nightclubs. He stands under six feet tall and boasts the 'cut' physique of a light-heavyweight or male model. He is twenty-six years old.

Mark has not been a working-class capitalist for long. He had taken part in a wide range of criminal activities, but only rarely profited from them. Mark's opportunity to enter a thriving and competitive illegitimate marketplace occurred after work one night, during a lock-in to watch a late night boxing bout on satellite television.

> *Mark*: Micky Smith was in the place. I knew he was doing a regular beer run so I'm wanting to see him, just to get a slab of beer. We get talking and he's asking do I want any wine, spirits, tobacco, fags, aftershave and that. So I say, yeah, get me as many fags, aftershave and that as you can get me. It's easy to sell them on. So that's it really.

Mark has always been a good person to see if you wanted something which may have 'fallen off the back of a lorry'. He would sell on fake designer menswear and anything else he had access to in order to supplement his meagre bouncer's income and occasional bouts of heavy manual work and window cleaning. Micky Smith had apparently been going over to the continent quite regularly to buy cheap alcohol and avoiding British duty payments, a relatively simple practice which can be very profitable. The market for cheap alcohol is considerable and Micky Smith seemingly had it down to a fine art. He started out by hiring a van and having two friends, usually unemployed and keen to earn some extra money, drive over to France and fill the van with a variety of items. Soon the number of vans and unemployed drivers was to increase and his base of operations moved in part from the North East of England down to Dover to speed channel crossings and lower expenses.

Mark was keen to take anything available, while Smith was apparently bringing over such large amounts of alcohol he found it tiresome to sell the slabs of lager and bottles of spirits individually, and therefore was keen to get rid of some of his stockpile in larger increments. Mark knew he could easily sell on alcohol to friends and acquaintances and also hoped to interest a number of landlords and pub managers with whom he was acquainted.

Mark quickly unloaded the alcohol and returned to Micky for more.

> *Mark*: Everyone wants cheap beer, don't they? Ask anyone, do you want a slab of Stella, ten quid, normally cost you eighteen, they're gonna say fucking yes, aren't they?
>
> Mostly I got those little bottles of French shit, five-and-a-half per cent stuff, which isn't bad really. Six quid a case. Three bottles of Lambrusco a fiver. Spirits, daft makes is like six quid. You can't beat that, can you? Gordon's gin eight, nine quid, fucking Smirnoff vodka. People buying it for parties, Christmas, whatever. People love a fucking bargain, don't they? Why would they not want some?
>
> The beer I mostly sold to mates and that, no bother. I asked the manager of the pub I work, does he want any spirits? Fucking right he does. He's only the manager so he can get a nice rake off without the brewery knowing. He puts up a bottle of gin on the optics and he's charging two quid a shot or whatever for a bottle that only cost him nine quid or something. Not even that if he buys a case of the stuff. That's fucking his. The brewery just thinks nobody's drinking vodka any more. I had a few blokes like that, making money out of it. I had one fella

who would buy the cheap stuff and then put it in an expensive bottle, Smirnoff or something. Most people can't tell if they're pissed. Makes no difference to me.

I was doing nice. It's fucking exciting when you've got the money in your hand and that. I had nothing to do after I'd flogged it and Micky Smith says, do I want to go on a run? He's got his nephew going over in a rented van. I thought I may as well. You should have clocked it – the van had like so and so rentals written on the side, it's not hard to fucking spot. Anyway we do it; coming back, the fucking back of the van is fucking dragging along the floor . . . We get pulled over off the coppers; they say the van's overloaded. The lad I was with gets done for it, and I'm just sitting there saying fuck all. I told them I was just hitch-hiking and got picked up. The poor kid's in the shit. I got back and I'm a bit pissed off like. I go and see Micky and he's like, that's just the way it goes. The kid's lucky really, he's not getting done for beer running, just over-loading a van . . . He came to me in the first place because he knew I could get rid of loads of gear, I can just tout it about at work and see landlords and that. He can't just walk into a place like ours [his place of work] and go up to the manager and ask if he wants anything, he needs me to do it . . .

The next time I go over I get back and say I'm taking half of it. I give him the money he's paid plus a bit extra and that's that. He's obviously pissed off but so fucking what? What's he pissed off for? He didn't even go over [to France]. All he's done is put up some money and he's getting that back, plus I'm selling most of the fucking gear anyway. I couldn't give a fuck, he's a fucking prick anyway. It's not like he's well liked because he's a slavery cunt and he's not going to do a fucking thing is he?

After that, obviously he's not going to ask me to go over to France again or get rid of any gear. I hire myself a fucking van, and not one that says fucking 'beer runner' on the side. I get along nicely. I pack in working as a window cleaner but I'm still doing a bit on the door. It's not bad. I was still a bit dodgy about getting caught for overloading so I mix things up a bit; I get a mate who's got a Sierra estate to go on a run and I rig up one of those pulley container things to the back or I might go around to a garage and get them to build up the suspension a bit. I get regulars who take beer and booze off me and I bring back duty free fags and that which I start knocking out at the pub.

The duty free fags Mark talks of earned him a significant income. On his arrival at work he would turn off the two cigarette machines on the premises and put up a sign saying cigarettes could now be purchased behind the bar. As cigarettes from a machine in a pub now cost at least three pounds fifty, this allowed him a consider-able profit margin. Two friends of Mark also succeeded in bringing two suitcases of cigarettes back from a holiday in Tenerife, which they later sold to Mark for a good profit. These products were also dutifully passed on to the unsuspecting clientele at Mark's place of employment.

Demand for Mark's cheap alcohol remains high. His supply of cigarettes, rolling tobacco and aftershaves and perfumes varies. He brings back all the cigarettes and tobacco he can on his frequent forays over the channel, and his efforts are bolstered by those of two air stewardesses who pass on their duty free allowances and all the aftershaves and cigarettes they can bring back from countries outside the European Union. He keeps his job as bouncer on because it allows him to remain on the spot to watch his investments and places him in ideal location to find buyers for his various consumer items. He tells me he also finds his job appealing:

> *Mark*: The place I work isn't really that bad for bother so it isn't bad that way. You get your days off to do whatever the fuck you like – maybe you sign on [the dole] and do a bit of fiddle or you can get a job. If I wasn't doing it I'd just be out in the same pubs and that, and it costs you like fifty, sixty quid to get pissed these days, so I'm earning money while the lads are spending it and it's just like being out on the piss anyway half the time. It's not like anyone could do it. You've got to be a bit known, be able to have a fucking fight like. Some of the bouncers in the town centre just have to look hard, you know? The place where I work, there's three of us, but in the town there's pubs with like seven, eight doormen. Some clubs have got over ten, so it's the numbers as well. I do OK because loads of the lads come in so if there's any bother there might only be three of us, but we've got maybe twenty lads in at any one time who'll jump in. That's another thing. After a while it's just work and you don't even think about it. It's just a place to see the lads and that.

Mark Revisited

I still see Mark from time to time. We don't talk about the research I conducted but then that research is over and our relationship has returned to its initial state. Mark is still a bouncer, and still engages the deviant marketplace within the region. However, his import earner became problematic shortly after completing this piece.

Mark was somewhere on the periphery of a cigarette importation scam that recently found its way into the criminal courts. To cut a long story short and help hide the specifics of the case: customs discovered a smuggling route between Tenerife, where cigarettes can be bought extremely cheaply, and the North East of England. Mark apparently helped sell on a significant amount of cigarettes, but was not caught up in the specifics of the case. He had not commissioned the importation of the cigarettes, though he had profited from their importation, and could have therefore been dragged into the prosecution, which actually included a number of other associated criminal charges. Some of those central to the prosecution received significant prison terms.

Mark's various business dealings over this period dwindled. His almost continuous supply of cheap alcohol slowed significantly as the number of people willing to conduct business with him declined because of an affair he had had with the wife of a local bouncer. Later, he also became involved in a dispute with another businessman over a seized consignment of cigarettes from Tenerife. Mark's various disputes go some way towards endorsing Polanyi's (1957) argument that there is an incompatibility between the logic of the market – which incorporates free exchange between egotistical players – and social relations, which are based on trust and reciprocity (see also Scott 1997: 8–18).

Mark is intimately aware that the dog-eat-dog world of deviant business is a dangerous place to seek a living. He has come close to receiving a spell in jail, and recently come into direct competition with men who are just as willing to embrace their masculine heritage and resort to violence in order to expand and defend that which they consider to be theirs. Mark is still a trader but is also seeking pastures new: The market for illegally imported alcohol has shrunken significantly due to recent government initiatives and cost-cutting by large supermarket chains.

He doesn't ask a lot. He is not in the same mould as Michael, who seeks riches along with his consumer and cultural dream. Mark just wants a living. He tells me the Child Support Agency is after him, and so is destined to a life on social security and in hiding his extra incomes to prevent the courts seizing his money and giving it to his ex-girlfriend and child. He doesn't want a job – well not a job where he would have to work – for he gets up in the morning and negotiates his post-modern reality, a world of risky profits, hidden meanings and complex cultural understandings, and of doing whatever it takes to get by. At the moment he is attempting to revive his fortunes; he is continuing his work as a bouncer and will continue to keep his eyes open for market opportunities.

A Note on the Importance of Location

> One of the most genuinely appealing things about crime to career criminals and part-timers alike . . . is that for most crimes the working hours are both short and flexible.
>
> (Polsky 1969: 103)

Jimmy and Mark are bouncers who have taken part in an entrepreneurial criminality ideally suited to their occupation and to the locations this occupation provides. As Mars has noted, 'it is not accidental that pubs have long been traditional places in which to do amateur business. Custom is predominantly local and customers can . . . be positively vetted . . . relationships are informal' (Mars 1982: 174). As bouncers are employed to police these environments ideally suited to deviant business, they are in an ideal position to spot and exploit gaps in the market, to profit by allowing the deviant business of others to transpire and, given the violent abilities and cultural importance of many bouncers, simply to impose the power of their identity on deviant marketplaces in order to grab a market share or even a monopoly. As in the case of Jimmy, competing market forces can simply (in actuality it is rarely simple) be denied entry to the immediate trading milieu. For the doorway to pubs and nightclubs provides a particularly fruitful location at which to promote goods to potential customers, as can be seen by Mark's use of his occupation to find buyers for bootleg alcohol. Being a bouncer can also bring about money-making opportunities, as illegal traders recognize the cultural and situational importance of bouncers and attempt to circumvent their influence by offering them fees or profit-sharing arrangements.

The macho status so often granted to, or earned by, bouncers seems to allow people engaged in this occupation a multitude of options for transgression into criminality. The potential rewards can be substantial, and this adds to the problematic nature of a leisure industry prone to drug markets and protection rackets.

Slick's

Introduction

Slick's is one of the numerous bars I worked in as a bouncer during the course of this research. I have included an ethnography of this bar in particular, for it incorporates many of the characteristics I noted elsewhere, and my employment there as a bouncer led to incidents that pertain more closely to criminal activity and therefore to issues central to this book. Moreover, in looking back, I find I quite enjoyed the experience, for *Slick's* provided the most entertaining working environment I encountered. Something was always happening, and consequently I never became bored, as I did in other establishments. I have restricted the account to two nights in particular, the reasons for which I hope will become evident. However, I must make it perfectly clear that the focus of this piece of ethnography is on the criminal activity in and around a working environment that I have categorized as peculiarly post-modern (Chapter 3: 237–51). I include other incidents in the hope of portraying a working environment that is inherently problematic, but the focus of this piece is the threat and application of violence and the criminal opportunities that exist in this post-modern bar and club milieu. This is certainly not intended to be an exhaustive investigation into the social, cultural and economic organization of bouncing as a career; however, I am adding this ethnographic detail to further authenticate the theoretical points made elsewhere, and to give the reader a sense of what these environments to which I have continually alluded are actually like.

Location and Environment

Slick's is a bar in a major North-Eastern conurbation. It forms part of an extensive pub route around the town centre, where masses of young people with a disposable income congregate to do what young people do when they go out to get drunk. It is one of the more popular bars in the town centre, and has been open for some time despite the highly competitive nature of the bar and club scene. Almost immediately next door to *Slick's* lies another bar. Another two can be found across the street, and altogether there are seven bars on the short street where *Slick's* trades.

Associated services capitalize on the influx of money and market opportunities that occur in these dark but crowded streets. For when they get drunk, many people want to eat, hence the proliferation of fast-food outlets in and around the city centre, usually in close proximity to some popular bar or nightclub. A good many of these properties remain closed during the day, for sober shoppers seem much less likely to fall victim to the unusual attraction of a greasy kebab than a ravenous teenager feeling the effects of twelve bottles of lager. Limited opening hours do not necessarily limit profitability, however, and most takeaways are crowded between 11.00 p.m. and midnight, and then between 2.00 a.m. and 3.00 a.m. on Fridays, Saturdays and Tuesdays (the latter being a popular evening out in this particular town on which many bars and clubs offer cheap drink). On Sunday nights the same fast food venues are only busy between 10 p.m. and 11 p.m., for licensing restrictions means the nightclubs are closed on Sundays, and consequently there is no 2.00 a.m. to 3.00 a.m. rush.

Other trades also latch on to this alcohol-fuelled economy. After midnight at the weekend the streets are awash with a multitude of taxis speeding between fares, failing to keep up with the almost constant demand for their services despite the number of men turning to this trade since the decline of mass industrial employment and the steady rise of the night-time economy. Word has it that their drivers can make between two and four hundred pounds a night across a busy weekend. The only other motor vehicles on the roads in the early hours are police vans filled with officers on overtime, and the occasional ambulance. Other legitimate businesses that are keen to cash in on this economic explosion includes hotels, some of which now rent rooms by the hour to cope with a particular type of late-night client, the late-opening restaurants staffed by abuse-resistant waiters, and traders selling plastic roses for the newly found love of your life.

On top of such legitimate reactions to this supply-and-demand situation come those equally energetic entrepreneurs who are willing to overstep the boundary between lawful and unlawful business practice. The dogged search for hedonistic fulfilment by the young drinkers helps to bolster a manufactured environment of quick-fix pleasure seeking, the offshoot of which is a ready market for all that disposes one to happiness or is believed to possess properties that will create that emotional state. It is here that all forms of late youth culture are slowly beginning to merge in the old industrial cities of the north. Bars and nightclubs are increasingly where concepts of self are formed and reinforced, where ideas of fun and hedonism are believed to lie, and no matter what music you like or what type attire you choose to exhibit, bars are progressively becoming the field on which youth is played out.

Notwithstanding other social and cultural influences upon post-modern modes of gratification, it is this search for a 'good night' that also contributes to a drugs market brimming with various gradations of stimulation and simulation, and a continuous interplay between use and sign value. Simulation can be found in the selling of fake drugs, and the mistaken consumer belief that fake drug experiences constitute the real thing. Anecdotal evidence suggests that some users of Ecstasy new to the experience believe the effects of adulterants to be the actual effect of the drug, and actively seek out the this particular experience, believing it to be the real thing.

The interplay between use and sign value in this culture can be witnessed in the search for a drug sensation, and in the potentially favourable cultural reaction to those seen taking drugs. As has been the case for some time, drug use need not be a retreatist form of deviance, but can be an activity that in fact, can be a route into mass youth cultural acceptance. For example cocaine, at around forty to sixty pounds a gram or 'wrap' (which is literally wrapped in paper), can be seen not only to denote the favourable devil-may-care attitude of the party animal, but also a measure of financial power and the potential to create a big-spender image. Linked to this, the user may also, or may instead, wish to get 'off his face' (experience the drug to its fullest, to the extent that its effects are obvious), and thus will go to some lengths to stop others learning that he has drugs, and in consequence forestall a situation in which he feels compelled to share.

Drug supply in this environment, becomes not only a straightforward process of consumer–supplier exchange, but creates niches where market strategies are employed and new products are made available for the up-for-anything hedonist. Multi-level supply systems are employed to maximize profit and drive the market forever forward. Masses of drugs of varying quality are now available, some of which are branded with the hope of creating customer loyalty, only to be consequently copied by other eager entrepreneurial criminals. What is real can become less important than what is immediate, and the starting point becomes irrelevant to those engaging at any point in this drug market. Drugs become another consumer choice, to go along with the designer shirt, car, house and neighbourhood, all of which are becoming increasingly important to the way we perceive the social world and our involvement in it.

This night-time economy, fuelled primarily by consumers attracted to the network of bars and clubs, has created a situation where its component industries, legal and illegal, become to some extent mutually dependent. Your night out can now take you in numerous different directions, and the pleasure derived from it becomes increasingly dependent on access to the full marketplace and its continued mutation so that now, having succeeded in attracting a member of the opposite (or even same) sex and bought a plastic rose, the discerning consumer can locate a friendly drug dealer and buy some cocaine or speed to keep himself awake, as well as some Viagra (male impotency pills) for the obvious. Then if he can avoid being arrested or beaten up and taken to hospital, he can grab a taxi to a hotel and seek personal nirvana. He might even stop for a kebab on the way.

There are plenty of alternatives. He might venture to an after-hours drinking club, a tiny microcosm of market driven capitalism, where a plethora of further services will be offered him. He could well buy some cannabis or pay for it by the joint if he can't be bothered to roll his own. And if that is not to his taste, he need not venture home just yet, but perhaps go on to a rave or house party, with a choice of venue to suit his musical tastes. If the evening has failed to yield female accompaniment, he may perhaps move on to a strip club or even hire a prostitute; discretion guaranteed.

This is the current state of the night-time economy in the mid-1990s in the north, of which *Slick's* bar is a small but successful part. This, in conjunction with other social and cultural forces noted elsewhere, is why people come here. There is violence, the doormen can be intimidating, there is the threat of arrest and almost constant physical danger, it is expensive (expect to spend at least £50 on alcohol alone on your average lads' night out) and sexual success is far from guaranteed, but people keep coming back. It is what this environment offers rather than what it delivers that attracts the young and the restless to return. God forbid you should stop in and miss something.

To gain entry to *Slick's* you must ascend three flights of steep stairs. On Fridays, Saturdays and Sundays a queue will often form, the length of the staircase and out on to the street, especially in the busiest hours between 9.00 p.m. and 11.00 p.m. in the evening. Before nine the bar is all but deserted, but after that it is crammed full, testifying to the route nature of the town's night-time economy, where herds of young men and women stagger from bar to bar, consuming one drink in each as they slowly progress around the city centre. In other bars around the town centre the busiest trading times will vary as the crowds slowly but surely edge their way around the established drinking route, finishing in or around the area of *Slick's* before heading for a kebab and a taxi, or going on to a nightclub.

Approaching *Slick's* you will hear the dull thud of loud dance music, blending with similar sounds being emitted from other nearby bars. Arriving at the staircase you will have to shout to make yourself heard. Having gained admittance (see later), you find that the environment you enter has a slightly surreal atmosphere. Deprived of natural and more mundane forms of artificial light, the customer finds his or her way with the help of masses of stringed neon, glitter balls, spotlights in a variety of pastel shades, bar lights to aid the bar staff who are either idle or overwhelmed, and the powerful light emitted from large, rectangular refrigerators displaying bottled beers, alcopops and the like. The bar has recently benefited from considerable refurbishment, and the new décor hints at 1980's minimalism. The carpets are black, as they have to be, and still possess and admirable thickness, a huge departure from the pre-refurbishment flooring of matted carpeting of indeterminate colour with a consistency resembling that of chewing gum.

There are five bar areas around the interior, staffed overwhelmingly by attractive females under the age of twenty. Unlike other bars on the route, these barmaids are fully dressed. The two barmen wear ties. A raised section takes up perhaps a quarter of the total area, and many groups make for this vantage point in order to see and be seen. A large DJ stand is adjacent to this raised section, and this overlooks a small circular dance floor. A short walk along a narrow corridor takes you to a small bar area where the toilets are situated. Here the music is loud, but not as loud as in the area surrounding the DJ stand, dance floor and raised section.

When the bar becomes busy no floor space remains, and customers are packed tightly together, reminiscent of a football crowd. It is impossible to take a step without having it obstructed, and consequently customers tend to shuffle to their desired locations, producing conga-style snakes of people weaving their way through the assembled masses. The music prompts many to dance wherever they stand, but the crowd restricts individual and flamboyant self-expression to the music. The most one can hope for is to dance from the chest up, nodding one's head and perhaps accomplishing a slight shoulder movement, usually with drink clasped in hand. Move your feet and you run the risk of being 'eaten alive' by the unmerciful crowd. Attempting to get on to the dance floor usually entails a circuitous and time-consuming shuffle and, on arrival, patrons will often find it equally crammed with drinkers attempting to lay claim to floor space.

The DJ plays all the favourites, and sections of the crowd sing along. Apart from the odd serious face, everyone appears to be having a good time. There is laughing and shouting and singing, drinking and merriment. Occasionally fake disco-style smoke is pumped into the atmosphere, creating a distinctive odour that mixes with the more recognizable smell of stale beer and cigarette smoke.

Slick's tends to attract the younger end of the under-thirty market. This would appear to be due to the dance music and the self-perpetuating nature of peer congregation; young people want to be with others of a like mind and disposition. Linked to this, it is the fact that success breed success in the bar trade. If yours is a popular bar, customers will be attracted by the fact that the bar is busy and has a good atmosphere. No one wants to stand in an empty bar in these environments. The chance of getting a good seat means nothing and the quality of the beer is only a minor consideration, especially as most males drink bottles or cans. Access to members of the opposite sex and a chance to see and be seen by as many people as possible are the deciding factors when it comes to choosing which bar you will attend and at which time (again witness the influence of the drinking route).

The size of *Slick's* and its pervading atmosphere resemble those of a nightclub rather than a pub, and with this comes associated difficulties.

Meet the Boys

On a busy Friday or Saturday five bouncers are employed at *Slick's*, whereas only four are employed on a Tuesday, and three on a Sunday owing to the sliding scale of the bars' busiest periods. A local security company, which runs numerous other doors in the area, provides all the bouncers employed in the bar. There are five regular bouncers who work a rotation system governing which nights they work in any given week. Usually they work three nights a week each, for which they get around £30 a night (circa 1998). Supporting these five are two regular doormen who fill in as and when necessary, and numerous other bouncers employed by their security company who can be called upon if need be. The regulars are:

- *Dom*, aged twenty-five. He stands around five feet ten inches tall and has a muscular physique. He is not hugely muscular, but is clearly a regular weightlifter. He has a sunbed tan and a short but not shaved haircut. In my estimation he weighs around thirteen to fourteen stones (slightly under 200 lbs). Dom has been working as a doorman for three years and likes his job. He supplements his income by working part-time at a local gym where he also teaches occasional classes in martial arts. Dom likes the lifestyle his occupation affords. He is not well off, but for the most part his days are free so that he can either seek some kind of financial remuneration, or indulge his passion for martial arts, boxing and weights. He is quite young in comparison to his colleagues at *Slick's* and other members of his security firm, but is considered 'well up to it', and clearly enjoys his employment in *Slick's* and the ambience and fringe benefits it provides. He is good company, usually jovial and entertaining, and is clearly good at his job. He gives a good deal of attention to the female customers, and receives a good deal from them, but never appears distracted enough to miss anything. When he makes a decision he sticks to it; he seems never to be intimidated, and enforces company and bar rules strictly, though without being pedantic or lacking the foresight to predict situations where those rules need to be bent slightly. He is thorough in asking young looking patrons for proof of age, which can be repetitive work, and he can be effectively violent when need be.

- *Gary* is twenty-eight years old. He has a completely shaved head and has tattoos down both arms which he is asked to cover up at work with the bar sweatshirt or a padded bomber jacket. Gary was the least talkative when I began working at *Slick's*, but later became more at ease with my presence. He is just under six feet tall and weights around fourteen to fifteen stones (just over 200 lbs). He is not as muscular as the other doormen but provides an equally intimidating presence. He has a badly broken nose and a large scar running through one eyebrow. Gary works on an assembly line at a local factory, and brings with him an established fighting reputation gained during his younger years. He takes his job seriously, and seems to considers any misbehaviour in *Slick's* a personal insult. Fights occurring in the bar when he is working infuriate him, and he broods and swears about the protagonists for some time after the problem has been resolved. Violence is something he takes seriously, although he never attempts to exaggerate his skill or bring up violent incidents of the past, unlike many of his colleagues. He rarely involves himself in group discussions and gives little away about himself. Occasionally he will smile and laugh at some joke or witticism but he seems slightly uncomfortable with this display of emotion and enjoyment. He clearly holds his job and his colleagues in high regard, and I am informed by Dom that he is fiercely loyal to his friends and 'will do anything for you'. Gary also runs the lottery syndicate operated by the door staff, making sure everyone pays up and knows the numbers. Occasionally his long-term girlfriend, to whom he is clearly devoted, will come into *Slick's* and station herself close to him for the entire evening.

- *Malcolm* is the head doorman, and I would guess he is approaching forty years of age, although I never asked. Malcolm has been working in *Slick's* for eight years, which, he tells me, is a long time in bouncer years. Malcolm seemingly knows everybody, and is greeted warmly by many customers. Women, often highly attractive ones, run to greet him and embrace him warmly, which he loves – not least because it pisses off his colleagues. Malcolm stands around six feet, two inches tall, and is big but not particularly muscular. He has thick, closely cropped ginger hair and sported a goatee beard until recently, before moving on to a mous-tache, which lasted all of a week after having to take a significant amount of abuse from his *Slick's* colleagues. He acts as unappointed meeter and greeter, and is always happy and talkative. His company is guaranteed to lighten the mood of his colleagues in what can be an exceptionally boring occupation. Rather than telling jokes and being funny, Malcolm strings together a stream of witty observations, piss takes and generally amusing conversation. Malcolm absolutely cracks Dom up, and often has him on the verge of tears. When the two of them get together any potential problems that the night holds fade into the distance as everyone begins to have fun.

  Malcolm is capable of violence, but his contribution to keeping the peace at *Slick's* usually lies elsewhere. Because Malcolm is so well known, the number dissuaded from being violent in *Slick's* is considerable. This happens with all doormen to varying degrees. Men who may be violent are more likely to curtail their activities if they have a friend, or someone they consider to be their friend, working on the door. Malcolm is also skilled at placating drunken customers and persuading them to stagger out quietly, along with those customers known by the door staff to be skilled at violence, men with a large and potentially dangerous friendship network, or notable criminals. Malcolm can talk to these people and persuade them that it is in nobody's interest to fight in *Slick's*, and also employs tactics of a similar kind in order to remove trouble from the bar out on to the street. The reader will see how Malcolm's skills, and those of his colleagues, manifest themselves in problematic situations over the coming pages.

Malcolm's regular job as a chef contrasts sharply with his role as a bouncer, and is an occupation that occasionally prompts others to poke fun, which Malcolm is quite capable of dealing with. He has a strangely paternal role with regard to some of barmaids, despite being exceptionally young at heart. He is twice divorced and single, has two school-aged sons he still has contact with, and lives alone in a relatively middle-class area on the outskirts of town. It is usually he who organizes trips for the *Slick's* staff to restaurants or out-of-town nightclubs, and persuades the other door staff to go out for a post-work beer at one of the local nightclubs. He dances along with the music at the doorway to *Slick's* and ogles attractive young women. Despite this, he is happy to jump in between two groups of brawling men if need be. He determines strategy, appears supremely confident that nothing will happen that cannot be dealt with, and is constantly checking the safety of his colleagues. Though to the outsider Malcolm may appear to be an unusual doorman, he acts as a figurehead to the rest of the door staff and is highly valued by his colleagues and employers alike. What he brings to the job may not be the typical violent reputation and physically intimidating appearance, but the skills he does possess are recognized by those in the know to be significant.

- *Gordon* stands around six feet-four inches tall and weighs around nineteen stones. No description of Gordon could adequately describe him, although I will attempt a loose portrayal. Gordon is simply one of those men whom people stare at, but from whom they quickly avert their gaze if he looks their way. Many would say he is 'not the kind of person you want to run into on a dark night', and without wishing to be overly dramatic, he seems to personify violent menace. A female acquaintance described him as resembling a walking fist.

Weighing in at around nineteen stones (about 270 lbs), he has recently lost over a stone and now, according to Dom, has a body 'like a condom filled with walnuts'. With little fat and a great deal of muscle, Gordon is what is called 'ripped'. Coupled with this physique are an almost completely shaved head (he keeps a little spiky tuft of fair hair right at the front of his head), a mass of large, gold coloured, sovereign style rings taking up six of the eight available fingers, a considerable amount of facial scarring and a disfigured ear, partially bitten off in a brawl some years ago.

Gordon is thirty-three years old. He is not from the town where *Slick's* is located, and is new to the local door scene, although he has worked as a bouncer since his teens. Over the short time he has been working at *Slick's* however, he has become very well known to the town's bouncers and bar customers alike. He is closely linked to notable criminals in the area, is a close friend of Derek, one of the owners of the security company contracted to mind *Slick's*, and has established what appears to be a large protection racket throughout the region (see later).

Despite these facts, and contrary to what we might think from his appearance and occupation, Gordon possesses a friendly demeanour and is happy to joke around with his colleagues. Despite his status and links to some of the regions most important criminals, he does not pull rank or hand out orders. Malcolm remains head doorman, and everyone gets along very well. Despite the nature and the seriousness of his activities, Gordon conducts himself much like the other doormen and is more than willing to take part in the usual banter, and I found him remarkably open about what he does for a living. Despite initial indications to the contrary, I got on very well with Gordon and our budding friendship provided much of the information central to this piece.

Gordon's appearance obviously provides an element of intimidation useful to the deterrence of potentially problematic situations at *Slick's*. His body and bearing transmit a coded but easily decipherable message which patrons undoubtedly take to mean, 'You don't want to fuck around in Slick's, because if you do, look who's going to have to sort it out.' His presence alone goes some way to making people think twice about misbehaving in *Slick's*, and this message is amplified by the presence of his colleagues. Gordon's implicit violent potential has a clearly noticeable effect on customers' behaviour; on occasions he only has to glance over at a group guilty of some minor infraction of the rules in order to persuade them to desist.

Some, talking privately, have expressed the belief that people who look that hard cannot be as hard as they look. The information I have gathered seems to indicate the contrary. Gordon never caused trouble himself and would not become violent unless the occasion demanded it, and although I did not see him in full swing, as it were, I was left with the impression that he was perfectly capable of backing up his appearance with actual violence. Tales filtered back of his awesome power and skill in violent situations, and despite the unlikely stories of conflict against insurmountable odds and notable foes, I never doubted Gordon's credentials as an exceptionally hard man.

- *Neil* is thirty-two. He has worked at *Slick's* for four years and works as a security guard during the day. Neil, a father of two, is divorced, lives with a girlfriend, and is a regular weightlifter, although he has only recently taken up the pastime seriously for the second time after a long layoff. His regaining of lost size is nearly complete, and he weighs around sixteen stones (around 225 lbs). He stands perhaps six feet tall, is shaven headed but not completely bald, and sports a goatee beard. He is a very close friend of Gary, and they usually appear and disappear together.

Over the course of my research at *Slick's*, I got to know Neil the least well. The reason for this is that I filled in for Neil while was off work – for reasons I never discovered.

These are the bouncers I worked with at *Slick's*. Each possessed his own persona, his own specialisms and his ways of dealing with the general and specific problems that arose. I will not go on to detail all aspects of these, for this is not the focus of this section. Some individual characteristics and ways of doing things will, however, be discussed peripherally as I describe the specific environment and discuss the more central concerns of description, violence and crime. I shall now go detail the course of one especially violent evening at *Slick's*. This, I hope, will further illuminate my theoretical points regarding masculinity, post-modernity and change in the North East of England.

Naked Women and Plenty of Claret

I arrive at *Slick's* just after eight o'clock, fashionably late. I have on my black trousers, white shirt and padded bomber jacket, the kind favoured by the majority of bouncers who belong to the Doorkind Security Company, for whom I work and on whose orders I am here. The jackets offer a means of defining colleagues, and despite the fact that you may never have met some of your Doorkind brethren, when you and another Doorkind employee meet you can immediately recognize each other. Often another bouncer known to both of you will make the introductions, say you both work for Derek and Trevor, the Doorkind bosses, and tell the other where you work. These introductions, of which there are many, display a ritualistic element not unlike Mafia greetings (Pistone 1988), but this is 'our thing', and there are few outsiders. On meeting, the two newly acquainted colleagues are expected to show each other the respect due to someone worthy of working for Doorkind, to look out for each other, to provide further introductions and, if need be, to help in a violent confrontation. Once you are in, the security company provides friends, status, a lively social life, free access to nightclubs, introductions to women and a system of mutual defence for those who want to take advantage of these and other benefits.

The place is deserted except for around ten scattered staff. The DJ is already at work and I immediately make my way to a back room to fill in my name and door-man's registration number on the provided pad. Malcolm, Gordon, Gary and some of the male glass collectors are gathered around one of the bars watching a boxing match on satellite TV. I notice Gary is drinking a beer, so I order one myself, which I am not really supposed to do. I have to pay, but I get free soft drinks. I say 'all right' to everyone and shake hands with Malcolm, Gordon and Gary. I ask where Dom is and one of the barmaids informs me he's gone to order a pizza. I start to watch the fight.

It's after eight and strictly speaking we're all supposed to be at work. We should be stationed at the door and around the bar, but in fact we won't actually start work for another hour at least. Lenny, the manager of the bar, is unlikely to say anything. We're the bouncers, and already I have become aware that if anyone is going to give orders it is not going to be him.

Our security company has the contract for this door, and no matter what, that contract will not be going to another security company for the foreseeable future. In this town a rival company will not bid against ours because of friendships and agreed-upon territories, and if the manager or owner were actively to seek another security company, Doorkind would be unlikely to go meekly along with it. Your bar could be burned down, fights could break out every time the doors were opened for business, the new bouncers could well be intimidated, beaten up or worse; the manager could be attacked after closing time, the owner might find his window shattered, the place could be robbed; anything could happen. Despite the unspoken understanding between Doorkind and the manager and owners of *Slick's* concerning such matters, this area of uncertainty does not pervade the environment in which the staff have to work; and on the surface everyone is genuinely friendly towards each other. The bouncers provided by Doorkind take their job seriously and, despite slacking off during quiet periods, they do it well. Doorkind wants to do a good job. It is in nobody's interests not to. Derek and Trevor, the owners of Doorkind, simply cannot allow word to get around that his doormen are weak in any way, as weakness always provokes others to try to take over, and once one door goes, the rest can quickly follow in this social-Darwinian milieu.

Despite the fact that everyone likes Lenny, the bar manager, I am left under no illusion that I am answerable to Derek and Trevor, who both have a good working relationship with the owners of *Slick's*, and are contracted to mind a number of other doors owned by the same company. Nobody wants any ill feeling and the owners are happy with the service Derek provides. Doorkind provide a valued service and their predominance in this locale is unquestioned. There is no need for threats if business continues to go smoothly, but it is clear that the owners and managers of *Slick's* and other venues are aware of the possible consequences of a change to another security company.

Derek

Although *Derek* is part owner of Doorkind Security, he still comes in to check on the smooth running of all the bars he and Trevor are contracted to protect. He is a regular at *Slick's*, especially during busy periods, and provides a welcome addition to the bar's security. Derek may be the part owner of a successful company, but in this business company owners are unlikely to wear business suits and carry briefcases. Derek has risen to his present position by cultivating advantageous friendships, being well known and respected within the bouncing scene, being business minded and, most of all, being exceptionally hard.

Derek is around six feet tall and weighs in at around sixteen-and-a-half stone (around 230 lbs). His head is completely shaved, as is the fashion among many bouncers, and he possesses the powerful physique of a regular weightlifter. His life is devoted to his work and the constant threat of extreme violence that surrounds it.

When he is not at work, he is in training to protect his market share. He works out at least twice a day, six days a week; however, even Derek rests on a Sunday. His daily regime includes a gruelling session of weights, Monday to Saturday, and at least one session of boxing and kick-boxing, jujitsu or some other form of martial art. Derek works on his body from nine to five, and takes his training and business extremely seriously, for there are no shortage of hard men in this town and a good many of them would like a shot at running a successful and highly profitable security company like Doorkind. To get business in this town, however, you would have to get rid of Doorkind's virtual monopoly if you are to earn real money. Moreover, 'hard' men in some way associated with Doorkind are linked to a flourishing protection racket and other money-making ventures. So although Derek is now at the top, or near to it, many want to knock him down. In consequence, just as the bouncers he employs must perform well to ward off potential rivals, so Derek must win any violent confrontation he finds himself in, and he finds himself in many. If Derek were to lose a fight, word would find its way throughout the town within hours, no doubt prompting some to attempt to capitalize on this show of weakness. Furthermore, Derek's near mythic capacity for violence would come under more intense scrutiny, and others who had previously been deterred, and those who hold grudges, might feel the time was right to challenge him. Alliances would quickly form and if Derek failed to act quickly his position and status would be quickly diminished. Numerous groups would no doubt soon be scavenging the remains of Derek and Trevor's legitimate and illegitimate businesses, recruiting his doormen, and bidding for his security contracts.

The consequence of this situation, of which Derek is clearly aware, is that he must be as hard as he possibly can. Always prepared to the extent that he rarely drinks and has stopped taking drugs, Derek now strikes first at the slightest threat, and always makes sure the man stays down. If someone were to beat him in a fight, the last punch would not be the end of it. He has too much to lose; and they would find Derek outside their house first thing on a morning, waiting at their workplace, in their local, or around at their mother's house. It goes without saying that he would also have a number of tough-looking friends with him, just in case his opponent was not alone.

The possibility of someone like this turning up at your door while you're rubbing the sleep out of your eyes first thing on a morning is not an attractive thought, and the knowledge that he cannot afford to be seen to be beaten is a clear indication you've moved up a league when you're dealing with someone like Derek. Even if you beat him again, he is still going to keep coming back, and may well arm himself the next time. People like this and those others in the subculture I have described previously know that civilians with day jobs cannot win with the likes of Derek, even if initially they appear to have gained the advantage. Ultimately defeat of some sort must come unless they also are willing to raise the stakes to ever-increasing levels. It doesn't matter how hard you are, for you have to know that he will be getting up every morning with nothing else on his mind other than how to do you harm and even the score; and will continue to do so until a satisfactory conclusion is reached, or one of you is dead or in jail. This is perhaps the one crucial difference between being hard and being hard for a living.

Trevor

Trevor is Derek's partner in Doorkind Security. He generally deals with the business side of things, and compared to Derek he is seen far less often. Perhaps because of this he is a far more mysterious figure, even to those who work for him. He is around fifty years old and comes from a major city in Northern England, some distance from *Slick's* and the other bars and nightclubs his company protects. He is a member of a family allegedly involved in serious crime throughout the region. Over the period of my research I only saw him on one occasion: he was dressed casually, almost scruffily, stood around five feet nine inches tall and was of a slight to medium build. Sporting a deep tan, badly broken nose and what looked like expensive jewellery, his appearance contrasted sharply with Derek, his business partner, and those he paid to protect the local bars and clubs. On the occasion I saw him, he spoke to Gordon at length about matters unknown and best not enquired about. As is often stated by ethnographers, one must know when to keep your mouth shut, and when dealing with men such as these this knowledge seemed to transcend cultural awareness and become almost instinctual.

Back at Work

We watch the boxing and offer opinions on who will win and in what round. Malcolm is convinced the boxer in the flashy red shorts will win within three rounds. I disagree and bet him a fiver the other boxer will win within six. I even offer to name the winning punch: a right hook. Everyone laughs at such a bold prediction, and I have to enduring a bit of piss taking until the boxer I backed stops Malcolm's nominated fighter with a right hook in the fourth round. There are roars of laughter and Malcolm swears a lot, saying he is not going to pay up because the fight must be a repeat and I'd seen it before. I protest I hadn't, and claim I'd noticed that Malcolm's flashy boxer kept his left hand very low after throwing the jab. More laughing and piss taking as Malcolm still refuses to pay up. I let it go.

For the next half an hour or so we joke around and flirt with the barmaids. Malcolm offers advice to a particularly lovelorn barmaid, Gary phones his girlfriend and endures some piss taking in the process, and Dom returns with his pizza, which Malcolm and Gordon attempt to greed off him. Gordon relates a story about a fight with a group of football hooligans in a bar also protected by Doorkind Security. There is more conversation about assorted violent incidents. Violence is a regular topic for discussion, and not simply because it is central to their working lives. They like violence, or at least are involuntarily drawn to it and what it can mean in terms of status, identity and self-perception. It intrigues, excites and beguiles them in equal measure despite their intimate knowledge of the potential downsides to violent conflict. They like to talk about it in minute detail, act out scenarios in order to display the full magnitude of their tales, construct vague hierarchies and guess at the victors in imaginary match-ups (see Chapter 1). Dom, especially, loves to impart tales of fights he has witnessed. He offers sound effects and thick description and plays up the comic overtones. His fighting narratives are reminiscent of a football fan recalling a great piece of skill he has witnessed, full of drama and enthusiasm. He is also more likely to describe his own violent battles, none of which he appears to have lost, and to go into detail about how he overcame various foes and what their injuries looked like afterwards.

Gordon is clearly in a good mood. Tonight *Slick's* is playing host to a group of strippers, and everyone is looking forward to this, although it is expected to cause extra drunkenness and perhaps some violence. Malcolm, Gordon, Gary, Dom and I make our way over to the top of the stairs, partly blocking the entrance. This is us easing into work mode. The music is turned up a notch and Malcolm and Gordon begin to sway to the music. Everyone is having fun, and I feel relaxed. By nine o'clock I've usually been working for a couple of hours and I'm beginning to deal with the first drunkenness and violence of the night.

The first real surge of customers begins to enter. We watch them closely as they ascend the stairs, with one of us, usually Dom, deciding whether or not they will be allowed in by the time they get to the entrance proper. If you're young looking and have no identification with proof of your age, you will not getting be in. Dom's line is, 'ID? You're not getting in', all the while pointing back down the stairs. He does not offer politeness, nor allow for extenuating circumstances. Dom is not interested in any story you may wish to concoct about why you have no ID. If you haven't got ID it is a waste of time arguing and it pisses the bouncers off. If you continue to protest, Malcolm might say, 'look, you're blocking the stairs, you may as well go', whereas Gordon or Dom is more likely to say. 'Look, you're not getting in, you may as well fuck off.'

Gordon enjoys this part of the job. He likes listening to the protestations, the appeals to the other doormen, and the reasoning as to why customers should be allowed in. If one of the other doormen does not intervene on your behalf if you have been denied entrance, no matter what, the decision will not be reversed. Gordon likes watching men climb all the way up the stairs, and then be denied entrance just because they've got trainers on. He likes the fact they have to walk all the way up to him just to be told 'no'. The stories people concoct in order to get the doormen to reverse a decision can be quite imaginative, and friends will often petition the doormen for leniency. Tonight, however, the doormen are expecting the bar to be extremely busy and they can therefore afford to be choosier.

It should be noted that it is often very difficult to tell the age of potential customers. Younger patrons attempt to look older and older patrons attempt to look younger, and the most the door staff can hope for is to keep out those who are obviously too young. They do ask what they consider to be borderline cases for identification, and if you haven't got any you won't get in. Generally speaking, borderline females are more likely to get in. This is not simply because they tend to be more capable of disguising their true age but because of an understandable element of sexism on the part of the bouncers. Often, when a highly attractive female is climbing the stairs the bouncers are likely to be staring at her for reasons other than that of attempting to determine her age. Moreover, no one wants to disappoint an attractive female, and attractive females tend to look over eighteen. A good percentage of the female clientele is aware of this bias and will attempt to use it to their benefit. A clear example of this would be shameless flirting in order to attempt to avoid paying an entrance fee, should one be levied.

As they watch the procession of customers climb the stairs, the bouncers are also on the lookout for people who are unsuitably dressed, for large groups of men, for men with a violent reputation, for those who have been previously barred from the premises and/or other Doorkind bars, for drug dealers and those people attempting to smuggle their own drink into the bar. The latter activity happens quite often and mainly involves men who have failed to finish their drinks in the previous bar by the time their friends leave, and consequently attempt to carry it in to the next bar rather than leave it. Occasionally people will also attempt to smuggle in bottles of spirits, and in one incident I am aware of, a huge bottle of cider.

By 9.30 p.m. the bar is packed. The bouncers have spread out to their usual locations around the bar: Gary is stationed on one side of the raised platform, Dom is on the other and Gordon is behind the DJ stand, leaving myself and Malcolm to mind the door. Who stands where will usually be rotated over the course of the night to prevent boredom. Tonight I have also been given the job of walking the strippers out onto the dance floor and preventing them from being attacked in the process.

The staircase is now packed and I am forced to walk down and ask those waiting to enter to push against one wall so there is enough room for those wishing to leave to do so. When this job appears to have been completed successfully, I station myself on the landing at the bottom of the upper flight of stairs before moving back up to the doorway to *Slick's* bar proper. The place is absolutely packed and the first fight of the night occurs.

From the door I catch glimpses of two girls arguing. I then catch the attention of Dom, who by now is making his way down from his perch to address the problem. Established tactics at *Slick's*, formulated by Derek, decree that the two bouncers at the door are not to leave the door area unless there is an emergency. Malcolm and myself watch from the door, but also control the heavy flow of bodies in and out of the bar. Just as Dom is approaching the scene of the mild disturbance, it steps up a gear. Two men, presumably boyfriends of the arguing girls, are now pushing and shouting at each other and people have begun to move away. This is an emergency and I make my way over. As I force my way through the crammed bodies the first punches are thrown. All the doormen, except for Malcolm, are now making their way to the scene (this is all happening very quickly). The sheer number of customers means that the bouncers must push people out of the way in the event of a fight. There is no time to ask people to move, and as a consequence drinks are spilt and customers annoyed. Most are used to this turn of events and at least make some attempt to get out of the way of the charging bouncers.

Dom arrives first and gets one of the combatants in a bear hug. I can see him talking to the man, presumably telling him it is a bouncer who has hold of him in case the man believes it is someone involved in the fight. Women are screaming and I can hear the sound of breaking glass over the loud music.

I arrive next on the scene and grab the other principal involved in the fight. I get him in a headlock and drag him roughly towards the door. As I do so I can hear him saying 'OK, OK', presumably to let me know that he knows it's over. At the door I let Malcolm deal with it. By now the man has slumped to the floor and is covering his face as if he expects a beating. Malcolm calls him a 'daft cunt', drags him to his feet and pushes him down the stairs. I run back towards the scene to find that the other doormen appear to have dealt with the situation. I see Dom struggling with the man he has grabbed and I help out by grabbing an arm and dragging him to the door. Dom is considerably bigger than the young man and could easily have dealt with the situation, but I offer my assistance. Just as we arrive at the door, the struggling man attempts to butt Dom and just misses. Again the situation changes. I can see the expression change on Dom's face; his look of surprise quickly changes to one of utter hatred. Dom lets go his grip of the man and with extra-ordinary speed has hit him twice in the face. I grab the man before he has time to fall to the floor and again force him toward the door, mindful that Dom may not be finished with him. I force him down the stairs, and from somewhere a group of men have appeared, friends of the man I am now throwing out. To my relief they are telling him to stop acting up and drag him towards the door. He has a rapidly closing eye and a badly bloodied nose. At the top of the stairs Dom is laughing and shouts 'go on you daft cunt, get the fuck out before I give you a proper beating'. Malcolm is also laughing and shouting insults. One of the young man's friends apologizes. I am speechless, having expected Dom to be furious. Gordon arrives with another youth whom he grips with one hand around the back of his neck. The youth's face is bright red and he is obviously in pain, but he says nothing. Gordon is laughing and roughly pushes the youth down the stairs. He says 'fucking kids these days' and walks back off towards the scene of the fight. I follow him. Dom arrives behind me and points out the two girls who were involved. One is arguing with an amused Gary. She's crying and pulling her arm away from him, pleading for mercy and trying desperately to stay in the bar. She doesn't seem too worried about her bleeding boyfriend outside. Dom says 'throw the bitch out' and Gary steps up his efforts to get the girl to the door. All her friends are pleading with Gary and Dom to let her stay, and they are amused by the girls' inordinate wish to stay in what is, after all, one of many bars. The arguments continue all the way to the door and various females are offering versions of what happened and whose fault it was. None of the bouncers care; they've heard it all before and it just serves to piss the bouncers off even further. Both the females are thrown out and around five or six friends go out with them, some crying. The queue of people waiting to get in find it all very amusing. Dom decides he is going to throw out a group of men involved on the periphery of the incident. I walk over and he asks me if I recognize any of them; I say no. He asks the group which one threw a punch at him. Nobody did, but the group of young men visibly pale at the thought of the potential repercussions. Gordon arrives and joins in the joke. I can see they sense an imminent flurry of punches, and seem happy when Gary turns up and tells the lot of them to 'get the fuck out'. The whole incident has taken no longer than two minutes.

Dom, Gary and Gordon stand at the door for a short while, joking and offering different versions of what happened with Malcolm and I. Everyone thinks it was very funny. Malcolm is highly amused by the state of the young man's face, and says he thought it was me who hit him. I tell him it wasn't and this provokes further laughter and story telling. To these more seasoned doormen the incident almost amounted to nothing. Those involved were simply young men, and I begin to realize they never represented much of a threat to these men. Still, these young kids have had the affront to start a fight in their bar, and the bouncers all consider that they showed a great deal of restraint in dealing with the incident. These men take it as a personal show of disrespect to fight in *Slick's*, and all express the belief they should have given the young lads a good slapping, just so they know they cannot fight wherever they like – they have to show some consideration. Malcolm puts this down to their age; they didn't know who or what they were dealing with and would quickly learn. I estimate those involved were all under the age of twenty.

Gordon, Dom and Gary return to their stations and the night continues. Malcolm is really having fun now, and dances along with the music and greets a succession of stunning females with hugs. Men known to both of us come in, pump our hands and offer some form of greeting and accompanying witticism. A poster next to the door promoting tonight's strippers brings in extra customers and keeps them there longer as they wait for the show. There will be both male and female strippers, and for the last hour or so we've been telling customers the show will begin in about ten minutes. Lenny, the manager, comes over and is clearly panicking about the where-abouts of the strippers. He tells me these are high class, not your usual slappers. The male strippers will be on first in order to keep the men waiting and drinking longer.

A short distance away I can see an attractive girl dancing provocatively in front of Dom. I point this out to Malcolm and we laugh and get Dom's attention. Dom does his trademark eyebrow wiggle and we crack up. A hen night party comes in with around ten women dressed in French maids' outfits. They're all pissed and are having a good time. The bride-to-be is more drunk than the rest and has a twenty-inch fake phallus attached to her head. Her friends are rubbing it in the faces of passing men, most of whom seem not to find it amusing. She also has car 'L' plates attached to her back and chest and has a vibrator stuck in the top of her stockings. I'm asked to give her a pre-wedding kiss but decline. Malcolm is happy to go along, and amuses the masses of people on the steps by bending her over into a passionate kiss, and then lifting her short skirt a little.

Inside I spot a youth sitting on the floor, seemingly fast asleep. I go and wake him and ask him to leave. Moments later, another young man staggers towards the door and vomits, missing me by inches. I swear a little and push him towards the door. I look around and see Dom, Gary and Gordon in hysterics, prompting me to see the funny side.

Every minute or so Malcolm will walk a short way into the bar and give all the door staff a thumbs-up sign, to check everything is going OK. If something has come up, a bouncer will point it out, and one or more, depending who is closest, is dispatched to deal with whatever the problem is. This happens virtually every ten minutes. Dom, or whoever, will signal to Gordon or Gary that someone behind them is standing on a chair, or whatever, and the closest bouncer will solve the problem. Once this is done everyone gets a thumbs-up sign.

At about 9.30 p.m., a slightly different problem arises. A girl, who Malcolm knows vaguely, approaches him at the door and complains that a male customer has thrown a glass at her. Gordon is called over and he and I are dispatched to investigate.

In situations like this, the bouncers in *Slick's* never attempt to intervene by them-selves. Even if a fight breaks out right next to you, you are advised not to intervene until another bouncer knows what is going on and where you are. On an evening like this, however, this is unlikely to happen, for the doormen can see right across the bar and constantly pick each other out and confirm that everything is going as planned. Experience dictates that it is better to be safe than sorry. Malcolm has previously told me of an incident in which a *Slick's* doorman, now retired, attempted to stop a fight in the men's toilets only to have the two sides turn against him and one man to try to bite his left index finger off, provoking a pitched battle outside *Slick's* when the bouncer rallied and was able to summon help.

Gordon and I make our way over to the place of the incident, following the female complainant. Malcolm, Dom and Gary are doubtless watching us from their various positions. When we arrive I recognize a local boxer and a group of his friends. I know him, but not well. The girl indicates to Gordon that these men tossed the glass, which seems a little unusual, given that it takes only one person to throw a glass. Gordon asks the boxer about the incident and he protests his innocence. He claims it was one of his friends who has since left the premises and says that he hadn't thrown the glass violently. He continues, telling us that she, in fact, caught it and that the glass didn't break. The boxer's friends begin to gather around. There are more of them than I had at first believed. I estimate there are at least twelve men and that these indeed are men, not boys. Gary, who is stationed nearby, comes over and stands directly above the unfolding incident. Gordon returns to the aggrieved female and asks for more facts about the incident. Everybody is taking this very seriously. It is becoming apparent that this group is unlikely to walk quietly from the bar if Gordon deems it necessary and if they don't this is going to be a huge battle. Gordon is clearly angered at having to mediate between the two parties. He asks me if I know who the group are and I tell him. He tells me to watch his back. I reply, 'no problem'. Dom is at the door talking to Malcolm. I overhear two of the group commenting on Gordon's size and reputation to which another replies that he 'doesn't give a fuck'. I find this slightly amusing given the size difference between Gordon and the issuer of this bold statement and his obvious inebriation. Experience tells me that violence is not far away. People are putting down drinks, extinguishing cigarettes, hands are coming out of pockets, posture and position change. Gordon is also clearly aware of this, knowledgeable as he is about the choreography of imminent violence. The girl is now shouting at Gordon who is quickly becoming angry. His face is beginning to redden. Soon Malcolm is on the scene. He talks to both parties, and decides the girl is complaining about nothing. (He later tells me the root of the incident has something to do with a broken romance and the resultant ill feeling.) He knows the boxer and some of his friends and quickly smoothes things over but not before Gordon has the last word. He says, 'if Malcolm says its OK then I'll let it go, but don't ever think you can fuck around in here. I don't care who you are, all right?' The implication is clear to all who hear it. The boxer might not have done anything too severe but Gordon clearly felt the boxer and his friends had challenged his authority and this could not be allowed. The boxer says 'no problem' and offers his hand to Gordon, who looks at it for a long moment before engulfing it in his mighty paw and turns quickly away. Gordon makes the boxer look tiny, even though he fights at light heavyweight. Everyone except Gordon looks happy that the conflict has been resolved without violence.

In incidents such as this Malcolm proves his worth. He mediates and plays the role of friend to the masses, keeping everyone happy when need be. Despite the fact the boxer and his group appeared to be worthy adversaries, easily outnumbering the door staff, I was always confident that if things turned violent the bouncers would triumph. We were sober and they were drunk and we had the organization if not the numbers. Again, experience suggests that not all of the twelve potential foes will want to fight and some will search for ways to avoid conflict, by making excuses, by mediation, or seeking to escape. Some will be fearful of taking on bouncers, especially these bouncers. Some will know the individual reputations of Gordon and the others, and some will be influenced by the dark spectre of Doorkind Security and its two shadowy bosses. Having earlier witnessed Dom throw two of the fastest punches I have ever seen outside of a boxing ring, and on a previous occasion having seen Gary demonstrate an aptitude for extreme violence, as well as knowing Gordon's reputation and the esteem in which he is held by some very hard men, I had faith in the abilities of my colleagues. Regardless of this, however, the relaxation I felt earlier in the evening has disappeared. I am here, I remind myself, to conduct research, even though I take this job seriously. Indeed, I realize, it is impractical to pretend; for to all intents and purposes I am a bouncer, and I will do whatever protocol and circumstances demand of me. At this point, however (and on many previous occasions) I was crucially aware of the potential repercussions on my academic endeavours.

Immediately after this incident Derek turns up. As always he is wearing tracksuit bottoms, trainers and his bomber jacket emblazoned with the Doorkind logo. He shakes my hand and asks if everything is OK. I say it is. He seems happy and joins Malcolm in ogling some passing females before setting off to greet his other employees around the bar. After talking to Gordon I see him make his way over to the boxer. Again all the bouncers pay close attention and are ready to jump into action. Derek is clearly having words with the boxer and I can see him pointing at him. The boxer is avoiding eye contact, and I momentarily empathize with him. Having Derek talk to you in these terms must be terrifying. His friends are close by but are also examining their pints and staring into the distance. Gordon gives the thumbs-up indicating to Malcolm and myself at the door that everything is OK and there is nothing to worry about.

The strippers arrive. I escort the men to the manager's office and then to a storage area where they are to get changed. The females will use the manager's office to change in. Another hen party arrives and Malcolm jokes with them. The bar is now busier than I have ever seen it.

Derek returns to the door and tells me to make sure nobody gropes the girls on the way to the dance floor, which is going to serve as a stage. He says he 'doesn't give a fuck' about the men, but to give them an escort if they want one. He tells me to look out for a drug dealer he has caught earlier in the evening at another one of his doors, who is wearing a bright orange puffa jacket. He then says his goodbyes and leaves.

Lenny, the bar manager, comes over and asks if some of the bouncers can clear the dance floor, as the male strippers are ready to begin their act. Malcolm tells me to do it and to get Gordon to help me. The DJ aids matters by turning the music down and asking the assembled masses to clear the dance floor, and slowly but surely we manage to get it done. Already people are pushing to get a vantage point and I begin to sense the difficulties the strippers are going to create. Members of both sexes are already baying for naked flesh. I talk to Gordon and it is agreed we will stand on each side of the dance floor to make sure nobody invades the show and that the crowds allow the strippers enough room to perform. To compensate for this shift of manpower, Gary joins Malcolm at the door where still more people are attempting to gain entry.

I make my way over to the storage area where the male strippers are getting changed. One emerges from the door dressed as a cowboy, complete with hat, guns, boots and chaps. And baby oil. He tells me he'll be able to make it on to the floor by himself just as the DJ announces the beginning of the act. Women scream. I wander past the door and share a joke with Malcolm and Gary. Malcolm calls the male strippers a bunch of puffs, and drags a female friend over to ask who she would rather see naked, them or us. She says them, and makes a joke at Malcolm's expense. We continue to joke around, and poke fun at the desperate women waiting to get in, queuing down the stairs. They're edging their way forward in order to try to see some of the action, but the packed-in mass of bodies makes it impossible. People are now standing on chairs and tables, but Malcolm says to let them get on with it until the show ends. The song ends and the stripper bolts back to his changing area clasping a ten-gallon hat over his genitals. One of the drunken members of the hen party grabs his arse before he disappears behind the door. She turns, shouts and raises her fist in the air in triumph, much to the amusement of the door staff and the customers at the front of the queue.

Shortly after this, another male stripper, dressed as a sailor, emerges from the storage area. He comes over and asks me to escort him on to the dance floor. Malcolm looks at him incredulously and then openly laughs at him. The DJ announces the next act and I and my new friend make our way on to the dance floor. Once there I fend off a group of girls who have spilled on to the dance floor. Gordon is laughing so hard his face is bright red. On the raised platform I see Dom shouting at a group of young girls who have climbed on to the railings overlooking the dance floor; eventually he gets them down. All over the bar, women are screaming.

When male stripper number two finishes his act he bows quickly and sprints past me in the direct of the storage area. I follow him at a slower pace. Again women make desperate grabs, but the baby oil aids his escape. Another male stripper comes and goes, but this time I am not required to provide an escort. I remain at the door with Malcolm, where a girl taps me on the shoulder and tells me a fight has broken out at the main bar. I had been distracted by the general goings-on around the door and had not noticed Dom signalling as he and Gary hurry toward the incident. Gordon, despite his size, remains hidden from view in the clearing on the dance floor and cannot tell what is going on. I rush towards the fight, which I can now see quite clearly. One man is standing with his back towards the main bar, head down, trading wild punches with a more skilled adversary. People are trying to give them room but the sheer size of the crowd is preventing them from backing up too far. The barmaids are looking on in horror, backed against the shelf holding the tills. Customers have forgotten their difficulties in ordering a drink and watch the spectacle. I get there first just as the man with his back to the bar catches a punch squarely on the nose and another flush on the mouth. He stops swinging and although he doesn't go down he seems defeated. I grab the victor from behind, swear at him and drag him to the door. Dom joins me, swears at him, grabs him by the collar and yanks him so hard I lose my grip and he falls to the floor. While he is down another customer kicks him in the ribs. Dom then drags him along the floor towards the door. I once again join in, stand him up and drag him towards the door. He is now saying something to the effect of, OK, he'll go out quietly. Dom pushes him down the first flight of stairs; he looks back briefly as if about to say something, and then makes his way out. I notice his right hand is bleeding quite badly. Around five of his friends quickly join him in leaving. A friend of mine waiting in the queue shouts, 'go on fuck off, you stupid fucking pricks', and I tell him he can come straight in. Dom and I make our way back to get the man who kicked the victor when he was on the floor. He protests his innocence, as do a group of nearby females, but we're not in the mood and he gets roughly dragged to the door, while Dom swears and threatens him repeatedly. He puts up no resistance.

Gary is at the scene of the initial disturbance, and is being harangued by a group of upset females, one of whom is crying. The man who was fighting and who lost is leaning against the bar, nursing his wounds. A concerned friend is telling him to put his head back to stem the blood-flow. His nose is clearly broken and he is bleeding from a gash on the bridge of the nose as well as from his nostrils. His top lip is also bleeding and it appears he has lost some teeth. Again Dom grabs him roughly by the collar of his shirt and drags him to the door. The group of girls protest, and Gary explains that he was fighting and therefore he has to leave. He also tells them that we can't have people bleeding all over the bar. It doesn't look good.

The friend who was helping the defeated fighter is now covered in his blood and I tell him he has to leave. He doesn't argue, and on the way out he asks me if he will be barred from *Slick's*. I tell him no. I then walk over to Gary. He points to the floor, which has a large pool of blood gathering on the tiled section immediately in front of the bar. It mixes with the broken glass, fag butts and discarded cans and bottles.

Again I return to the door. The queue is getting smaller as females leave the bar after the male strippers have done their thing, allowing others in to take their places. It is mainly men who now populate the bar. A short while later an embattled glass collector comes up to the door and tells Malcolm that a man has just taken a piss against the fruit machine. Malcolm pulls a pained expression, and nods in the direct of the glass collector, indicating he wants me to deal with it. The packed-in crowd has prevented many people from seeing the incident but the glass collector has witnessed the man in action. I walk toward the fruit machine and the man is pointed out by the glass collector. He is clearly very drunk. I grab an arm and tell him he will have to leave. He just manages to slur the words 'what for?' before allowing me to steer him towards the door. I hold him at arms' length in case he pukes. His friends look on through half-closed eyes before going back to watching one of their number play on the fruit machine. They all look under twenty.

At the door Malcolm grabs him, calls him a dirty bastard and begins to issue warnings before realizing the man is too drunk to take in what he is saying. A few minutes pass. I am sweating under my thick bomber jacket, but can't take it off as I have not been given a *Slick's* sweatshirt and I need to be quickly identified as a bouncer. My bouncer registration card is attached to my jacket zip. A few moments pass and I talk to Malcolm and some customers at the front of the queue. Gary has returned to his station on the raised platform.

Malcolm is happy and is enjoying the atmosphere of the busy night. We talk about the female strippers, whom he says are gorgeous, although I have not yet seen them. Lenny comes over and seems truly overjoyed. He says business is through the roof and the cost of the strippers was well worth it. He too says they are gorgeous before asking if I am ready to begin my escort duties for them. All right then.

I make my way towards the manager's office and notice one of the male strippers, dressed now, surrounded by a flock of excitable young girls. A glass collector is attempting to clear the blood from the floor with a mop and bucket, all the while fighting a losing battle with the eager crowds waiting to get served at the bar. He looks harassed and exhausted. I stop to shake hands with a group of friends and they take the piss out of my intervention in the recent fight. One friend tells me I should have just 'knocked them the fuck out'. One comments on the size and reputation of Gordon and calls him a 'fucking animal'. I tell him not to let Gordon hear him say that, and tell them duty calls and I have to go and hang around with a bunch of naked women. They swear a little as I walk off laughing.

I knock on the door and wait for an answer. None comes so I knock again and enter. Five women are in various states of undress and are not in the least distressed by my sudden arrival. One asks when they are expected on and I say we are just waiting for the DJ to make the announcement. She then asks if it's all right if I walk them on to the dance floor. I say no problem, just as the door opens and a young male flies into the room. He has clearly been pushed. I grab him, push him out, and tell him and his friends to 'stay the fuck away' from the door. The group are all laughing and I try not to join them. They apologize and say it will not happen again and I let it go.

The DJ gives his introductory spiel, and the music starts. The door opens and the emerging stripper grabs my hand and off we go. I push through the crowds and shout for people in front to move. The route to the dance floor is crowded and men line the route shouting, basically, 'whey-hey!' and the like. At the edge of the dance floor I have to shout at the top of my voice and push to get the crowd to open up and allow her in. Once again men are balancing on every available perch in order to catch a glimpse of the show. Gary and Dom making desultory attempts to regulate just what they stand on, but I can see they're having fun as they fight back laughs and try to get a look themselves. Gordon and I are now stationed on each side of the dance floor to keep the crowd back and have the best view in the bar. Gordon beams and laughs out loud. He claps along with the show and occasionally bellows 'get the fuck back!' to the encroaching crowd. Gordon dances along with the show, which amuses me. We look at each other and laugh out loud. Malcolm is stuck by the door, up on tiptoes, unable to see anything.

Without my knowing, another of the strippers has made her way to the dance floor. She shouts to me and I part the crowds to allow her in. The two girls launch into a dance routine. They are dressed in bikinis designed to resemble the American flag. They do their dance and then take off their bikini tops to a huge cheer. I see Gary drag a man down who has attempted to get on to the bar to watch the act. Gordon points at an older man right at the front of the crowd who is standing open mouthed. We laugh. The girls finish up and make their way back to the office with me attempting at least to keep the majority of men at bay. One makes a grab and I fend off an arm. As we arrive I see a group of men waiting by the office door. I push them out of the way and the girls enter. They laugh hysterically. The next girl emerges and the crowd descend. Again I force my way through and manage to get her on to the dance floor. Gordon is pushing men back and shouting. Yet another girl emerges and tells me another is on her way. I head to the office to pick her up and do my best to offer some protection. She doesn't seem to mind too much and gets involved in some banter with a section of the crowd. She's dressed as a nurse. I head back to the office and ask if there will be any more. One of the remaining strippers is in the middle of a costume change and informs me they will all be going on again.

I return to the dance floor, fight my way through, and see a man stripped to the waist, sitting on a stool in the middle of the dance floor. Soon one of the strippers is covering him in baby oil and whipped cream and rubbing it in. The music is loud, and, given the shouts of the audience, conversation is unlikely. The strippers have launched into a complicated dance routine and Gordon ushers the drenched man back into the crowd. The strippers are now rubbing each other with feather dusters. Once again I escort the strippers back to the office and take the next troop back to the dance floor. When I return once again one of the girls tells me that's it. The DJ announces the end of the show and, to my relief, the crowd begins to make its way outside in dribs and drabs. After a few minutes all the strippers emerge topless from the office and walk to the dance floor. They are available for photographs. For five pounds you can have a Polaroid picture taken surrounded by the topless girls. The DJ attempts to drum up business but many people have left for nightclubs. It's ten to eleven and last orders are sounded. In an effort to get the ball rolling, the photographer asks if I want a photo at no charge. Shy, but of generous spirit, I agree. One girl sits on my knee while the other four surround me. Gordon laughs loudly and slaps me hard on the arm when I'm finished. He's really having fun. Three other customers follow my lead. Gordon and I remain on hand to monitor proceedings. A drunken customer is attempting to chat up one of the girls. He doesn't seem a danger so I let him get on with it. I joke around with Gordon and the girls and some of the customers who remain. At that moment one of the strippers tells me another fight has started.

Gordon and I have been so distracted that a fight has started only a few metres away from us. I turn to see two men exchanging punches, and one catches a head butt full in the face. Gordon and I rush to the incident. Malcolm has arrived already, having seen the fight before us. He grabs one of the fighters and pushes him against a pillar close to the female toilets. I notice the other fighter is the boxer who caused problems earlier in the evening. He is clearly very drunk and seems not to grasp what has happened. Gordon has arrived and the boxer is protesting he didn't do anything, now more worried about Gordon than his original adversary. He is becoming angry and shouting across the bar at his adversary. Gordon is calmer than I thought he would be, and tells the boxer to go outside and that we'd throw the other man out and he can sort it out there. The last head butt has opened up a cut around the boxer's left eyebrow and a trickle of blood is making its way towards his mouth. He whips at the cut and on seeing blood becomes angrier still. His eye is already swollen. Gordon once again tells him to sort it out outside. The boxer asks if we'll throw him out. Gordon confirms that we will and the boxer says 'Right. Cheers', as if Gordon and I are doing him a favour. Gordon releases his grip but stays close to him as he walks out on wobbly legs. The boxer's friends follow him out. The other fighter is still pinned to the pillar by Malcolm, with Gary in close attendance. Dom is waiting at the door. The bar is now quite empty with only groups of drinkers dotted around the place. Once again friends of the fighter are attempting to explain what happened. Malcolm has waited until the boxer and his friends have left the bar before throwing this one out. He walks to the door under pressure from Gary and appears to be bleeding slightly from the mouth. Malcolm has released his grip and is talking to Gordon. I look around the bar; the strippers have retreated to the manager's office. For the first time in hours it is possible to see a good portion of the floor. The place is a mess. The glass collectors are pushing large blue wheelie bins around collecting the masses of empty bottles that cover every available surface and are scattered round on the floor among the pools of spilt liquid, broken glass, cigarette packets and other assorted debris. The DJ is packing up his records and chatting to a girl who has made her way into the DJ stand.

I look back over towards the door and see that the latest fighter has yet to leave. Girls look around for someone to explain the proceedings to. Malcolm walks over and tells the man he has to go outside. The man says he isn't going because there are people outside who are waiting to give him a kicking. He has no male friends with him. Malcolm is annoyed by this, grabs the man and says, 'I don't give a fuck. You can't stay in here you daft cunt. Fucking fight in here and think you can stay in? Are you daft or what?' Malcolm's anger clearly increases as he says it. A girl who knows Malcolm in some way begs for mercy, but Malcolm is annoyed now and says there is nothing he can do. Dom joins in and they push the man down the stairs towards the exit. Dom adds, 'Go on, get out, fucking dopey cunt.' Females continue to plead but it's too late now. Dom goes back up the stairs and I join Malcolm to watch the fight. The circle that almost naturally encompasses a fight forms quickly. The boxer is clearly more drunk than his opponent, who is bouncing up and down in an exaggerated boxing style. The boxer has his hands on his hips and is waving his foe towards him. His friends show no sign of intervening. The two begin to fight, but it is a poor spectacle. The boxer is too drunk to perform and his punches miss by a distance. The whole thing descends into a wrestling match, until one of the boxer's friends kicks his opponent in the face as they struggle. This prompts Malcolm to act, and I accompany him out in to the street. Malcolm starts to drag the two fighters apart, telling them the police are on their way. They pay little heed, so Malcolm makes do with stopping others from intervening. A woman shouts at me to do something, but I tell her it's none of my business. She looks at me with contempt. As a police van turns the corner Malcolm and I make a final attempt to break up the fight, this time aided by the boxer's friends. The police approach, Malcolm and I run back into *Slick's*. As I retreat, I notice a bystander stripped to the waist for some reason; and his companion is singing football songs. I'm not sure if the police arrest anyone.

It's now around ten-past eleven and well past closing time. Dom, Gary and Gordon are walking around the bar shouting for people to finish their drinks and make their way outside. Gary asks what happened outside and I tell him. I show Malcolm my photo with the strippers and his mood brightens. Gordon comes over and we discuss their act. Everyone is in a good mood again. Malcolm tells me he'll go and get my wages and disappears, leaving the rest of us to usher away the remaining customers. By twenty-past eleven they have all left, apart from a group of young girls who are waiting for some of the barmaids to get changed before heading off for a nightclub. Dom goes across and Gordon, Gary and I watch as he chats up one of the girls. He returns with a phone number.

Malcolm returns with my wages and asks if I want a drink. All except Gary get a bottle of lager. Gary says his goodbyes and leaves. His girlfriend is waiting outside in the car.

The strippers emerge from the manager's office and we talk for a while. They seem friendly enough. Their photographer asks if one of us would walk the girls outside to make sure they're all right. One of the girls says that won't be necessary, they'll be OK. They leave accompanied by their male colleagues.

We sit around among the debris of the night's trade and discuss the evening. The remaining barmaids and glass collectors join in. Gordon is still amused by the activities of the strippers, Malcolm mentions the male stripper who wanted to be escorted on to the dance floor and Dom brings up the subject of the drunken customer who nearly puked on me. I get out my photo again and they all agree I'm a lucky bastard.

The manager emerges and seems very happy with the night's business. Dom asks if I want to join him and Malcolm who are going to a nightclub. I tell him no, I can't be bothered. Dom protests and tells me a gorgeous girl he knows was asking who I was and seemed interested. I again decline. I am tired and need a decent night's sleep to recuperate.

'Some Gangster Shit'

Derek has phones me on Sunday afternoon and asks me to work at *Slick's* that evening. It's short notice, but he says he would consider it a personal favour. I've had a few drinks that afternoon but I say OK, no problem. Given the short notice, he says I needn't bother getting there before nine, and says he will be in *Slick's* himself after ten o'clock.

Sundays are quiet in *Slick's* between seven and around quarter to ten, and then, after that, until last orders at half past ten, the place is packed. Only two doormen are required for this restricted business, and tonight I will be working with Gordon.

I arrive at *Slick's* at around quarter to nine. As expected the place is deserted except for the bar staff, who are trying to find something to do, cleaning glasses and filling up the fridges. I sign my name and registration number as required. Lenny greets me and makes conversation before heading off to deal with his assorted duties. Gordon has yet to arrive so I pull a stool up to the bar and order a beer. I watch the television and talk to the barmaid. She tells me of her recent trip to a famous nightclub and her boyfriend difficulties. Another Doorkind bouncer comes in around nine looking for Gordon. We shake hands and I tell him he hasn't come in yet. I take a message, to tell him to phone Tony before ten.

At just after nine Gordon turns up. He goes to sign the book and hang up his coat. When he returns I pass on the message. He turns his nose up at it and ignores it. He tells me about his new car, an Audi, and we go outside to look at it. It's bright red, has a personalized licence plate and is covered in sports trimming. I congratulate him on his purchase, of which he is obviously immensely proud. We go back inside and he begins to tell me of his other money-getting activities.

He mentions a notable criminal, reputed to be a close associate of Trevor's, who is currently in jail. He tells me he has been looking after a few things for him. I don't push him for more details and he seems to presume I know more about these matters than I do. This is a very delicate area. I am not really here to gather information about professional and organized crime in the region and any real involvement in such matters is further than I am willing to go in the name of research. I have already discovered that all is not well in gangland, and that there may well be a conflict between two notable groups. If this does happen, door security in the area is likely to be one of the main staging grounds for the unfolding conflict. As if this wasn't enough, working for Doorkind and being friendly with someone like Gordon clearly identifies me as having taken a side in the dispute. This is tricky; however I am naturally curious and I am keen to curry friendship with Gordon.

Gordon tells me of a fight he recently had in one of the pubs he 'minds'. Again I don't press. Apparently he and Derek had taken on around twenty men and gained a satisfactory result. He then goes on to discuss an associated incident in which one of the men was caught by a friend of Derek in a nearby bar and beaten up. The story involves a good deal of movement so Gordon stands up in order to fully describe the incidents involved in the story. Gordon tells the story as it was told to him, in the first person, by Derek's friend. Apparently Derek's friend had the man against the wall and was beating him around the head. After he had given him his best shots, Derek's friend had apparently backed up, for the man had not yet fallen to the ground. The aggressor, it appeared, had begun to worry about the potential of this man, who, it seemed, could not be knocked out. That was until he noticed the victim's coat had become caught on a coat hanger directly behind him and he was already unconscious but could not fall to the floor as his coat was holding him up. The story is much more amusing than can be conveyed here, and it amuses Gordon all over again and he laughs loudly.

We talk for a while about nothing in particular and two glass collectors join us at the bar before being told to get some work done by Lenny. Gordon tells him jokingly to leave them alone. The first customers begin to enter and we make our way over to the entrance.

We talk to certain customers who enter and Gordon half dances, half stands still to the music. Again he talks about trouble in his business. Apparently he has been told that a gang from another area of town are going to attempt to beat him up in order to seize a section of the protection racket he and others run in their area. Gordon knows exactly how they will do this. He expects to get a call on his mobile phone from a landlord informing him that a fight has broken out in one of the pubs that he protects. This, he says, will be a setup, and on his arrival the real trouble will start. He says he knows who his opponents are but so far has been unable to locate them. Apparently the group includes a once-notable local 'hard' man who has faded from the scene. Gordon doesn't seem too worried, and I hope his phone doesn't ring while he's in my company.

The evening progresses without incident. We have to turn away a few drunks and a few underage kids, but that's it. Derek turns up, says 'hello' and once again thanks me for filling in at short notice. Gordon tells him of the information he has received. Derek appears unconcerned, and brings up an upcoming trial in which he and Gordon know the defendant. I know of the case. Derek mentions having talked to one of the witnesses. This man had come to him, scared that some action would be taken against him, and promising to give testimony that would not damage Derek's friend's case. He mentions the man's Christian name, but struggles to recall his surname. I know it and tell him. He asks if I know the man and I say I do. I sense Derek knew this all along.

He asks me what he's like. I give an opinion, and tell Derek the man used to be a drug dealer. Derek brushes the conversation off, saying that it seems to be sorted out anyway. Customers coming in and out of the bar attempt to shake Derek's hand; some he greets warmly, some grudgingly. He then makes his way into the bar, dressed in his usual attire.

Before long it's closing time and the DJ is telling the assembled masses to please drink up and leave. Sundays are a good night to work because nobody comes in until late in the evening, and only a minimal amount of work is necessary, especially as last orders are filled at half-past ten instead of the usual 11.00 p.m. The bouncers therefore only have to stand by the door for an hour at most, and the pay is the same.

Shortly after last orders Derek leaves and tells me he'll give me a ring during the week. Gordon and I give the drinkers five minutes before we start to harass them into leaving. The only bad thing about working a Sunday is that the customers are not always quick to leave because the nightclubs are closed and there isn't really anywhere else to go except home, although a good number of customers go on to local restaurants where they can eat and drink until later in the evening.

Meet Matty

Two weeks after this brief discussion of protection rackets with Gordon I receive a phone call from a friend who informs me there is the possibility of accompanying a friend of Gordon's, Matty, as he does a few rounds on their protection racket route. This is a considerable break for my research and, although I'm apprehensive,

I find it difficult to say 'no'. I'd seen Matty about many times previously with Gordon and Derek in bars and clubs in the region, and he'd often hang around the bars protected by Doorkind Security, seemingly as a vaguely sinecured quasi-bouncer, there to help if need be, but ostensibly just hanging around and enjoying himself. I'd presumed that he was being paid for this service, and the subterfuge was necessary to avoid licensing problems: Matty had been released from prison a year or so earlier after having served a sentence for a serious charge, and thus he was unable to get a license to legitimately work as a bouncer. More recently I had come to believe he also served some other function for Trevor and Derek, but was unable to work out quite what it was. It now became clearer, that Matty was in some way involved with protection rackets, but I was still far from being in possession of all the necessary information to work out just what was going on who was linked with whom and in what way. It was possible Matty was working by himself, or in conjunction with Derek, Gordon, Trevor or some combination of those involved in the illegitimate aspects of the security business. Matty had always seemed peripheral to what I had imagined was going on, based upon various bits of gossip I was able to pick up and what I was able to surmise from watching these men at work and play. Matty did, however, possess what appeared to be a shadier circle of friends than others involved in the scene. Most criminals would be recognized by bouncers knowledgeable about the locality in which they lived and worked, and certainly this was true of the bouncers in *Slick's*; Matty however seemed to be on first-name terms with nearly all of them, and would often leave whatever bar he happened to be in to talk privately with them.

Aside from this, Matty had always been polite and talkative, but rarely revealed much about himself, certainly not to the same degree as Gordon, who seemed to think of it all as legitimate business that need not necessarily be hidden from public debate. He was no more than average height and weight, standing around five feet and ten inches tall, and didn't look obviously dangerous – no visible tattoos, no bulging muscles, no especially significant facial scars. He nonetheless came across as a man to be reckoned with: his nose had obviously been broken, but this is no more than par for the course in these circles; he spoke quietly, but in an assured tone, and always held eye contact with whoever he was talking to or listening to. The indefatigable quality of utter confidence in any situation, and the almost unsettling disregard for broadcasting the fact, helped to bestow Matty with an almost tangible aura of danger. He would discuss football, which many of the bouncers who I worked with were not interested in, and generalities about friendships, nights out and women. One thing about working as a bouncer is that it gives you plenty of time to get to know your colleagues, due to the sheer amount of time you spend standing around together. Matty did, however, remain somewhat aloof, which didn't seem unusual at the time because it was never made clear that he was part of the team; he was just there, part of the regular social scenery at *Slick's* and other local bars and clubs.

I meet Jason, my friend who has set up this fortuitous research opportunity, outside *Slick's* before continuing on to another local bar to meet up with Matty. Upon arrival he shook both our hands before resuming a conversation with a man seated at the bar. When Matty returned his attention to us he seemed unaware that I would be accompanying him and Jason on the journey around the bars and pubs that he, and/or others, were protecting. He presumed I was there to accompany Jason to some unmentioned activity after the rounds where made, and I was just killing time until they were finished. Neither my friend nor I thought it necessary to inform him otherwise and we were informed that our trip wouldn't take more than an hour. Rather than an exciting piece of illegal activity, it all seemed strangely mundane, as if Matty's sideline was holding up our night out.

Matty's previous knowledge of me in my role as bouncer served to temper his natural urge to be circumspect and he had seen me for around long enough to know that we had many mutual friends and acquaintances. What we were about to do or why wasn't mentioned at any stage, although there was the tacit assumption that I had some knowledge of what would come to pass and the various circumstances that surrounded this particular trip. Some information had been passed on through my conversations with Gordon, a major player in the recent gangland turmoil, and I had other contacts immersed in these criminal circles, but still much relied on the ability of those on the periphery to piece things together with the various snippets of information they had at their disposal.

Jason had done this before, and told me it was nothing to get excited about. Just some bloke talking to some other bloke in a bar, with rarely anything happening outside of polite conversation, a handshake and the exchange, sometimes although not always, of a small sum of money. I'm informed that there really isn't any need for us to be there, Matty usually does this stuff by himself, but tonight he had asked for a lift and Jason didn't mind doing him the favour. I ask him about the spate of trouble in some of the bars protected by Gordon, and presumably Matty, and rumours of a take over bid by another group. Jason shrugs, pulls an exaggerated frown, and says nothing. I press the subject. 'Probably just a load of bullshit. Just gossip and stuff. It'll be nothing' he says, before finishing with his familiar 'what-do-I-know?' shrug.

It's getting dark outside and young men and woman wander around the streets in various states of inebriation. Before getting into Jason's car we watch two men wrestle with two police officers who are trying to put one of the men into the back of an unmarked police car. The police are alone and seem to be a bit nervous about the number of bystanders who are gathering. The man who is being forced into the car clearly isn't keen to get in. One of the policemen begins to punch him in the stomach in order to get the man to bend and thus aid his entrance into the car. His friend is protesting loudly and asks the crowd to bear witness to the assault. Some begin to shout at the policemen, telling them to leave the man alone. The police begin to panic further, but gain added encouragement by the sound of approaching police sirens. By the time the police backup has arrived, the punching has succeeded, and the first man is in the back of the unmarked car. Around ten officers spill out of two cars and a van and arrest the man's friend and another man who has been offering vocal support.

The spectacle over, Matty, Jason and I continue to the car. Inside, Jason voices hatred for the police and his belief in the idea that the police think they can just go around doing whatever they like. He clearly isn't happy that the policeman repeatedly punched the arrested man. After this he goes on to discuss his love life and bemoans the plight of a bouncer's relationships, for having had to keep unusual and unpredictable hours has affected his current relationship. After this we discuss women and he questions me as to why it is that women automatically assume that you're promiscuous if you are a doorman. We then discuss the phenomenon of 'bouncer groupies' and we trade stories, which serves to lighten the mood somewhat. Jason puts on some loud dance music, and Matty mocks his musical taste, saying they are both too old to be listening to kids music, forcing Jason to relent and put the radio on.

A short while later we approach Matty's first 'pick up'. He tells us he is seeking information about the gang that is apparently planning to take control of some of the bars on Matty's and/or Gordon's route. He does this casually, without adding the note of drama that had been present when Gordon had offered information about these matters two weeks earlier while working at *Slick's*. We enter a small local pub. I remain silent while Matty shakes hands with the publican and ignores a group of what appears to be regulars sitting beside the bar. The publican offers Matty a drink and Matty immediately turns to ask if we want a pint. I say 'yes', as does Jason. Gordon doesn't bother. I get my pint and nobody asks for the money.

The locals, apparently having 'after hours' drinks [known as a 'lockin'], stare into their pints and are unnaturally quiet. They avoid looking at Matty, Jason and myself and try not to seem interested in what is being discussed.

Matty asks the publican if he has heard anything about this supposed gang and asks for details, which range from if they've been in for a drink to whether they've been in trying to drum up business. The publican claims to have heard a few whispers, and infers that he knows what's happening, but also says the gang hasn't been in, even for a drink. Matty asks if he's sure. The publican flushes slightly and says, absolutely, he wouldn't lie to him. Matty tells the publican that he's heard that the gang are going to try to set him up. The publican nods along before saying he knows who the gang are and that they ought not to scare Matty. Matty looks directly at the publican and tells him he wants him to find out what he can. He also adds that if there is trouble he wants him to think long and hard before phoning him, and the publican replies, 'of course'. Matty then starts all over again with the same questions and the atmosphere becomes more strained. Again the publican offers protestations and promises until Matty appears satisfied. Matty reinforces his points about wanting information and to think twice before phoning him in the event of trouble. He also says that if anyone else pitches him (the landlord) for business he's to get straight on the phone, any time of the day or night. The discussion has lasted around five minutes and neither Jason nor I have said a word. Both my pint and Jason's are nearly finished, and Matty says 'goodbye' before leaving. Once we get inside the car, Matty says he has forgotten something and goes back in, emerging moments later.

We drive off, and Matty asks if I'm hungry. I say 'yes' and he asks what kind of food I would like. I say I don't care. He then pulls up at an Indian takeaway and asks if that's OK. Jason says he isn't hungry, which I know to be untrue. He's actually on a diet to try and lose some of the surrounding fat from his muscular physique. We go in and Matty asks what I want. I say I don't know anything about Indian food, so he says he'll just get me the same as him. He greets the owner who takes the order and makes small talk. Matty asks how business is going and the owner says not bad. Gordon calls him a lying bastard and says they always do well in here. After a short wait our food emerges from the back room. There's a lot. We have a rice dish, a curry dish, some chicken and some popadoms. We say goodbye and walk out without paying.

Back in the car Matty appears in relaxed mood and tells me that I never pay for food around here when I'm with him. We pass a Chinese takeaway and a pizza shop and he tells me he's 'got' them as well. I wish I'd specified Chinese food but decline to mention it. Matty again takes the lead in conversation and mentions Doorkind's recent employment at a newly developing nightclub. The place has been open for years but has recently been refurbished and is hoping to attract a younger clientele with dance music and big name DJs. He suggests I come to the opening night if I'm not working. He'll get me plenty of free drink vouchers. He says he isn't sure who else will be working there but he'll try to get me on if I like. I say that would be great. Matty says the only drawback is having to wear bow ties, but apart from that it should be a laugh.

We arrive at stop number two. The pub appears to be shut, but Matty knocks on the door until the landlady arrives and lets us in. We stand in the hallway of the pub, shut off from the bar area where I can hear people are still drinking. Immediately I regret having brought in a huge popadom. I hold it uncomfortably in my hand while Matty begins to question the landlady, whose pub Matty is clearly also employed to protect.

The landlady admits that a man has been in and has offered to mind the pub. She says he was polite, and when she said no thank you, that matter was already taken care of, he accepted it and said to get in touch if she ever changed her mind. Matty doesn't look happy. He wants to know what his name was, what he looked like, and wants to know, to the exact last word, what the man said. This questioning goes on for some time and the landlady goes over and over her answers. Having the popadom in my hand is now making me feel even more uncomfortable. A middle-aged man emerges from the bar area, prompting a sudden halt to the conversation. He says hello to the landlady and to Matty before going into the toilet, through another door in the hallway area. Matty's mobile phone rings; he takes a brief call, then returns to business. Conversation continues. Matty tells the landlady the information he has picked up, and what the gang have planned. For the third time the landlady pledges her loyalty and the man emerges from the toilet and goes back into the bar area.

After further questioning Matty seeks to bring me into the discussion. Amazingly he asks what I think. I say the landlady should make sure that any fight is exactly what it appears to be before getting on the phone to Matty, and to watch out for little things, like groups of men shouting and causing a disturbance unnecessarily, or perhaps a group of men she hasn't seen before lighting up joints, things like that. I tell her these things might be done on purpose in order to set Matty up. I also tell her that if the man comes in again she should watch him closely and inform Matty. Matty seems greatly pleased by what I have said and seeks to finish my sentence. He says if the man comes in, it may be he will attempt to stop any trouble whilst on the premises, and thus put himself in a position to ask for payment. Jason remains silent throughout this discussion, apart from the occasional disinterested sigh. Matty makes it clear that the man will have set up the trouble in the first place and that the landlady should be aware of this.

Throughout this discussion the landlady has been nodding her head. I don't doubt she has heard it all before and knows the gang's game plan and what to look out for. Once again Matty asks some more questions before allowing a gap in conversation to develop where we might be expected to make our departure.

Back in the car we start to eat and I discard the now cold popadom. Matty tells me it's 'just the usual shit', and both Jason and I agree. Jason tries to move the conversation forward by asking Matty if he wants to accompany us to a nightclub.

Matty clearly believes my knowledge of these matters is greater than it is. The only knowledge of protection rackets I have has come from a drunken conversation that has proved to be well wide of the mark, from 'true crime' books and from the academic literature available on the matter. As we eat, the man who recently interrupted our discussion in the hallway of the pub comes out. Matty lowers his window electronically. The man says 'hello' to Matty, using his first name (Matty later tells me he has never seen the man before), and goes to some pains to get his hand through the window and shake Jason's hand across in the drivers seat. He makes do with a little wave to me in the back. The man says the gang had been in the bar and that the landlady told them they weren't needed. He also says some of the gang have been hanging around more than usual, and offers Matty another name from the gang. He says he knows the gang has also pitched other local publicans for business, and confirms that they intend to set Matty up.

Matty thanks the man for his help, and the man says to give his best wishes to a friend of Matty's, currently in prison. We then depart. It is now around half-past midnight and he stops to make a final call. On this occasion Matty asks us to stay in the car. In his absence Jason moans about his hunger and desire for a few pints. A few gentle questions about the night's proceedings fails to yield any noteworthy response from Jason, who clearly has more important things to think about; he mentions his latest work in the gym, a steroid new to the area that appears to be all the rage, a recent sexual conquest and his hatred of aerobic exercise. After a long fifteen-to-twenty minutes, Matty returns to the car, jogging a little to avoid the worst of the rain that has just begun to fall, and with his phone clasped to his ear. I can clearly hear his side of the conversation, but it amounts to little more than a few 'yeses' and 'nos' and the occasional grunt. When he's finished he informs us 'that's it', and asks Jason to drop him off beside the bar where we picked him up. I had expected there to be more bars and pubs to visit, but I'm later reminded by Jason that this is a full-time job for these people and they can make these visits whenever they want, free as they are from the regimentation of legitimate employment. We drop off Matty, who now seems a little distracted and keen to be somewhere else. He says 'thanks for the lift' to Jason, and says he'll see us both later.

Jason and I progress to a nightclub where we bump into Gordon. He already knows where we've been and with whom. He immediately launches into a detailed question-and-answer session, wanting to know all that had been said and seen. Jason can't drink much because of his diet and he seems a little moody because of it and consequently it is me answering most of the questions. After recounting the minutiae of the evening's developments, Gordon seems to wants to talk further about the protection situation; we should over the loud music to make ourselves heard. He certainly doesn't seem as relaxed about recent developments as Matty had been, and I offer consoling words, which seem to keep him happy. Before leaving he tells me he'll try and get Derek to sort me out with a regular job at that new night-club Matty mentioned. Once again I thank him and say I'll see him next week before heading home.

Comment and Discussion

The above ethnography of two nights in and around *Slick's* bar is not, I stress, intended to be a complete analysis of how and why the bouncers act in the way they do. I offer it in order to portray elements of the formal and informal night-time economy that exists in the North Eastern region at the time of writing (circa 1998). The reader should also consider these environments in relation to the points I have made about the destructuring of traditional forms of masculine employment and expression and the various contexts of post-modern working-class masculinities.

I have already offered an analytical discussion of the nature of these problematic leisure locations and of the status-providing and criminal opportunities that have arisen for those who police and regulate these environments. As I have previously argued, violence has become both a legal and illegal career option for those skilled in its deployment and manipulation.

Gordon's and Matty's activities would certainly be deemed illegal by the courts of law, but from what I have been able to gather his services are valued by many of his customers and his business enterprise is, for the most part, informal rather than of a completely criminal nature. As with aspects of the black economy, neutral-ization, symbolism and economic rationality blend to offer a viable means of engaging the market and deriving from it a diversity of meanings and understandings, as well as cold, hard cash.

Gordon and Matty's connections and violent reputation allow them to earn money (I would estimate not an inconsiderable sum of money), through methods that, as I have argued previously, were, for the most part at least, not available to 'hard' men during the industrial modern era in the North East. To some extent, Gordon and his thriving business represent the contemporary incarnation of Tommy and his small protection activities as detailed in Chapter 1. Gordon and Matty have what it takes to engage in what can be a deadly but profitable business, as did Tommy. The difference between them and Tommy, and the different levels and understandings of success they achieved, derive from changing economic, social and cultural realities in the North East of England (see Chapters 1 and 4).

Gordon's violence has given him access to both legitimate and illegitimate markets for protection and intimidation in a night-time economy awash with money-making opportunities, and Gordon has the ability to tailor his role to fit his employer's needs. As well as his admirable aptitude for straddling legitimate and illegitimate business spheres, Gordon now has the capacity to shift the market to suit his needs by creating business where none is needed. Although I did not see Gordon or Matty apply any pressure to his various customers at any stage, the threat of violence is ever present, if seldom expressed. It is now possible for Gordon and Matty to offer their services to bars and pubs whose managers may feel they, and their local repute, are not needed, but who will negotiate terms with them because of implied or imagined threats, perhaps mixed with an understanding of the value of their services, even if they will rarely be used. Nobody likes to consider themselves as being weak and open to intimidation and it is likely that some publicans who subscribe to Gordon's and Matty's service would employ market logic rather than admit to this. One publican I talked to explained he dealt with Matty because trouble may one day occur in his pub, and in that event he could at least call on Matty. The publican also mentioned that in over a year he has yet to use Matty's services.

In some cases Gordon's and Matty's service is highly valued and is highly effective, for though he may not be in the bar or pub regularly, word quickly gets around as to who 'looks after' which pubs and this, correspondingly, influences the behaviour of those who may be likely to cause some kind of trouble. In these cases Gordon or Matty's name is often enough. In others Gordon may have to talk to troublesome elements among the pub's clientele and in others still, someone may have to take a beating. During the course of my research I witnessed one example of this, which I describe below.

Getting the Phone Call

The following events are offered as an example of what can happen when the mobile phone rings for someone like Matty. This is the dirty end of a dirty business, and it is Matty's stock-in-trade.

It's Saturday, and I have been working at a Doorkind venue (not *Slick's*) with a friend. It has been a long, tiring and uneventful evening and I am again bemoaning the ethnographer's lot. Kevin, a long-time friend of mine, who actually helped get me the job, is my companion and we have arrived at *The Pleasure Dome*, a Doorkind venue and hangout for its bouncers once they have finished work.

The Pleasure Dome employs seven Doorkind bouncers on a Saturday. You can expect to find another ten Doorkind doormen dotted around the club, drinking, dancing and propositioning women, or standing at the door with their friends and colleagues, talking about violence, work, women and the night's events. Doorkind bouncers, of course, get in free, and as a result *The Pleasure Dome* probably possesses the most wide-necked clientele in northern England.

Tonight Kevin and I are here to pick up wages from Derek, who can usually be found holding court at the door on a Friday and Saturday. Kevin is around five feet nine inches tall and weighs around fifteen stone. He used to be a serious bodybuilder and is still a big man, although he is now becoming fat through lack of exercise and the wrong diet. He has an eighteen-inch neck and is a renowned, although not legendary, street fighter. I have known him for around two years, and he's been a bouncer for at least five years, work for which he is highly suited. He has built up the useful bouncing commodity of experience and has seen most things over the years. He has an unusual-shaped scar running underneath his left eye, a wound inflicted two years previously in a glassing incident. Kevin used to be in the Army and is still a member of the Territorial Army, a pastime that he talks about often. He also used to be a football hooligan but his passion for this form of violent engagement is beginning to wane. Many consider him to be a little bit mad and he has been known to become violent with little reason, although the arrival of a live-in girlfriend and baby son appear to have mellowed him somewhat as he eases into middle age.

We are both wearing our thick bomber jackets and weave our way through the crowds of pissed-up youths who have congregated around a pizza shop and taxi rank close to *The Pleasure Dome*. The occupants of a police van look on as couples fumble, and men and women eat, puke and piss. I can't be bothered with it tonight, and I'm looking forward to getting my money and a cold beer. Kevin is his usual jovial self. He likes his evening job in every way, likes playing the tough guy; he likes the female attention and the money comes in very handy for his new family.

As we arrive at the doorway of *The Pleasure Dome* we are greeted by Gordon and three others who are running in the opposite direction. He shouts something I can't quite make out, but I guess he wants me to follow. Kevin and I set off in pursuit. I recognize Chris, another Doorkind bouncer who works at *The Pleasure Dome*, and Matty, but I can't yet work out who the other the other man is. He isn't dressed in the usual Doorkind attire.

We arrive in a car park and Gordon informs me he has had a phone call from a pub he minds. There's been a fight, and some furniture has been smashed. The licensee has told Gordon that at least one of those involved is still standing outside the pub.

The six of us squeeze ourselves into a black Volkswagen owned by Chris, who has had to take a set of tools and a baby seat out of the back of the car to fit us all in. We are going to *The Owl,* a pub some distance away. Matty and his friend, whom I have been unable to identify, are clearly pissed and are talking about what we're going to do to the troublemakers when we get there. Gordon asks if anyone has 'got anything'. He's talking about weapons. Chris says he's got some Mace and a bat in the boot of the car. Gordon tells him to be careful where he sprays the Mace and look out for which way the wind is blowing. Kevin says 'shit', he's come out without his knuckle duster, and asks if Chris wants to take a detour so that he can pick up some further weaponry. I say nothing, but think, 'oh shit'.

Matty says, 'no time', and asks Chris to speed up, which he does, occasionally slowing down for speed cameras and traffic lights. The man I haven't seen before tells Chris that he should smear some mud on his plates to prevent this type of inconvenience. Kevin is sitting on my knee and my leg is going numb. The un-identified man says 'all right?' He introduces himself as Frankie, says he's seen me around and asks how long I've been working the doors. I tell him and there is some nervous conversation. Kevin is getting into the spirit of things and is including himself in the talk of upcoming violence. He apparently knows the other man in the car, and they talk about the wellbeing of Kevin's cousin, whom the man apparently knows.

Some way into the journey Chris speaks for the first time, asking which is the quickest way to *The Owl*. Matty says, take a left, it's quicker. I know this is the wrong way but don't say anything. Frankie says bullshit; we should have gone straight ahead. I feel under pressure to join in the conversation, so I say, he's right, he should have gone straight ahead. Matty uses my opinion to back up his point and he and Frankie exchange mild insults. Gordon asks them politely to 'shut the fuck up'.

We are now going in the wrong direction, but eventually things are worked out and we pull up outside the pub. About ten men are standing around outside the pub, one of whom is bleeding from the mouth, clasping a toilet roll to the wound. They purposely look away as we skid to a halt and spill out of the car. Right away I get the sense that my companions are going to start hitting people. Frankie, Matty and Kevin are on their toes while Gordon knocks on the front door of the now shut pub. I stand next to Chris, who seems the calmest and the least likely to maim somebody.

From where I'm standing I can see a group of young girls inside the pub eagerly looking out of the window at the spectacle. We've made quite an impact. The licensee opens the door and talks quickly to Gordon. I make out there has been a fight, that some furniture has been smashed, and that one of those involved was a man named Reddy. It's not a name you hear often. Matty talks to Frankie in hushed tones. I can't hear what else is said but I see the licensee point at a nearby man. Gordon immediately turns and starts walking urgently towards the identified man. Frankie however beats him to it, runs the short distance and punches the identified man in the face. The man falls to the ground.

The realities of this kind of violence cannot be understood if incidents such as this haven't been witnessed. The sounds, the movements, the immediate wounds and the effects of such violence certainly aren't captured by most media portrayals, and the uncensored realities would be considered extremely disturbing by many. Frankie is a big, powerful man and his knowledge of violence is considerable. When a man like this pulls his arm back and delivers a punch he intends to do extreme harm and it is not unrealistic to envisage death. If the initial punch doesn't do it, the victim may well bang his head on the pavement and die.

Gordon immediately advances on the now prone man, preparing to launch another onslaught. He begins to kick the man and is joined in this by Frankie and Matty. They aim kicks at the man's head, the way you would shape up to strike a football with the utmost force. Frankie is swearing, calling the man a bastard. I see the man role into the foetus position and cover his head with his hands. Matty, clearly drunk, is also swearing and is now raising his foot to stamp on the man's head. Gordon gives up and walks away.

Frankie and the Matty, and now Kevin, kick the man for a while longer, and then ease up for a moment. The wounded man, lying on the ground, has stopped moving and I consider seriously the possibility they've killed him. However, he then sparks back into life, rolls on to his other side, re-covers his head and the kicking recommences.

Against all instinct I tell the men to stop. I don't want to, but I feel compelled. I know what doing this can mean. I'm not naïve about what these men can do.

My stomach is turning as I say, leave him alone, he's had enough. I can feel Matty looking at me. There is an uncomfortable moment of silence before Chris joins in and tells them to leave him alone.

Gordon tells Kevin to see if he can get any names out of him. Kevin drags the badly injured man to his feet. He is still covering his face and I can hear him sobbing. I bring myself to look and see his face is in a bad way. Kevin is asking the man where Reddy lives. The man is crying and saying he doesn't know. Frankie makes his way over and shapes to throw a punch but doesn't. Again the man flinches, before saying he doesn't know anyone called Reddy and beginning to offer his version of events.

Gordon walks back over. I look round and see the assembled crowd are watching, but trying to hide the fact. Gordon cuts to the chase. He tells the man that if he ever hears of him coming near the pub again he'll break his legs; 'no one', he says, 'repeat no one, fucks around in this pub, right?'

Matty, breathing heavily from his exertions, asks the licensee to point out any other troublemakers. Everyone appears nervous, on edge. It is possible to sense them praying that she doesn't point them out. She says no, the others have gone. A younger man says something to another bystander and Frankie makes a move for him. He grabs him but the licensee is now screaming 'Not him, he didn't do anything.' We go into the pub.

The place is indeed a mess. A group of young men and women are sitting in a lounge area drinking. The atmosphere lightens somewhat. Gordon asks the licensee if there is anyone in she doesn't want there. She says 'no, these lot are all right'. A barmaid makes a joke about how we all fitted into the car. I don't feel like laughing. The licensee asks if we want a drink. Everyone says no. Kevin asks the people in the lounge area what happened and around five girls rush to give their version of events. When they are finished Kevin goes outside with Frankie and Matty to question further witnesses. I lean against the bar and wait with Chris.

When Gordon is finished talking to the licensee Chris and I follow him outside towards the car. Kevin and Frankie are still interrogating witnesses and asking for names (I can see Kevin is enjoying being a gangster for a night). Suddenly Frankie butts a man in the face, and the sound of flesh and bone on flesh and bone startles some of those present and forces them to pay attention to what is going on. It is not a pleasant sound. Matty holds him back. Frankie swears at the man he has butted, who has remained standing but is now covering his face. Frankie is saying, 'don't fucking ever look at me like that.' Gordon tells Frankie, 'just leave him', and we squeeze back in the car.

The journey back is awash with competing conversation. Everyone is talking and few are listening. Frankie is telling me you haven't got to fuck around, you've got to get in there and bang a few heads. If you don't, they keep coming back. Take it from me, he tells me, he knows. I explain that there was no sense in killing the kid, but I can see what he's saying. Frankie has now got his arm around me, and is talking into my ear, telling me it's business and you can't fuck around. I say anything to him that I think will stop him from continuing the conversation.

Matty is now slurringly relating a story of how, armed with a knife, he had waited by himself for a rival to come into a bar and he clearly takes his rival's non-appearance as a sign of cowardice. I've never known Matty to be so open and talkative – clearly the effects of mixing alcohol with extreme, adrenalizing violence. The man he is talking about is a noted gangster and I wonder if he's exaggerating the tale. Gordon joins in and says that someone should 'do away with the cunt' because he's a liability and just creates trouble for everybody. Frankie agrees. These men are now talking about serious criminality, about gangsters and issues I do not want even to know about. The gangster they have mentioned again indicates the likelihood of a serious conflict between two rival groups.

Kevin is joining in the conversation and appears to be attempting to ingratiate himself with the men in the car. There is more talk of gangsterism and violence before we arrive back at *The Pleasure Dome*. We are greeted warmly by the other bouncers and are forced to answer searching questions about the recent events. Dom, whom I worked with in *Slick's* is in, and he asks me if I enjoyed it. I say that I did.

I later found out Matty had asked Kevin the same question, and also asked him if I enjoyed myself. Thankfully Kevin said that I did, that I liked a bit of trouble the same as the next man, and that I would be 'straight in there' if there was any further trouble. I was pleased with Kevin's answer for I want to appear just like the rest of the Doorkind staff and the various men around Gordon and Matty, not because of what they do but because it is my job to be like one of them. Moreover, I do not want to unnerve Gordon or Matty, not simply because it would suddenly end my research but because I don't want him to become annoyed at me. Matty's questioning of Kevin made me believe he was checking out my reaction to the violence, especially given the fact that I had asked them to leave the victim alone. Kevin's answer no doubt went some way towards making him believe I could still be trusted and that I was one of them, that I belonged. However there were other circumstances that I used to my advantage to bolster my credibility and at our next meeting Matty and Gordon were just as they always had been and I continued to be treated as a friend, by Gordon especially.

The Monday following this incident I was in the more comfortable confines of Durham University. I spoke to my academic supervisor and we agreed it was time for me to start negotiating my withdrawal from the field.

−4−

Summary and Conclusion

As soon as it begins to speak and convey meaning, the bird has flown, the rain has evaporated.

Foucault, 'This is Not a Pipe'

Summary

This book has been about changing masculinities and changing crime in the North East of England. The evidence and arguments presented in these pages should indicate that the social upheavals of de-industrialization and post-modernity, and all that these two phrases entail, have prompted huge changes in the region's working-class masculinities. As economic, social and cultural transformation has fundamentally affected men and masculine identities, so has it changed the breadth and nature of criminal practice in the North East.

As traditional structures have been eroded and the world has changed, North-Eastern working-class men have been forced to develop and recognize new means of masculine expression. As Brod (1987: 195) has pointed out, 'men both form and are formed by their conditions, or as Marx put it, men make their own history, but not in circumstances of their own choosing.'

Contemporary working-class men in the North East no longer have the established structures that provided such reliable bases for identity and behaviour throughout the modern age. Sons no longer follow their fathers into specific industrial trades, and they may not follow them into manufacturing at all. Working-class working lives do not have the structure that allowed men in the modern era to predict their future employment. Class position may change as downward mobility grips re-dundant working-class trades and generations; the nuclear family has become more of an ideal than a prevailing familial structure and forms of working-class leisure and pleasure become less beholden to historical cultural inheritance as new influences initiate a remodelling of cultural meaning and understanding.

The destructuring of working-class life in this locale is multifaceted, and the working-class manifestation of criminality has also been jettisoned from the modern order. As Chambliss (1987) has stressed, 'crime . . . takes its character from the economic institutions that exist at a particular point in time' and we can clearly see how crime in the North East has undergone a process of substantial restructuring as global, cultural and economic imperatives fuse with local interpretations of market and status concerns. The economic institutions of the modern era that suggested such predictable characteristics for criminality are now gone, and while the remnants of these structures linger on to inform contemporary criminality, new global influences, notably entrepreneurship, have been drawn into criminal culture, redrawing boundaries and recategorizing concerns. Gone are the days when crime was, for the most part, restricted to petty pilfering and conflict-orientated crime. Men such as Tommy (see Chapter 1) are now relics of a bygone age as money and entrepreneurship entwine themselves around the local criminal culture and economy. Criminal careers have emerged and successful criminal role models now exist whom the next generation can revere and aspire to emulate; a new strange ladder of social mobility is beginning to establish itself (Sutherland 1937).

Crime, especially in its entrepreneurial embodiment, seems to have taken on new seductive qualities that do not solely reflect upon immediate gratification or cultural understanding but fix on wider social aspirations and hidden knowledge. The human embodiment of professional crime is sexy and daring; he flouts convention, he gets all the best girls and pulls the strings to which the world dances (Bell 1960). Or at least he does so in the movie version, in the myth; and this is far more inspiring and just as available as the actuality.

The transition from industrial to post-industrial work and masculinities, and from conflict to entrepreneurial criminal foundations has not been smooth, and much is left unresolved. What remains of the old structures is scrutinized for relevance and remoulded to fit the new, while simultaneously being imbued with more diverse global understandings. As the market imposes its influence upon criminal activity, not all criminal stimuli are financial. A complex of reasoning still exists and violence as a means of status advancement still has relevance.

It is not my intention to portray this world as being inhabited solely by successful criminal entrepreneurs because it most certainly is not; however, what has changed fundamentally with regard to criminality is *opportunity*. The chance to gain financially from crime and violence is now available, and is currently being grasped by a growing number of young males who have little interest in cultural continuity, communal belonging or methodological application; what counts is the immediacy of one's own lived existence, the chance to live 'life as a party' (Shover and Honaker 1991) and the opportunity to attain and maintain relevant status goals and experience the illicit stimulation that deviancy so often provides.

I do not see the arrival of opportunity with regard to entrepreneurial and professional crime as a particularly liberating development. The word 'opportunity' is used to depict entrepreneurial crime in terms of what is now available but was not previously. I do not wish to imply that contemporary North-Eastern criminals have been emancipated from the shackles of an industrially informed criminality, because that would indicate that, in some sense, criminals are 'better off' in contemporary criminal culture. They are not. Opportunity and potential financial reward may be welcomed by those committed to contemporary criminal life, but had industry and the modern economic order survived the lack of this opportunity would not be lamented. Criminals of the age did not consider themselves in some way disadvantaged in this regard, because one does not miss that which one does not experience. The conflict-orientated criminal culture, which existed during the industrial period, was just as relevant to those who valued its content as those who attempt to engage the contemporary criminal marketplace. A particularly apt truism here is that you can only work with the tools you've got. Criminals in the modern industrial period were equally committed to the complexities and component parts of their criminal culture as contemporary criminal entrepreneurs; they just didn't wear Ralph Lauren shirts and fake Rolex watches.

The case studies in this book illustrate this change in criminal opportunity and practice when taken as a whole. Tommy (see Chapter 1) was a violent man who was unable to capitalize financially on his abilities because he was situated in a time and space that restricted criminal entrepreneurship. This failure to earn financially was not, however, a failure *per se*. He did not stop being violent because this failed to open up business opportunities. In his time and space it simply was not a particular consideration. Violence held other benefits; violence was (and is) culturally valued and thus status was bestowed upon those who were skilled in its intricacies. This was a form of success that Tommy valued and, as such, was reward in itself.

Michael and Artie are young enough to have been freed from the criminal and opportunity restrictions imposed by the industrial modern era in the North East of England. Business has become the order of the day, along with other considerations. In Michael's case, violence provided the catapult to launch him into a highly competitive criminal marketplace, an environment in which he seems to have thrived. Violence still holds other seductions for Michael but it also provides a significant business advantage, which can be brought to bear in a highly problematic environment. Violence, in these places, and among these men, is a highly valued commodity that must be recognized, nurtured and defended at all costs; 'maintenance of a credible threat of violence' (Daly and Wilson 1988: 128) is essential and its power reaches beyond purely business concerns. Violence here 'runs like a bright thread through the fabric of life' (Sykes 1958: 102) and its centrality to Michael's character and identity is certainly not a new cultural development. The use of violence and the hidden power of a violent reputation travel with Michael everywhere. These are tools that can be drawn on to his benefit in a vast number of social interactions, both in business and leisure. Yet violence also dwells in his deeper recesses and can burst forth unexpectedly, even when there is seemingly no benefit to accrue. This propensity is staggering to behold and adds a layer of unpredictability to the myth, forcing others to recognize the complex social strictures of doing business with, or merely encountering, the man.

Artie, while not being particularly skilled in violence, still found himself in a position in which he could use a knowledge and skill of violence to benefit financially from the market. He has no industrial trade; he can't come around and sort out your dodgy boiler or washing machine, nor can he tell you enthralling tales of the funny and unusual characters with which he shared his working life, in a shipyard or down a coalmine. However he can sort you out with a nice chunk of dope or a rap of dynamite Charlie (cocaine), a skill highly valued by his peers. Artie's complex and highly stressful existence is centred around his interpretations of criminal business in the region, and his understandings of this environment have as much to do with global concerns as they have with his masculine cultural inheritance.

Jimmy and Mark serve here to depict the continued transformations of masculinity and criminal opportunity. Even as they find themselves in a legitimate occupation in which they can capitalise upon violent capabilities and repute, they also benefit from the criminal opportunities which that occupation provides. I have also used the studies of Jimmy and Mark to explore the development of bouncing and door supervision as a career, and the numerous issues associated with changing masculine identities and ideologies. Topics such as bodybuilding and its meanings and the development of a diverse night-time economy have also been discussed with the aim of shedding further light on economic, social and cultural changes and the advent of post-modernity in the North East of England.

To visit the places I have visited during the course of this piece of research is to enter an environment that immediately reinforces understandings of cultural and economic change in the North East of England. The differences between the industrial North East and the area today is apparent and there is no better place to observe these changes than in the gyms, bars, nightclubs and drugs dens of the region. Here 'new men' exist: not the kind who would do the ironing and are not afraid to cry, but neither are they the men who inhabited the region in the not-too-distant past.

In Sunderland much of the old industrial scenery on the Wear has disappeared. The shipyards, for the most part, have been transformed into other commercial ventures, and the riverside is now a place to walk your dog or go for a life-affirming jog through newly planted parkland. If these scenes still existed they would have cast an imposing shadow on the city's burgeoning night-time economy where Baudrillard and his peers would have a field day examining stages of simulacra, pontificating on the sign value of the bouncers' muscles, bottled beers and the designer and post-designer (fake) shirts, before commenting on a peculiarly working-class form of hedonistic consumption.

The Global, Local and Glocal

Local criminal organisation was always deeply entrenched in the cultures of the urban working-class, and de-industrialization and the consequent fragmentation of traditional communities has resulted in their transformation into disordered mutations of traditional proletarian culture.

(Hobbs 1998: 408)

As I have repeatedly stressed, the destructuring of traditional working-class culture and community has resulted in new means of cultural expression based on new global influences and local and historical interpretations which are still within reach. As Wilk (1995: 130) has pointed out, 'the same processes that destroyed autonomy are now creating new kinds of locality and identity'. This dialectical relationship between the local and the global has been stressed by numerous writers (see Giddens 1990, 1992; Robertson 1992; Friedman 1994). What we are seeing is local and global influences merging and mutating into different forms of cultural expression, with the result that the point of origin of all these influences becomes lost, meaningless, in a process of reconstitution and simulation.

Contemporary working-class culture in the North East is largely a varied mix of local, global and personal influences as differential association and media messages penetrate and mould young minds, and the industrial economy becomes a fading memory, a 'nostalgic paradigm' (Robertson 1995) of culturally informed action.

While this culture appears to be set adrift on the choppy seas of global culture, caught in an environment of continuous flux, it has not completely cut its ties to locality and history. Local history and culture, and aspects of these, serve as reference points and offer viable means of interpreting global influences. Cultures and localities do not blindly accept colonizing global culture (see Jalan 1997; Gurnah 1997; Tao and Wai-Nang 1997); interpretations and modifications are made. Locality and local culture offer means of deciphering messages and clarifying and reconstituting meaning and understanding.

As Hobbs (1998: 409) points out 'the new rhythms of consumption and circulation . . . determine social incorporation, and are a direct consequence of the emergence of the marketplace as a primary societal dynamic', yet even the global marketplace is imbued with local flavours (see, for example, Tao and Wai-Nang 1997). Professional and organized crime in the North East still possesses peculiarly North-Eastern facets even as it adopts global entrepreneurial and financial imperatives.

Sunderland, still considered a mixture of rural backwater and urban slum by many, now has a serious crime community (Block 1991a; 1991b) and very *professional* professional criminals. Tales of large-scale drug importation within the city have begun to emerge, while organized gangs, prison breaks, protection rackets and money laundering are now incorporated into the city's and the region's criminal culture and milieu. These professional criminals are working without a locally and historically informed template for professional criminal action and identity but are acquiring a semblance of order through the adoption and transformation of national and global cultural and criminal inputs, rearticulating them across time space (Giddens 1991: 17). Parallel to and incorporated into this process is the necessity to mould and work with those elements of historically informed local criminal structures that are still available in their original and simulated form. The resulting synthesis is in sharp contrast to the masculine criminal culture and practice that achieved dominance during the industrial modern age.

The idea that Sunderland has produced criminals capable now of masterminding (and that is an appropriate term) the importation of large quantities of illegal drugs is a massive change in itself. Furthermore, the fact that so much money has been made that it needs to be laundered ideally portrays the gulf between the criminal practices of then and now. Sunderland, for so long indicative of the industrial modern period and its associated structures, has changed to such an extent that criminals now have access to global markets, serious criminal action, established criminal cultures and vast financial profits.

Contemporary North Eastern criminals are not trapped in space. They traverse the globe and make contact with like-minded individuals, broadening their access to markets and influence, creating new business opportunities and tailoring the old. Previously, in the era of Tommy (see Chapter 1), 'hard' men rarely knew their contemporaries in nearby cities, towns and villages, and were not certain to know other noted 'hard' men outside of their own neighbourhood. Today, North-Eastern criminals can travel to Spain, arrange relevant meetings and buy and import tons of cannabis. They can go to Holland and buy Ecstasy and amphetamines. They can even get the Colombian cartels to sort them out with a load of cocaine.

If we add to this picture other aspects of an emerging entrepreneurial criminal ethic, such as money laundering, contract killings and a merging of legitimate and illegitimate business, the division between the industrial modern and the post-modern eras can be seen being enacted in working-class North-Eastern criminal practice. Crime and criminals have adapted to their changing cultural environment and have absorbed the influence of the global, while not entirely casting off the historical and local. Media portrayals of professional and organized crime, of criminal success, of gangsters and idealized forms of masculinity, now merge with the global market and its corresponding entrepreneurial thrust to remodel local criminality in conjunction with local economic and cultural upheavals. Today the North East has its own gangsters. Not men of fighting repute with significant cultural influence (although this role continues, with modifications), but professional, goal-orientated criminals with national and global links. Huge amounts of money are being made, and the men who are making it are not simply an aberration – a completely new form of masculine and criminal expression; they are the present incarnation of changing working-class masculine deviancy in the North East (albeit with varying business competence). The contemporary working-class criminal entrepreneur represents a synthesis of historical and local cultural influences, global inputs and the post-modern world, and, as such, is a complex hybrid of the old and the new.

As I have pointed out, successful criminal role models now exist in the North East, but they are not restricted to the local pub and neighbourhood. The media, in their quest to present crime as a form of public drama, offers a multitude of deviant achievement goals for the budding gangster, and in the course of this research these influences were made plain. For example, I witnessed young males strive to be Robert De Niro in *Goodfellas*, where the gesticulation, the language and the use of violence in a business context were highly seductive, and were visibly translated into locally informed action. In one case a group of respondents attempted to steal a delivery truck after watching Joe Pesci and Ray Liotta perform the same act in *Goodfellas*. Even in the cloudiest moments of the research, reality seemed open for continual manipulation and transformation as the global and the local merged before my eyes.

Gangsterdom and the real gangsters in their own environment clearly held the attention of many of the respondents I spent time with over the course of this research. To be a gangster, a 'movie star with muscles' (Pileggi 1987), represents an idealized form of masculinity to elements of the male working-class, with the money, the women, the esteem and respect, the fear, the lack of mundanity and regimentation, the battle with convention, all comparing favourably with the blunt reality of life in the working-class northern city. Professional crime *is* highly seductive, and working-class men in the North East can now strive towards these modified success goals and embrace these powerful status concerns.

Simulation and Glocality

Artie is what you'd call a music lover. Music accompanies him wherever he goes, usually at a very high volume, and it is one of the few things he is truly passionate about. Today he is in a flashy racing green BMW as he cruises the northern city with no particular destination in mind. It's not his car, but that doesn't matter. His musical selections have been carefully chosen, labelled and stacked in a highly personal system incorporating style, mood and perceived quality.

His personal appearance clashes slightly with his sophisticated transport. He appears younger than his years and wears a designer sweat top and jeans over expensive trainers. He seems happy and shouts across the car to make himself heard.

Artie is listening to rap music, hip hop, and has an encyclopaedic knowledge of its generating milieu and superstars. He has formed his own opinions about their music, but to many of his peers and contemporaries he might as well be talking another language. Few in Artie's circle share his current musical interests or can understand his engrossment in this foreign and other-worldly musical genre.

To friends of Artie's who find themselves subject to his musical tastes, the rhymes and raps, when they can be deciphered, mean little, and are tales from another world, another time. They know the rap music that makes it into the charts but this is the music disdained by Artie as he seeks *real* rap music: hip hop from the underground – the constantly metamorphosing and diversifying culture and state-of-the-art. Artie listens closely to the rhymes and understands what is said. He knows all the seemingly incomprehensible jargon and vague lexicon of the music. Artie is not just listening to the bass of the music as we drive, nodding his head in time with the music: he knows the words and raps along with the music in an impressive display of remembrance.

Artie knows all the words, and they and the music clearly mean something to him, yet he is not black and has never been to America never mind South Central LA, Harlem or the Bronx. He has never participated in many of the activities recounted in the music, and knows little of the black experience in America and the social and cultural change that created his favoured musical tastes. But Artie is not playing and he is not feigning interest to appear cosmopolitan. Nor is he pretending to come from the culture from which rap music developed or its present generating and sustaining climate. His clothes and attitude are only partially linked to hip-hop culture, and links between his culture and that portrayed in rap music are tentative and vague to say the least. Yet, 'the music industry is . . . at the forefront of a move towards global standardisation of cultural products' (Malm and Willis 1993: 7) and the music and the culture it carries with it are as available to Artie as they are to others.

Perhaps Artie is not rap music's imagined audience, but his access and subscription to it allows him in. He is, after all, a paying customer. As he raps along with *Method Man* in his heavy Northern accent, it appears he is transforming the culture and context of his lived environment and that of a colonizing musical genre into an entity in which the two seemingly mutually exclusive influences interweave and mesh together. The music informs his knowledge of the global and the local as he becomes aware of other cultural outputs and facilitates their transposition onto and into his locality, offering new means of action and expression and a complex interpretation of outcomes and meanings.

People look into the car, drawn by the dull thud of the bass-heavy rap music. Peter, Artie's companion today, tells him to 'turn that shit off' and put on some house music. Peter takes exception to the stares of pedestrians, responding with a menacing look and a clenched fist; everyone attempts to ignore the spectacle invading this quiet suburban street. Peter isn't getting the music, but Artie is bound up in it and isn't turning it off. He closes his eyes and nods his head.

Artie's new-found love of rap music has added to his complex lexicon of expression. A joint has become a 'blunt' or 'chronic', women or 'lasses' have become 'bitches' and 'whores' and so forth. Rap music and its rivalries, gang allegiances and affiliations, big earners and sellouts are known to Artie for he reads everything he can about the scene. Artie knows about these things and has no compunction about informing others, letting them work out linguistic mutations and developments as he goes. Expressions from rap music are already finding their way into everyday use and are lost amid local phrases, dialect and other global influences, becoming part of what is used and passed on to the next generation who, in turn, will also add to and reject elements of cultural language structures.

Artie's love of rap music is only one small example of the merging of the global and the local to produce the contemporary cultural environment in the North East. It is only recounted here because the afternoon in which I made the above notes and observations was memorable for other reasons. Vast numbers of equally convincing anecdotes and examples can be found among my research notes on the culture I observed. Tiny fragments and huge chunks of influence are up for grabs in a maelstrom of continual cultural transformation, and seemingly everything is affected. For example, for some, the factory overalls of well-paid local industries have become status symbols, a designer label of employment rather than a sign of a lower class status. These factory overalls have become a symbol of gainful employment (occasionally reasonably lucrative), of a secured and disposable income, of masculinity, provision and reflection upon industrial heritage. Go to the pub in your overalls and let the neighbourhood girls see that you are a viable life partner, still in possession of those seemingly lost elements of downwardly mobile working-class masculine imagery, such as providing for one's offspring and working with your hands. And just as your Paul Smith suit spells financial security, a commitment to consumerism and a reflexive relationship with culture, so, in this local milieu, do certain overalls. Providing easy-to-decipher codes they reveal who the wearer is and what is his place in the world, and offer clues to consciousness, values and outlook in a post-modern culture where sign value has often come to replace use value as a means of cognitive understanding.

The Future

> It is this order of interweaving human impulses and strivings, this social order, which determines the course of historical change; it underlies the civilising process.
>
> (Elias 1982: 230)

Predictions as to what the future holds are rarely positive yet I make no attempt to place any predictions in either a negative or positive light. As I am unsure about much that I predict, I shall leave it up to the reader to form his or her own opinions. Importantly, as the central thrust of the book has been to describe a transforming culture destructuring and recomposing itself in the light of old and new, local and global influences, the only real predictable certainty is that change will continue. Aside from that we can only make informed guesses.

As I have stressed, the arrival of entrepreneurial crime in the North East has not replaced all forms of non-entrepreneurial criminal activity, and not all entrepreneurial criminal activity is successful. For every Michael or Artie there are masses of young men who have engaged the market and failed, or have not become fully committed to its intricacies or have remained in purely conflict-orientated pursuits.

Petty crime and non-profit-making crime will not disperse with the arrival of a criminal entrepreneurial ethic. Car crime, burglary, shoplifting, vandalism, violence and other assorted crimes are, in themselves, all potential testing grounds for formative and fragile masculinities. Some of those engaged in these activities in their youth might become committed to criminal life and leave behind the trivialities of youth to seek financial reward. Others may drift out of crime as these activities lose their attraction, the pain of capture starts to outweigh potential rewards, or as non-criminal structures assume greater significance in their lives.

Obviously, this is not an exhaustive structural model of how and why petty criminals may 'move up' to professional crime, drop out of crime altogether, or negotiate a middle route, but that is not the point here. What should be taken from this is that the opportunity to enter professional crime now exists. Many may not find their way into these activities for a plethora of highly personal reasons, but the crime-ridden estates of the North East are still the breeding grounds for delinquency and the eventuality of serious professional crime. Crime is one of the few traditional trades that still offers an apprenticeship in the post-industrial North East.

Professional crime itself, I believe, will continue to embed itself in North Eastern working-class masculine culture. However, I am not predicting the rise of hierarchical organised crime structures, because, as I have pointed out, locality and history still have a considerable input into criminal masculinities no matter how often working-class males watch *The Godfather*. Instead, I believe we will see an amplification of the competition between criminal and law enforcement strategies and technologies (Hobbs 1995) and the continued establishment of national and global links with other serious crime groups, which will increasingly be centred on the provision of drugs and knock-on business opportunities (Hobbs 1995). Professional and organized crime in the North East will move out of the shadows of an industrial heritage and become recognized by the media and law enforcement alike as a subject for increased attention.

With regard to wider concerns, despite the fact I have repeatedly used the term 'working-class' as a means of generalization, referring to them now as a mass social class is clearly impractical. Subdivisions are considerable, and in the future I believe the most important differentiation will be between the working and the non-working. Aside from the working-class, the polarization of high-income, technical and skilled employment and low-wage casual labour will continue and become increasingly apparent. Excursions into the expanding black and grey economies will reinforce these divisions as legitimate employment opportunities rapidly decrease and the nine-to-five working day loses its relevance for large sections of the lower classes. Traditional employment patterns have already undergone massive destructuring and increasingly people will be forced to forage for incomes in a wide range of legal and illegal environments.

I believe that, as unemployment and poverty become increasingly intergenerational and locked into specific locales, the amplification of non-conformative social action is bound to continue as the cultural capital of the poor is passed on to the next generation, and that they will modify it slightly in the light of continual cultural change. Crime is partially a symptom of this process and I believe the numbers of the underclass will grow in conjunction with its level of dissociation from conventional, employed society. In this scenario those who are employed and have secured consumer-viable incomes are likely to flee these dangerous locations and seek a refuge from the demonized inner and outer city.

Hitting People

Violence will never go out of fashion or lose its perceived uses, or its aesthetic and seductive qualities. Violence may now be used as marketable asset, but this development has not replaced other violence-related considerations. Much of this book has focused on changing cultural dynamics and characteristics, yet violence has been central to lower class existence since the dawn of time. All of those discussed in detail in this book live in a violent world, where violence is always on the agenda, for a multitude of reasons, and yet violence is not the affliction of their environment. Most of them like it. They like the way it looks, sounds and ends; they appreciate quality, ferocity, cunning and cool conduct. Violence is an aspect of their lives that is comforting in its familiarity, a behavioural characteristic that everyone in this environment understands and respects, even if their involvement in it is minimal and they want to keep it that way.

Despite all this, I have no wish to portray the North East in a negative light. It is not all violence and crime, and not everyone in this region is working-class or subject to the cultural understandings I have taken pains to stress. Moreover, during the industrial modern age the North East was not filled with sturdy, morally minded men incapable of evil thoughts and deeds. History and human society does not work like that. Nor is every criminal on the contemporary scene a budding entrepreneur. In essence, I hope I have portrayed huge cultural, social and economic change, and their effects in more complex terms than that. I have attempted to provide a means of accessing the cultural world I have described, albeit briefly, and to offer ways of understanding how those discussed set out to negotiate and formulate their lived environment. Descriptions and analysis of society and culture are always, necessarily, complex, but they are not for those who live in these spaces. Those discussed here and those with whom I have spent time during the course of this research do not see their cultural environment in the same light or use the same terms as the academic community. They do not recognize or care about de-industrialization, post-modernity or notions of glocality and transforming cultures and social class. They negotiate the day and are concerned with the trivialities that clog up the majority of human lives. Structure and macro influences may define or frame the immediacy of their social action and individual agency, but, as this is primarily a work of ethnography, I have aimed to portray the lives of those studied on their terms, employing those theoretical observations that I believe fit best. I hope I have done justice to those who gave up their time to talk to me and who allowed me into their lives.

Bibliography

Adler, P. (1985), *Wheeling and Dealing: An Ethnography of an Upper-Level Drug Dealing and Smuggling Community*, New York: Columbia University Press.

Adler, P. and Adler, P. (1980), 'The irony of secrecy in the drug world', *Urban Life and Culture,* Vol. 8.

Akers, R. L. (1977), *Deviant Behaviour: A Social Learning Approach,* 2nd edn, Belmont, CA: Wadsworth.

Akerstrom, M. (1985), *Crooks and Squares: Lifestyles of thieves and addicts in comparison to conventional people,* New Brunswick: Transaction.

Albrow, M. (1992), 'Globalization' in T. B. Bottomore, and W. Outhwaite (ed.) *The Blackwell Dictionary of Twentieth Century Thought,* Oxford: Basil Blackwell.

Allsop, K. (1961), *The Bootleggers: The Story of Chicago's Prohibition Era,* London: Hutchinson.

Anderson, E. (1991), 'Neighborhood effects on teenage pregnancy' in C. Jencks and P. E. Peterson, (eds) *The Urban Underclass,* Washington DC: The Bookings Institution.

Anderson, M. (1980), *Approaches to the History of the Western Family 1500–1914,* London: Macmillan.

Appadurai, A. (1990), 'Disjunction and difference in the global cultural economy' in M. Featherstone (ed.) (1990) *Global Culture: Nationalism, globalization and modernity,* London: Sage.

Armstrong, G. (1998), *Football Hooligans: Knowing the score*, Oxford: Berg.

Baudrillard, J. (1975), *The Mirror of Production*, St Louis: Telos Press.

Baudrillard, J. (1975), *Simulacra and Simulation*, St Louis: Telos Press.

Baudrillard, J. (1981), *For a Critique of the Political Economy of the Sign,* St Louis: Telos Press.

Baudrillard, J. (1988), *Selected Writings,* Oxford: Polity Press

Bauman, Z. (1989), *Legislators and Interpreters*, Cambridge: Polity Press.

Bauman, Z. (1992), *Intimations of Postmodernity*, London: Routledge.

Bean, J. P. (1995), *Verbals: The Book of Criminal Quotations*, London: Headline.

Becker, H. and Carper, J. (1956), 'The development of identification with an occupation', *American Journal of Sociology* 6: 289–98.

Becker, H. (1964), 'Personal changes in adult life' in *Sociometry* Vol. 27 No.1.

Becker, H. S. (1963), *Outsiders*, New York: Free Press.

Belcham, J. (1990), *Industrialization and the Working Class: The English experience 1750–1900*, Aldershot: Scolar.

Bell, D. (1961), *The End of Ideology,* London: Free Press.

Benson, J. (ed.) (1985), *The Working Class in England 1875–1914*, London: Croom Helm.

Benson, J. (1989), *The Working Class in Britain, 1850–1914*, London: Croom Helm.

Berman, M. (1983), *All That is Solid Melts into Air,* London: Verso.

Blair, D. J. (1988), 'Sunderland 1945–1987' in M. Milburn and S. Miller (eds) *Sunderland: River, Town and People. A History from the 1780s to the Present day,* Sunderland: Thomas Reed.

Blauner, R. (1964), *Alienation and Freedom*, Chicago: University of Chicago Press.

Block, A. (1991a), *Masters of Paradise,* New Brunswick: Transaction.

Block, A (1991b), *The Business of Crime,* Boulder CO: Westview Press.

Blumer (1969), *Symbolic Interactionism,* Englewood Cliffs NJ: Prentice-Hall.

Bocock, R. (1993), *Consumption,* London: Routledge.

Bottomore, T. B. and Outhwaite, W. (1992), *The Blackwell Dictionary of Twentieth Century Thought,* Oxford: Basil Blackwell.

Bottoms, A. E. (1994), 'Environmental criminology', in M. Maguire, R. Morgan and R. Reiner, *Oxford Handbook of Criminology,* Oxford: Clarendon Press.

Bourdieu, P. (1979), *Algeria 1960*, Cambridge: Cambridge University Press.

Bourdieu, P. and Passeron, J. (1977), *Reproduction in Education, Society and Culture,* London: Sage.

Bourke, J. (1994), *Working Class Cultures in Britain 1890–1960: Gender, class and ethnicity*, London: Routledge.

Bowling, H. G. (1958), *The Land of the Three Rivers: The Tyne, the Wear and the Tees*, London: Macmillan.

Brannon, R. (1976), 'The male sex role – and what it's done for us lately' in R. Brannon and D. David (eds) *The Forty Nine Percent Majority: The male sex role,* Reading MA: Addison-Wesley.

Brannon, R. and David, D. (1976) (eds), *The Forty Nine Percent Majority: The male sex role,* Reading MA: Addison-Wesley.

Brittan, A. (1989), *Masculinity and Power,* Oxford: Basil Blackwell.

Brod, H. (1987) (ed.), *The Making of Masculinity,* Boston MA: Allen & Unwin.

Bryman, A. (1988), *Quality and Quantity in Social Research,* London: Routledge.

Byrne, D. (1989), *Beyond the Inner City*, Milton Keynes: Open University Press.

Byrne, D. (1993), 'Deindustrialisation, Planning and Class Structures: A Study in the Effects of Social Policy on Social Stuctures'. PhD thesis, University of Durham, Department of Sociology and Social Policy.

Byrne, D. and Parsons, D. (1983), 'The state and the reserve army: the management of class relations in space' in J. Anderson, S. Duncan and R. Hudson (eds) *Redundant Spaces in Cities and Regions*, London: Academic Press.

Burnett, J., Vincent, D. and Mayall, D. (eds) (1984), *The Autobiography of the Working Class: An annotated, critical bibliography*, Brighton: Harvester.

Callaghan, G. (1996), 'Women's experiences of Class and Gender in a Deindustrial-ised City'. Unpublished paper, University of Durham, Department of Sociology and Social Policy.

Callinicos, A. (1990), 'Reactionary postmodernism?' in R. Boyne and Rattansi, A. (eds) *Postmodernism and Society*, Basingstoke: Macmillan.

Callinicos, A. and Harman, C. (1987), *The Changing Working Class: Essays on class structure today,* London: Bookmarks.

Campbell, B. (1993), *Goliath: Britain's Dangerous Places*, London: Methuen.

Campbell, C. (1987), *The Romantic Ethic and the Spirit of Modern Consumerism*, Oxford: Basil Blackwell.

Carey, J. (1972), 'Problems of access and risk in observing drug scenes' in J. Douglas, *Research on Deviance,* New York: Random House.

Cater, F. and Tullett, T. (1988), *The Sharp End,* London: Grafton Books.

Cavan, S. (1966), *Liquor License: An ethnography of bar behaviour*, Chicago: Aldine.

Census Enumerators Returns (1851), cited in T. Corfe 'Prosperity and poverty' in M. Milburn and S. Miller (eds) *Sunderland: River, Town and People. A History from the 1780s to the Present day*, Sunderland: Thomas Reed.

Chappell, D., Grabosky, P. and Strang, H. (eds) (1991), *Australian Violence: Contemporary Perspectives,* Canberra: Australian Institute of Criminology.

Chambliss, W. J. (1987), *On the Take,* Bloomington, Ind.: Indiana University Press.

Chaney, D. (1996), *Lifestyles,* London: Routledge.

Chodorow, N. (1978), *Reproduction of Mothering: Psychoanalysis and the Sociology of Gender*, Berkeley: University of Califonia Press.

Cicourel, A. V. (1964), *Method and Measurement in Sociology,* New York: Free Press.

Clarke, J. F. (1988), 'Shipbuilding 1780–1914' in M. Milburn and S. Miller (eds) *Sunderland: River, Town and People. A History from the 1780s to the Present Day*, Sunderland: Thomas Reed.

Cloward, R. and Ohlin, L. (1960), *Delinquency and Opportunity*, New York: Free Press.

Cockburn, C. (1983), *Brothers: Male dominance and technological change,* London: Pluto Press.

Cohen, P. (1972), Subculture Conflict and Working Class Community Working Papers in Cultural Studies No. 2: 5-52 Birmingham: CCCS, University of Birmingham.

Cohen, S. and Taylor, L. (1976), *Escape Attempts*, Harmondsworth: Penguin.

Collison, M. (1996), 'In search of the high life: drugs, crime, masculinities and consumption', *British Journal of Criminology* Vol. 36 No. 3.

Commission on Urban Priority Areas (1984), *Faith in the City*, London: Home Office.

Common, J. (1938), *Seven Shifts,* London: Routledge.

Conlin, J. (1969), *History of Sunderland Borough Police Force*, Pub. Unknown Sunderland: Sunderland Public Library.

Connell, R. W. (1985), 'Masculinity, violence and war' in P. Patton and R. Poole (eds.) *War/Masculinity*, Sydney: Intervention.

Connell, R. W. (1987), *Gender and Power: Society, the person and sexual politics*, Cambridge: Polity Press.

Connell, R. W. (1995), *Masculinities*, Oxford: Blackwell.

Corfe, T. (1973), *Sunderland: A Short History*, Newcastle: Frank Graham.

Corfe, T. (1988), 'Prosperity and Poverty' in M. Milburn and S. Miller (eds) *Sunderland: River, Town and People. A History from the 1780's to the Present day*, Sunderland: Thomas Reed.

Corfe, T and Bowling, H. G. (1974), *History in Sunderland*, Sunderland: Sunderland Public Library.

Corrigan, P. (1979), *Schooling the Smash Street Kids*, London: Macmillan.

Craig, S. (1992) (ed.), *Men, Masculinity and the Media*, London: Sage.

Currie, E. (1997), 'Market, crime and community: towards a mid-range theory of post-industrial violence', *Theoretical Criminology* 1(2): 147–72.

Daly, M. and Wilson, M. (1988), *Homicide*, New York: De Gruyter.

Daunton, M. J. (1983), *House and Home in the Victorian City: Working-Class Housing 1850–1914*, London: Routledge.

Dennis, H., Henriques, F. and Slaughter, C. (1956), *Coal is Our Life: An analysis of a Yorkshire mining community*, London: Eyre & Spottiswoode.

Dennis, N. (1970), *People and Planning: Housing in Sunderland*, London: Faber & Faber.

Denzin, N. (1978), 'Crime and the American liquor industry' in N. Denzin (ed.) *Studies in Symbolic Interactionism*, Greenwich CT: Allen & Unwin.

Dibdin, T. F. (1838), *A Bibliographical, Antiquarian and Picturesque Tour in the Northern Counties of England and in Scotland*, [pub. unknown].

Ditton, J. (1977), *Part-Time Crime: An Ethnography of Fiddling and Pilferage*, London: Macmillan.

Donaldson, M. (1991), *Time of Our Lives: Labour and love in the working class*, Sydney: Allen & Unwin.

D'Orban, P. (1991), 'The crimes connection: alcohol' in Glass, I. (ed.) *The International Handbook of Addiction Behaviour*, London: Routledge.

Dorn, N., Murji, K. and South, N. (1992), *Traffickers*, London: Routledge.

Dougan, D. (1968), *History of North Eastern Shipbuilding*, London: Allen & Unwin.

Douglas, J. D. (1972) (ed.), *Research on Deviance* New York: Random House.

Douglas, J. D. (1976), *Investigative Social Research*, Beverley Hills CA: Sage.

Downes, D. (1966), *The Delinquent Solution*, London: Routledge & Kegan Paul.

Downes, D. and Rock, P. (1988), *Understanding Deviance*, Oxford: Oxford University Press.

Dubbert, J. L. (1979), *A Man's Place: Masculinity in Transition*, Englewood Cliffs NJ: Prentice-Hall.

Dunford, M. and Kaftalas, G. (1988) (eds), *Cities and Regions in the New Europe: The Global – Local Interplay and Spatial Development Strategies,* London: Belhaven.

Epstein, S. (1991), 'Sexuality and identity: the contribution of object relations theory to a constructionist Sociology', *Theory and Society* 20: 825–73.

Evans, C. (1986), 'Alcohol and violence: problems relating to methodology, statistics and causation' in P. Brain (ed.) *Alcohol and Aggression,* London: Croom Helm.

Evered, R. and Louis, M. R. (1981), 'Alternative perspectives in the organisational sciences: "inquiry from the inside" and "inquiry from the outside"', *Academy of Management Review,* 6(3): 385–95.

Fagan, J. (1990), 'Intoxication and aggression' in M. Tonry and J. Wilson (eds) *Drugs and Crime,* Chicago IL: University of Chicago Press.

Farberman, H. (1975), 'A criminogenic market structure: the automobile industry', *The Sociological Quarterly* 16:187–98.

Featherstone, M. (ed.) (1990), *Global Culture: Nationalism, globalization and modernity,* London: Sage.

Featherstone. M et al (1995), *Global Modernities,* London: Sage.

Field, S. (1990), *Trends in Crime and their Interpretation,* London: HMSO.

Fleisher, M. S. (1993), 'Burnout in violent criminal careers' paper presented at 1993 American Society of Criminology, Pheonix, Arizona, 3.

Ford, A. (1985), *Men,* London: Weidenfeld & Nicolson.

Foster, J. (1990), *Villains,* London: Routledge.

Foucault, M. (1983), *This is not a Pipe,* Berkeley, CA: University of California Press.

Foucault, M. (1986), 'Nietzsche, geneology, history' in P. Rainbow (ed.) *The Foucault Reader,* New York: Random House.

Fraser, F. in Morton, J. (1994), *Mad Frank,* London: Little Brown.

Freud, P. E. S. (1988), 'Bringing society into the body: understanding socialised human nature', *Theory and Society* 17(6): 839–64.

Friedman, A. (1977), *Industry and Labour: Class struggle at work and monopoly capitalism,* London: Macmillan.

Friedman, J. (1990), 'Being in the World: Globalization and localization' in Featherstone (ed.) (1990) *Global Culture: Nationalism, globalization and modernity,* London: Sage.

Friedman, J. (1994), *Cultural Identity and Global Process*, London: Sage.

Friedrichs, P. (1977), *Agrarian Revolts in a Mexican Village,* Chicago IL: University of Chicago Press.

Fromm, E. (1964), 'The psychological aspects of the guaranteed income' in Theobald, R. (ed.) *The Guaranteed Income: Next Step in Economic Evolution?*, New York: Doubleday.

Gans, H. J. (1967), *The Levittowners,* London: Allen Lane.

Garrahan, P. (1986), 'Nissan in the North East of England' in *Capital and Class* 27: 5–13

Garrahan, P. and Stewart, N. (1992), *The Nissan Enigma,* London: Mansell.

Giddens, A. (1976), *New Rules of Sociological Method,* London: Hutchinson.

Giddens, A. (1979), *Central Problems in Social Theory,* London: Macmillan.

Giddens, A. (1990), *The Consequences of Modernity,* Stanford: Stanford University Press.

Giddens, A. (1991), *Modernity and Self-Identity: Self and Society in the Late Modern Age,* Cambridge: Polity Press.

Gill, O. (1977), *Luke Street: Housing Policy, Conflict and the Creation of the Delinquent Area,* London: Macmillan Press.

Glassner, B. (1989), 'Men and muscles' in M. S. Kimmel and M. A. Messner (eds) *Men's Lives,* New York: Macmillan, pp. 310–20.

Goffman, E. (1963), *Behaviour in Public Places,* New York: Free Press.

Goffman, E. (1967), *Interaction Ritual,* New York: Free Press.

Goffman, E. (1969), *The Presentation of Self in Everyday Life,* Harmondsworth: Penguin.

Goffman, E. (1971), *Relations in Public: Microstudies of Public Order,* London: Allen Lane.

Goldthorpe, J. H., Lockwood, D., Bechofer, F. and Platt, J. (1968), *The Affluent Worker: Industrial Attitudes and Behaviour* Cambridge: Cambridge University Press.

Gorman, M. and Dunnett, H. (1950), *Inside the Pub,* London: Architectural Press.

Granville, A. B (1841), *The Spas of England and Principal Sea-Bathing Places,* [Pub unknown]: Sunderland City Libraries.

Guba, E. G. and Lincoln, Y. S (1982), 'Epistemological and methodological bases of natualistic inquiry' in *Educational, Communication and Technology Journal* 30(4): 233–52.

Gurnah, A. (1997), 'Elvis in Zanzibar' in A. Scott (ed.) *The Limits of Globalization,* London: Routledge.

Gutman, M. C. (1996), *The Meaning of Macho: Being a Man in Mexico City,* London: University of Califonia Press.

Hall, S., Winlow, S., Hobbs, D., and Lister, S. (forthcoming) *Daubing the Drudges of Fury: The poverty of the hegemonic masculinity thesis.*

Hall, S. and Jacques, M. (1990) (eds), *New Times: The Changing Face of Politics in the 1990s,* London: Lawrence & Wishart.

Hannerz, U. (1990), 'Cosmopolitans and locals in world culture' in M. Featherstone (ed.) (1990) *Global Culture: Nationalism, globalization and modernity,* London: Sage.

Harrison, T. (ed.) *Mass Observation: The Pub and the People: A Worktown Study,* London: Gollancz.

Harvey, D. (1989), *The Condition of Postmodernity,* Oxford: Basil Blackwell.

Henry, S. (1978), *The Hidden Economy: The Context and Control of Borderline Crime,* Oxford: Martin Robertson.

Henry, S., and Mars, G. (1978), 'Crime at work' in *Sociology*, 12 February.

Henwood, F. and Wyatt, S. (1986), 'Women's work, technological change and shifts in the employment structure' in R. Martin and B. Rowthorn (eds) *The Geography of De-industrialisation,* London: Macmillan.

Hitchin, G. (1962), *Pit Yacker,* London: Routledge.

HMSO (1970), *Ryhope: A Pit Closes; a study in re-deployment* Department of Employment and Productivity.

Hobbs, D. (1988), *Doing the Business,* Oxford: University of Oxford Press.

Hobbs, D. and Robins, D. (1991), 'The boy done good', *Sociological Review* 39 (3).

Hobbs, D. (1994), 'Professional and organised crime in Britain' in Maguire, M., Morgan, R. and Reiner, R. *The Oxford Handbook of Criminology,* Oxford: Clarendon Press.

Hobbs, D. (1994), 'Mannish boys' in T. Newburn and E. Stanko *Just Boys Doing Business?* London: Routledge.

Hobbs, D. (1995), *Bad Business,* Oxford: University of Oxford Press.

Hobbs, D. (1998), 'Going down the glocal: the local context of organised crime', *The Howard Journal,* 37 (4).

Hodson, P. (1984), *Men: An Investigation into the Emotional Male,* London: BBC/ Ariel Books.

Hopkins, C. H. G. (1954), *Pallion 1874–1954: Church and People in a Shipyard Parish,* Sunderland: Wearside Printing Co.

Horowitz, R. (1990), 'Sociological perspectives on gangs: conflicting definitions and concepts' in C. R. Huff (ed.) *Gangs in America,* London: Sage.

Horne, R. and Hall, S. (1995), 'Anelpis: a preliminary expedition into a world without hope or potential', *Parallax* 1, pp. 81–92.

Hudson, R. (1986), 'Producing an industrial wasteland: capital, labour and the state in the North East of England' in R. Martin and B. Rowthorn, *The Geography of De-industrialization,* London: Macmillan.

Huyssen, A. (1990), 'Mapping the postmodern' in L. Nicholson (ed.) *Feminism/ Postmodernism,* New York: Routledge.

Hyman, R. (1984), *Strikes,* Aylesbury: Fontana.

Ingham, M. (1984), *Men: The Male Myth Exposed,* London: Century.

Jackson, B. (1968), *Working Class Cultures in Britain 1890–1960: Gender, Class and Ethnicity,* London: Routledge & Kegan Paul.

Jalan, R. (1997), 'An Asian orientalism?' in A. Scott (ed.) *The Limits of Globalization,* London: Routledge.

Jencks, C. and Peterson, P. E. (1991), *The Urban Underclass,* Washington DC: The Bookings Institution.

Jenkins, R. (1983), *Lads, Citizens and Ordinary Kids: working class youth life-styles in Belfast,* London: Routledge & Kegan Paul.

Joyce, P. (1982), *Work, Society and Politics: The culture of the factory in late Victorian England,* London: Sage.

Katz, J. (1988), *Seductions of Crime,* New York: Basic Books.

Kelland, G. (1987), *Crime in London,* London: Grafton Books.

Kimmel, M. S (1987a), 'Rethinking masculinity' in M. S. Kimmel (ed.) *Changing Men: new directions in research on men and masculinity,* London: Sage.

Kimmel, M. S (1987b) (ed.), *Changing Men: New directions in research on men and masculinity,* London: Sage.

Kimmel, M. S. (1987), 'The contemporary "crisis" in masculinity in historical perspectives' in H. Brod (ed.) *The Making of Masculinities,* Boston MA: Allen & Unwin.

Kimmel, M. (1996), *Manhood in America,* New York: Free Press.

King, R. (ed.) (1983), *Capital and Politics,* London: Routledge & Kegan Paul.

Kirkpatrick, S. W. and Saunders, D. M. (1978), 'Body image stereotypes: a developmental comparison', *Journal of Genetic Psychology* 132: 87–95.

Klein, A. M. (1986), 'Pumping irony: crisis and contradiction in bodybuilding', *Sociology of Sport Journal* 3(2): 112–33.

Kray, R. and Kray, R. with Dineage, F. (1988), *Our Story,* London: Pan Books.

Landesco, J. (1929), *Organized Crime in Chicago,* Chicago IL: University of Chicago Press.

Lash, S. (1994), 'Reflexivity and its doubles: structure, aesthetics, community' in V. Beck A. Giddens and S. Lash *Reflexive Modernization,* Cambridge: Polity Press.

Lash, S. and Urry, J. (1987), *The End of Organised Capitalism*, Cambridge: Polity Press.

Lewis, J. (1986), 'The working-class wife and mother and state intervention 1870–1918' in J. Lewis (ed.) *Labour and Love: Women's Experience of Home and Family 1850–1940,* Oxford: Blackwell.

Liebow, E. (1967), *Tally's Corner,* Boston MA: Little, Brown.

Lipman-Blumen, J. (1984), *Gender Roles and Power,* New Jersey: Prentice-Hall.

McGrew, A. and Lewis, P. (1992) (eds), *Global Politics: Globalization and the Nation-State,* Cambridge: Polity.

Mackinnon, C. A. (1982), 'Feminism, marxism and the state: an agenda for theory' in N. O. Keohane, M. Z. Rosaldo and B. C. Gelpi (eds) *Feminist Theory: A critique of ideology*, Brighton: Harvester.

Mallier, A. T. and Rosser, M. J. (1987), *Women and the Economy: A comparative study of Britain and the USA,* London: Macmillan.

Malm, K. and Willis, R. (1993), *Music Policy and Music Activity,* Manchester: Manchester University Press.

Mann, K. (1992), *The Making of an English Underclass,* Milton Keynes: Open University Press.

Manning, P. K. (1977), *Police Work: The social organisation of policing,* Cambridge: MIT Press.

Markin, R. J. Jr. (1974), *Consumer Behaviour: A cognitive orientation,* New York: Macmillan.

Martin, R. and Rowthorn, B. (1986) (eds), *The Geography of De-industrialisation,* London: Macmillan.

Mars, G. (1982), *Cheats at Work,* London: Unwin.

Marshall, M. (1987), *Long Waves of Regional Development,* London: Macmillan.

Marwick, A. (1979), *War and Social Change in the Twentieth Century,* London: Macmillan.

Marx, K. (1972), *Capital, Vol. I,* Harmondsworth: Penguin.

Massey, D. (1980), 'Industrial restructuring as class restructuring' CSE Working Paper no. 604.

Massey, D. and Meegan, R. (1982), *The Anatomy of Job Loss,* London: Methuen.

Matza, D. (1964), *Delinquency and Drift,* New York: John Wiley.

Matza, D. (1969), *Becoming Deviant,* Englewood Cliffs NJ: Prentice-Hall.

McClelland, K. M. (1991), 'Masculinity and the representative artisan in Britain 1850–80' in M. Roper and J. Tosh (eds) *Manful Assertions: Masculinities in Britain since 1800,* London: Routledge.

Mearns, N. W. (1998), *Sentinels of the Wear: The River Wear Watch; A History of Sunderland's River Police,* Sunderland: Mearns.

Messerschmidt, J. W. (1993), *Masculinities and Crime: Critique and Reconceptualisation of Theory,* Lanham, M. D: Rowman & Littlefield.

Milburn, M. and Miller, S. (1988) (eds), *Sunderland: River, Town and People. A History from the 1780's to the Present day,* Sunderland: Thomas Reed.

Miller, D. (1995) (ed), *Worlds Apart: Modernity, Through the Prism of the Local* London: Routledge.

Miller, S. (1989), *The Book of Sunderland,* Sunderland: Barracuda.

Miller, W. B. (1958), 'Lower class culture as a generating milieu of gang delinquency', *Journal of Social Issues,* 14.

Mishkind, M. E., Rodin, J. Silberstein, L. R. and Striegel-Moore, R. H. (1987), 'The embodiment of masculinity: cultural, psychological and behaviour dimensions' in M. S. Kimmel (ed.) *Changing Men: New directions in research on men and masculinity,* London: Sage.

Mitchell, W. C (1919), *History of Sunderland,* Manchester: E. J. Morten.

Morgan, D. (1992), *Discovering Men,* London: Routledge.

Morton, J. (1992), *Gangland,* London: Little, Brown.

Morton, J. (1994), *Gangland 2,* Great Britain: Little, Brown.

Morris, S. (n.d), 'Clubs, Drugs and Doormen' Police Research Group; Crime Detection and Prevention Series, Paper 86.

Murphy, B. (1983), *The World Wired Up,* London: Comedia.

Murphy, R. (1993), *Smash and Grab,* London: Faber and Faber.

Murray, C. (1990), *The Emerging British Underclass,* London: IEA Health and Welfare Unit.

Murray, J. (1864), *Handbook for Travellers in Durham and Northumberland,* Sunderland Public Library.

Muthesius, S. (1982), *The English Terraced House,* New Haven.

Nettler, G. (1978), *Explaining Crime,* London: McGraw-Hill.

Nichols, T. and Beynon, H. (1977), *Living with Capitalism,* London: Routledge & Kegan Paul.

Nicholson, L. (1990) (ed.), *Feminism/Postmodernism,* New York: Routledge.

O'Brien, J. and Kurins, A. (1991), *Boss of Bosses,* London: Simon & Schuster Ltd.

Ogburn, W. F. (1950), *On Culture and Social Change,* Chicago IL: Chicago University Press.

Park, R. (1916), 'The City: Suggestions for the investigation of human behaviour in the urban environment', *American Journal of Sociology,* 20: 577–612.

Park, R. (1952), Human Communities, Glencoe IL: Free Press.

Parker, H. (1974), *View from the Boys,* London: David & Charles.

Parker, H. (1989), *Instead of the Dole,* London: Routledge.

Patrick, J. (1973), *A Glasgow Gang Observed,* London: Eyre-Methuen.

Patterson, G. (1988), 'Victorian working life' in Milburn M. and Miller S. (1988) (eds) *Sunderland: River, Town and People. A History From the 1780s to the Present day,* Sunderland: Thomas Reed.

Peterson (1992), 'The urban underclass and the poverty paradox', *Political Science Quarterly* 106: 639–56.

Pickard, T. (1989), *We Make Ships,* London: Secker & Warburg.

Pileggi, N. (1987), *Wise Guy* London: Corgi.

Piore, M. and Sabel, C. (1984), *The Second Industrial Divide,* New York: Basic Books.

Pitt-Rivers, J. A (1966), 'Honour and social status' in J. Peristiany (ed.) *Honour and Shame: The values of Mediterranean society,* Chicago IL: University of Chicago.

Platt, J. (1994), 'The Chicago School and first hand data', *History of the Human Sciences* 7(1).

Pleck, J. H. (1982), *The Myth of Masculinity,* Cambridge: MIT Press.

Plimsol, S. (1873. Reprinted 1980), *Our Seamen – An Appeal,* Original Pub unknown: Sunderland: Sunderland Public Library

Polk, K. and Ranson, D. (1991), 'Patterns of homocide in Victoria' in D. Chappell, P. Grabosky and H. Strang, *Australian Violence: Contemporary Perspectives,* Canberra: Australian Institute of Criminology.

Polsky, N. (1971), *Hustlers, Beats and Others,* Harmondsworth: Pelican.

Quinney, R. (1975), 'Crime control in capitalist society' in I. Taylor, P. Walton, and J. Young (eds) *Critical Criminology,* London: Routledge.

Raushenbush, W. (1979), *Robert Park: Biography of a sociologist,* Durham: NC.

Report of the Society for Improving the Condition of Merchant Seamen (1867). Cited in Patterson 1988 in M. Milburn and S. Miller (eds) *Sunderland: River, Town and People. A History of Sunderland from the 1780s to the Present day,* Sunderland: Thomas Reed.

Riemer, J. W. (1977), 'Varieties of opportunitistic research', *Urban Life* 5(4): 467–77.

Roberts, I. (1993), *Craft, Class and Control,* Edinburgh: Edinburgh University Press.

Robertson, R. (1992), *Globalization: Social Theory and Global Culture,* London: Sage.

Robertson, R. (1995), 'Globalisation: Time-space and homogeneity–heterogeneity' in M. Featherstone et al. *Global Modernities*, London: Sage.

Robins, D. and Cohen, P. (1978), *Knuckle Sandwich: Growing up in the Working Class City,* Harmondsworth: Penguin.

Robinson, F., Lawrence, M., and Shaw, K. (1993), *More than Bricks and Mortar?: A New Report on Urban Development Corporations,* Durham: University of Durham.

Robson, B. (1969), *Urban Analysis: Sunderland,* Cambridge: Cambridge University Press.

Roper, M. and Tosh, J. (1991), *Manful Assertions: Masculinities in Britain since 1800,* London: Routledge.

Rosaldo, M. Z. (1988), 'Women, culture and society: a theoretical overview' in Rosaldo, M. Z. and Lamphere, L (eds) *Women, Culture and Society,* Stanford: Stanford University.

Rose, A. (1962), *Human Behaviour and Social Processes,* London: Routledge & Kegan Paul.

Rose, G. (1968), *The Working Class,* London: Longmans.

Rowthorn, B. (1986), 'De-industrialisation in Britain' in R. Martin, and B. Rowthorn (eds.) *The Geography of De-industrialisation,* London: Macmillan.

Schoenberg, R. J (1992), *Mr. Capone* London: Robson Books.

Scott, A. (ed) (1997), *The Limits of Globalization,* London: Routledge.

Schutz, A. (1970), *On Phenomenology and Social Relations,* Chicago: University of Chicago Press.

Schutz, A. (1962), *Collected Papers I and II,* The Hague: Nijhoff.

Shaw, C. (1929), *Delinquent Areas*, Chicago IL: University of Chicago Press.

Shaw, C. (1930), *The Jackroller*, Chicago IL: University of Chicago Press.

Shaw, C. R. (1930), *The Jack-Roller: A Delinquent Boy's Own Story,* Chicago IL: University of Chicago Press.

Shaw, C. R. and McKay, H. D. (1972), *Juvenile Delinquency and Urban Areas,* Chicago IL: University of Chicago Press.

Shover, N. and Honaker, D. (1991), 'The socially bounded decision making of persistent property offenders', *Howard Journal* 31 Nov: 276–93.

Simmel, G. (1971), *On Individuality and Social Forms,* Ed. by Levine, D., Chicago IL: University of Chicago Press.

Sinclair, J. (1988), 'Industry to 1914'in Milburn M. and Miller S. (eds) *Sunderland: River, Town and People. A History from the 1780s to the Present Day*, Sunderland: Thomas Reed.

Smith, J. W. and Holden, T. S. (1953), *Where Ships Were Born: Sunderland 1346–1946,* Sunderland: Thomas Reed.

Soja, E. W. (1989), *Postmodern Geographies,* London: Verso.

Spangler, L. C. (1992), 'Buddies and pals: a history of male friendships on prime-time television' in Craig (ed.) *Men, Masculinity, and the Media,* London: Sage.

Spiegel, J. (1969), 'Problems of access to target populations' in Conant, R. and Levin, M. (eds) *Problems in Research on Community Violence,* New York: Basic Books.

Stone, P. Stevens, R. and Morris, L. (1986), *Economic Restructuring and Employment changes since 1971: Employment potential in Sunderland*, report by Sunderland Polytechnic for the EEC/Borough of Sunderland, Sunderland: Sunderland Polytechnic.

Street, J. (1997), 'Across the universe: the limits of global popular culture' in Scott, A. (ed.) *The Limits of Globalization,* London: Routledge.

Strinati, D. (1992), 'The taste of America' in Strinati, D. and Wagg, S. (1992) (eds), *Come on Down? Popular Media Culture in Post-War Britain,* London: Routledge.

Strinati, D. and Wagg, S. (1992) (eds), *Come on Down? Popular Media Culture in Post-War Britain,* London: Routledge.

*Sunderland Echo,*11 October 1984.

Sutherland, E. (1937), *The Professional Thief,* Chicago IL: University of Chicago Press.

Sutherland, E. H. (1939), *Principles in Criminology,* Philadelphia: Lippincott.

Sutherland, E. (1949), *White Collar Crime,* New York: Holt, Rinehart and Winston.

Swanton, O. (1998), 'Gangchester', *Mixmag:* February, pp. 68–76

Swyngedouw, E. A. (1992), 'The mammoth quest: "glocalisation", interspatial competition and the monetary order: the construction of new scales' in Dunford, M. and Kaftalas, G. (eds), *Cities and Regions in the New Europe: The Global – local interplay and spatial development strategies*, London: Belhaven.

Sykes, G. (1958), *The Society of Captives*, Princeton: Princeton University Press.

Tao, J. and Wai-Nang, H. (1997), 'Chinese entrepreneurship: culture, structure and enonomic actors' in Scott, A. (ed.) *The Limits of Globalization*, London: Routledge.

Taylor, I. (1994), 'The political economy of crime' in Maguire, M., Morgan, R. and Reiner, R. (eds.) *The Oxford Handbook of Criminology,* Oxford: Clarendon Press.

Taylor, I., Walton, P. and Young, J. (1975) (eds), *Critical Criminology,* London: Routledge.

Taylor, L. (1984), *In the Underworld*, Oxford: Blackwell.

Thompson, A. A. (1998), *Classic Murders of the North East,* London: True Crime Library.

Tolson, A. (1977), *The Limits of Masculinity,* London: Tavistock.

Tuck, M. (1989), *Drinking and Disorder: A Study of Non-Metropolitan Violence,* London: HMSO.

Urry, J. (1983), 'De-industrialisation, classes and politics' in King, R. (ed.) *Capital and Politics,* London: Routledge & Kegan Paul.

Wacquant, L. (1992), 'The Social Logic of Boxing in Black Chicago: Towards a Sociology of Pugilism', *Sociology of Sport Journal* 7(3): 221–54.

Wacquant, L. (1998), 'Review Article: Why Men Desire Muscles', *Body and Society,* 1(1): 163–79.

Wax, R. (1952), 'Reciprocity as a field technique', *Human Organisation* 11: 34–7.

Webster, D. (1988), *Looka Yonder: The Imaginary America of Populist Culture,* London: Routledge.

Wheelock, J. (1990), *Husbands at Home: The domestic economy in a post-industrial society,* London: Routledge.

Whyte, W. F. (1993), *Street Corner Society,* Chicago IL: University of Chicago Press.

Wilk, R. (1995), 'Learning to be local in Belize: global systems of common difference' in Miller, D. (ed) (1995) *Worlds Apart: Modernity, through the prism of the local,* London: Routledge.

Wilkinson, C. (1995), *The Drop Out Society,* Leicester: National Youth Agency.

Williams, F. (1989), *Social Policy: A Critical Introduction,* Cambridge: Polity.

Williams, T. (1989), *The Cocaine Kids,* Reading, Mass: Addison-Wesley.

Willis, P. (1990), *Common Culture,* Milton Keynes: Open University Press.

Willis, P. (1977), *Learning to Labour,* Farnsborough: Saxon House.

Willis, P. (1979), 'Shop-Floor culture, masculinity and the wage form' in J. Clarke, C. Critcher, and R. Johnson (eds.) *Working Class Culture,* London: Hutchinson.

Wilmott, P. (1966), *Adolescent Boys in East London,* London: Routledge.

Wilson, W. J. (1996), *When Works Disappears,* New York: Random House.

Wilson, W. J. (1987), *The Truly Disadvantaged,* Chicago IL: University of Chicago Press.

Wilson, W. J. (1992), 'Another look at the truly disadvantaged', *Political Science Quarterly* 106: 639–56.

Winlow, S. (1996), *Report on Young People's Attitudes in East Durham,* Durham: University of Durham/NACRO.

Winlow, S, Hobbs, D, Hall, S, and Lister, S. (forthcoming), 'Get Ready to Duck: Doing research on violence', *British Journal of Criminology.*

Wirth, L. (1928), *The Ghetto,* Chicago IL: University of Chicago Press.

Wirth, L. (1938), 'Urbanism as a way of life', *American Journal of Sociology,* 44: 8–20.

Wolfgang, M. E. and Ferracuti, F. (1982), *The Subculture of Violence: Towards an Integrated Theory in Criminology,* Beverley Hills, C. A: Sage.

Young, Lord. (1992), 'Enterprise regained' in Heelas, P. and Morris, P. (eds) *The Values of the Enterpirse Culture,* London: Routledge.

Index

Index

Index